P9-AGR-605

WHAT ABOUT THE BOYS?
Issues of masculinity in schools

EDITED BY
WAYNE MARTINO AND BOB MEYENN

Open University Press
Buckingham · Philadelphia

LIBRARY MSU-BILLINGS WITHDRAWN

Open University Press
Celtic Court
22 Ballmoor
Buckingham
MK18 1XW

email: enquiries@openup.co.uk
world wide web: www.openup.co.uk

and
325 Chestnut Street
Philadelphia, PA 19106, USA

First Published 2001

Copyright © Wayne Martino and Bob Meyenn and Contributors, 2001

All rights reserved. Except for the quotation of short passages for the purpose of criticism and review, no part of this publication may be reproduced, stored in a retrieval system, or transmitted, in any form or by any means, electronic, mechanical, photocopying, recording or otherwise, without the prior written permission of the publisher or a licence from the Copyright Licensing Agency Limited. Details of such licences (for reprographic reproduction) may be obtained from the Copyright Licensing Agency Ltd of 90 Tottenham Court Road, London, W1P 9HE.

A catalogue record of this book is available from the British Library

ISBN   0 335 20623 9 (pb)   0 335 20624 7 (hb)

Library of Congress Cataloging-in-Publication Data
What about the boys? : issues of masculinity in schools/[edited by] Wayne Martino and Bob Meyenn.
    p. cm.
  Includes bibliographical references and index.
  ISBN 0-335-20624-7 – ISBN 0-335-20623-9 (pbk.)
  1. Boys–Education.   2. Masculinity.   3. Sex differences in education.
 4. Gender identity.   I. Martino, Wayne.   II. Meyenn, Bob, 1944–

LC1390.W43 2001
371.823–dc21   2001021072

Typeset by Graphicraft Limited, Hong Kong
Printed in Great Britain by St Edmundsbury Press Limited, Bury St Edmunds, Suffolk

Contents

List of contributors   v
Preface   x

1 'What about the boys?' An overview of the debates   1
VICTORIA FOSTER, MICHAEL KIMMEL AND CHRISTINE SKELTON

2 The significance of teaching English boys: exploring social
change, modern schooling and the making of masculinities   24
CHRIS HAYWOOD AND MÁIRTÍN MAC AN GHAILL

3 Rethinking masculinities: new ideas for schooling boys   38
MICHAEL C. REICHERT

4 Pushing it to the max: interrogating the risky business of
being a boy   53
MARTIN MILLS

5 Challenging boys: addressing issues of masculinity within a
gender equity framework   66
LORI BECKETT

6 'Powerful people aren't usually real kind, friendly, open
people!' Boys interrogating masculinities at school   82
WAYNE MARTINO

7 Boyz' own stories: masculinities and sexualities in schools   96
DEBBIE EPSTEIN

8 'Learning to laugh': A study of schoolboy humour in the
English secondary school   110
ANOOP NAYAK AND MARY JANE KEHILY

9 'Sad, bad or sexy boys': girls' talk in and out of the classroom 124
VALERIE HEY, ANGELA CREESE, HARRY DANIELS, SHAUN FIELDING
AND DIANA LEONARD

10 Transgressing the masculine: African American boys and the
   failure of schools   140
   JAMES EARL DAVIS
11 'Someone has to go through': indigenous boys, staying on
   at school and negotiating masculinities   154
   LEE SIMPSON, MARK MCFADDEN AND GEOFF MUNNS
12 Naughty boys at school: perspectives on boys and discipline   169
   BOB MEYENN AND JUDITH PARKER
13 Boys will be boys (if they pay attention in science class)   186
   WILL LETTS
14 Maths talk is boys' talk: constructing masculinity
   in school mathematics   199
   ANNE CHAPMAN
15 Boys, books and breaking boundaries: developing literacy
   in and out of school   211
   CHRISTINE HALL AND MARTIN COLES
16 'I like smashing people, and I like getting smashed myself':
   addressing issues of masculinity in physical education and
   sport   222
   MICHAEL GARD

Index   236

List of contributors

LORI BECKETT is a lecturer in the Faculty of Education at the University of Technology Sydney, where she takes responsibility for the Graduate Diploma in Education. Recently she was commissioned to do research projects for the New South Wales (NSW) Department of Education and Training: Gender, Drug Use and Young People, and the evaluation of the Primary School Clusters project. Lori also worked on gender equity policy at the state and national level, being a member of the Ministerial Council of Employment, Education and Training's (MCEETYA) Gender Equity Taskforce 1993–1998, which developed *Gender Equity: A Framework for Australian Schools*, and the NSW gender equity consultative committee 1995–1998, which developed *Girls and Boys at School: Gender Equity Strategy 1996–2001*.

ANNE CHAPMAN is a senior lecturer in the Graduate School of Education at The University of Western Australia, where she teaches in the areas of pedagogy, mathematics curriculum and social semiotics. She has taught mathematics at secondary, TAFE and tertiary levels and is involved in the professional development of pre-service and practising mathematics teachers. Her research interests include language and learning, social semiotics, and the social construction of masculinities in schools. She has written numerous articles on the application of social semiotic theory to classroom education, and is co-author of *Literacy and Learning in Mathematics* (1996) and *Pedagogical Relationships Between Adult Literacy and Numeracy* (1996).

MARTIN COLES is a teacher and researcher within the Centre for Literacy Studies at the University of Nottingham, UK. He was a co-director of the Children's Reading Choices project, which produced detailed information about children's out of school reading habits. He has worked as a school teacher and is a frequent collaborator in research and writing about English teaching and literacy development. He is currently involved in leading teacher education programmes.

ANGELA CREESE is a sociolinguist at Leicester University, UK with a special interest in bilingual learners. She is currently writing a book on multilingual classrooms and is an active member of the British Association of Applied Linguists.

HARRY DANIELS is Professor of Special Education and Educational Psychology at the University of Birmingham, UK. Recent edited works include *Special Education Re-formed Beyond Rhetoric?* (2000).

JAMES EARL DAVIS is Associate Professor in the Department of Educational Leadership and Policy Studies at Temple University, USA. He previously taught at the University of Delaware and was a visiting scholar in the Institute for Research on Women and Gender at the University of Michigan. A former National Academy of Education Spencer Fellow, Professor Davis's research and teaching are in the areas of sociology of education, masculinities and schooling, and higher education policy. Professor Davis is co-editor (with Vernon C. Polite) of *African American Males in School and Society: Practices and Policies for Effective Education* (1999), and (with M. Christopher Brown) *Black Sons to Mothers: Compliments, Critiques, and Challenges to Cultural Workers in Education* (2000).

DEBBIE EPSTEIN is Chair in Educational Studies at Goldsmiths College, University of London, UK. Her research focuses on 'differences that make a difference' in the two key sites of education and popular culture. Her publications include: *Changing Classroom Cultures: Anti-racism, Politics and Schools* (1993); *Challenging Lesbian and Gay Inequalities in Education* (Open University Press, 1994); *Border Patrols: Policing the Boundaries of Heterosexuality* (with Deborah Lynn Steinberg and Richard Johnson, 1997); *Schooling Sexualities* (with Richard Johnson, Open University Press, 1998); *Failing Boys? Issues in Gender and Achievement* (co-editor with Jannette Elwood, Valerie Hey and Janet Maw, Open University Press, 1998); and *A Dangerous Knowing: Sexuality, Pedagogy and Popular Culture* (1999).

SHAUN FIELDING currently works in a private consultancy firm based in Birmingham, UK.

VICTORIA FOSTER is Adjunct Associate Professor in the Division of Communication and Education, University of Canberra, and is also a private consultant working in professional and community programmes. She is known internationally for her research on gender and education, civics and citizenship education, gender and literacies and professional development and curriculum change. She has published widely on these issues and is presently working on a book, *Space Invaders: Barriers to Equality in the Schooling of Girls*. She is also a frequent contributor to media discussions of gender issues.

MICHAEL GARD is a lecturer in physical education, dance and the socio-cultural foundations of sport and physical activity at Charles Sturt University, NSW Australia, where he is also a member of the Centre for Cultural Research into Risk. His teaching and research focuses on the social practice of physical education lessons and he has written and published on gender, sexuality and the human body.

CHRISTINE HALL is a teacher and researcher within the Centre for Literacy Studies at the University of Nottingham, UK. She was a co-director of the Children's Reading Choices project, which produced detailed information about children's out-of-school reading habits. She has worked as a school teacher and is a frequent collaborator in research and writing about English teaching and literacy development. She is currently involved in leading teacher education programmes.

CHRIS HAYWOOD currently works in the Faculty of Education at the University of Newcastle, UK. He has written on young people, sexuality and masculinity. His interests include research methodologies and the epistemology of identities.

VALERIE HEY is Research Professor of Education at Brunel University, UK. She is the author of *The Company She Keeps: An Ethnography of Girls' Friendship* (Open University Press, 1997).

MARY JANE KEHILY is a lecturer in childhood studies at the Open University, UK. She has a broad range of experience both as a teacher and a research in schools and universities and has written widely on issues of gender and sexuality, narrative and identity and popular culture.

MICHAEL S. KIMMEL is Professor of Sociology at SUNY at Stony Brook, USA. His books include *Changing Men* (1987), *Men Confront Pornography* (1990), *Men's Lives* (5th edition, forthcoming 2000) *Against the Tide: Profeminist Men in the United States, 1776–1990* (1992), *The Politics of Manhood* (1996), *Manhood: A Cultural History* (1996), and *The Gendered Society* (2000). He edits *Men and Masculinities*, an interdisciplinary scholarly journal, a book series on men and masculinity at the University of California Press, and the Sage series on men and masculinities. He is the spokesperson for the National Organization for Men Against Sexism (NOMAS) and lectures extensively on campuses in the US and abroad.

DIANA LEONARD is Professor of the Sociology of Education and Gender at the Institute of Education, University of London, UK. Her publications include *A Woman's Guide to Doctoral Studies* (Open University Press, 2001).

WILL LETTS, a former high school science teacher and coach, is a lecturer in science education and the sociology of education at Charles Sturt University, NSW Australia. He is also an associate director of the University's Centre for Cultural Research into Risk. His research interests include the cultural studies of science and science education, particularly in reference to sexuality, indigeneity, and gender.

MÁIRTÍN MAC AN GHAILL currently works in the Faculty of Education at the University of Newcastle, UK. His research interests include the sociology of racism and the cultural formation of gender/sexual identities. He is the author of *Contemporary Racisms and Ethnicities* (Open University Press, 1999) and has edited a collection on *Understanding Masculinities* (Open University Press, 1996).

MARK MCFADDEN has been a teacher, curriculum consultant, teacher educator and researcher. Until recently he was Head of the School of Education at Charles Sturt University, NSW Australia, and Director of the Group for Research in Employment and Training (GREAT). He is now a professorial associate of the University. He has published nationally and internationally on issues of access to and resistance to education.

WAYNE MARTINO lectures in the School of Education, Murdoch University, Western Australia. His research has involved an exploration of the impact of masculinities on boys' lives at school. He has also recently completed another book for Open University Press with Maria Pallotta-Chiarolli entitled *So What's a Boy?: Issues of Masculinity and Schooling*. Currently he is working with a team of researchers on a major research project for the Australian government entitled 'Addressing the educational needs of boys: strategies for schools and teachers'.

BOB MEYENN is the Dean of the Faculty of Education at Charles Sturt University, NSW Australia. He has served as President of the New South Wales Teacher Education Council (NSWTEC) and as the Secretary/Treasurer of the Australian Council of Deans of Education. He has made a significant contribution to the New South Wales Ministerial Advisory Council on the Quality of Teaching (MACQT). His research and teaching interests have centred on policy development in teacher education and issues of equity and social justice in education, especially gender equity. Bob is presently also Chair of the Board of Australian Volunteers International, having been a volunteer in the Solomon Islands in the 1960s.

MARTIN MILLS is a research fellow in the School of Education, The University of Queensland, where he also teaches in the social science curriculum area. He has published widely on the topic of boys and education. His other research interests include gender issues in education, social justice and education, teacher education, school reform and pedagogy. His book *Challenging Violence in Schools: An Issue of Masculinities* is being published by Open University Press in 2001.

GEOFF MUNNS is a senior lecturer in education at the University of Western Sydney and has a long association with Indigenous Australian communities as a teacher, school executive and researcher. He has conducted ethnographic research in schools serving Indigenous Australian communities and has published and presented at national and international conferences on issues of classroom relationships between teachers and Indigenous Australian students.

ANOOP NAYAK is a lecturer in social and cultural geography at the University of Newcastle, UK. His research interests are in race and ethnicity, youth studies and masculinities.

JUDITH PARKER worked at the Mitchell College of Advanced Education and then Charles Sturt University, NSW Australia until 1998 when she retired. She has served as president of the New South Wales Teacher Education Council (NSWTEC). She has also made significant contributions to the New South Wales Ministerial Advisory Council on the Quality of Teaching (MACQT). Her research and teaching interests have centred on policy development in teacher education and issues of equity and social justice in education, especially gender equity. The faculty's close association with the Solomon Islands led Judith to become a lecturer with Australian Volunteers Abroad at the Solomon Islands College of Higher Education.

MICHAEL C. REICHERT has been a practising child and family psychologist for the past 20 years. He currently practises as part of the multidisciplinary group, Bala Psychological Resources. He has consulted to independent schools for many years and is on the staff at The Haverford School, where he directs On Behalf of Boys, a centre for research on boys' lives. He also serves as Project Director for Peaceful Posse, sponsored by Philadelphia Physicians for Social Responsibility, which trains men to mentor boys at high risk as a result of their exposure to violence. He co-authored the book, *Bearing Witness: Violence and Collective Responsibility* with Sandra Bloom, MD, (1998). Dr Reichert is currently engaged in research on boys' development and learning. He has two sons of his own, ages 15 and 8.

LEE SIMPSON is Koori Teaching Fellow in the School of Education at Charles Sturt University, NSW Australia. She is passionate about and active in Aboriginal issues and works with students and teachers in the area of Aboriginal studies to develop shared cultural and social understandings.

CHRISTINE SKELTON is a lecturer in education at the University of Newcastle, UK. She teaches courses on gender and education at undergraduate and postgraduate level. Christine is joint editor of the international journal *Gender and Education*. She has written widely in the area of masculinities and primary schooling. Her most recent book, *Schooling the Boys: Masculinities and Primary Education* (Open University Press, 2001) is based on her doctoral research.

Preface

We believe that a book of this nature, which attempts to develop further understandings about masculinity within the context of current debates about the boys, is timely, given the continued moral panic that persists about boys regarding their disadvantaged status relative to girls. Even as we write this preface, a national inquiry into the education of boys is under way in Australia, initiated by the Federal Minister for Education, Dr Kemp. Not surprisingly, many of the submissions to that inquiry continue to promote the view that boys are victims and are attributed a disadvantaged status (see Lingard and Douglas 1999). This tends to support the need for a book of this kind which is committed to problematizing the simplistic conceptualization of boys as a homogeneous group whose interests are set against those of girls (see Collins *et al.* 2000; Martino and Pallotta-Chiarolli in press).

Research undertaken with boys spanning Australia, the United Kingdom and the United States is brought together in this collection. The focus for each of the contributors is addressing issues of 'what about the boys' in relation to their own research and informed perspectives on boys and schooling. Many focus on what boys (and girls) themselves say about their experiences of schooling and sexuality and use their voices as a basis for drawing out what the implications might be for those working in schools. In this regard the chapters are written with a broader audience in mind – particularly teachers and administrators in schools with the view to using research to illuminate the effects of masculinity in the lives of boys and girls at school.

All of the contributors are concerned to highlight the impact and effect of certain forms of masculinity on the lives of boys at school, but locate their research and/or discussion within the context of the boys' education debates outlined by Foster, Kimmell and Skelton in the introductory chapter. Many have also indicated what the implications of their research are for daily practice in schools and classrooms. In this sense, the research documented here has major implications for the professional development of teachers in schools and for student teachers in tertiary institutions.

Sociologists like Bob Connell (1987, 1995) have been particularly influential in drawing attention to how social, cultural and historical factors have influenced the various ways in which 'masculinity' comes to be defined and embodied by boys and men. We see the contributors of this book building on this work. They highlight that there are many forms of masculinity that are played out in the context of a complex set of power relations in which certain types of masculinity are valued over others. Many also draw attention to the role of a dominant form of masculinity, which comes to be defined in opposition to femininity, and highlight that association with the feminine for boys can often lead to other boys questioning their sexuality (see also Frank, 1987, 1993).

Other factors such as race, class, ethnicity and geographical location are also taken up to develop an understanding of the various ways in which boys learn to relate and behave in certain social situations and within particular educational institutions. In this sense feminist educators and theories also inform the perspectives on boys and schooling elaborated in this book. Such perspectives have contributed significantly to producing valuable insights into the links between gender and power (Davies 1993; Steinberg *et al.* 1997), specifically in terms of illuminating boys' social practices and ways of relating at school (Cox 1995; Davies 1995; Skelton 1996, 1998; Kenway 1997; Kenway *et al.* 1997; Pallotta-Chiarolli 1997; Yates 1997; Epstein *et al.* 1998; Gilbert and Gilbert 1998).

All contributors recognize that schools are important arenas of power where masculinities and femininities are acted out on a daily basis through the dynamic processes of negotiation, refusal and struggle (Giroux and McLaren 1994). In other words, these papers illustrate that there are indeed social constraints and power imbalances in educational sites, but that gender regimes are more shifting and contradictory than theorists supposed in the seventies and eighties (Jackson and Salisbury 1996; Kenway *et al.* 1997). In this sense, each chapter included in this collection builds on studies into boys at school which have been undertaken by Kessler *et al.* (1985), Walker (1988), Mac an Ghaill (1994) and Epstein (1994).

The contributors also suggest ways forward and beyond the popular and simplistic views which stress the need for boys to reclaim lost territory. There is a powerful discourse of neglect informing many of the popularist debates about the boys which continue to assert that provision for the educational needs of girls has been at the expense of boys (Yates 1997). Moreover, the idea or assumption that boys are somehow victims or 'losers' now competing with girls who have suddenly become the winners is also refuted strongly by the various positions that are taken up in this book. Compounding such a position is the view that biology needs to be given equal consideration in developing an understanding of boys' behaviours and learning orientations. This argument continues to be promulgated within the context of these debates about the boys (see submissions to Australian inquiry into boys' education at http://www.aph.gov.au/house/committee/eewr/Epfb/sublist.htm) as if appeals to biological sex differences and essentialism are somehow outside the effects of certain power relations (see Fausto-Sterling 2000). As Peterson (2000) has illuminated, appeals to biological determinism have been used historically to enforce a binary categorization of gendered behaviours always within the context of and in response to the perceived power gained by women. Moreover, as Lingard and Douglas (1999) have lucidly illustrated, the debates about the boys in the nineties have been characterized by a strong backlash against feminism and this continues to be the case as we enter the new millennium.

If we are indeed to encourage diversity and citizenship in multicultural societies it is crucial that issues of opportunity, access and distributed success be foregrounded in debates about gendered educational outcomes. Collins *et al.* (2000) have addressed this in a recent governmental report on the factors influencing the educational performance of males and females in school and their post-school labour destinations. In line with the positions taken up in that report, we believe that policy formulation and curriculum development in schools must avoid the popularist tendency to assert a binary oppositional and 'competing victims' perspective on the factors impacting on the social and educational experiences of boys and girls. This will only lead to homogenizing and normalizing boys and girls on the basis of biological sex differences and, hence, reinforce the very versions of masculinity which the research shows have detrimental consequences for both the former and the latter.

This book, therefore, is offered as an attempt to provide a more informed perspective on the social practices of masculinity impacting on boys' lives at school. We hope that it will have the effect of moving the debates beyond the feminist backlash rhetoric which persists in casting boys as the 'new victims'. If anything, as the contributors of this book argue, the issue that needs to be addressed is the investment that many boys, men and schools have in promoting a particular version of masculinity which is to their detriment in the sense that it limits them from developing a wider repertoire of behaviours and ways of relating. Until a commitment is made, particularly by men and boys themselves, to addressing the role that sexuality, homophobia and misogyny continue to play in how many of them define and negotiate their masculinities, we believe that very little will change.

Wayne Martino
Bob Meyenn

References

Collins, C., Kenway, J. and McLeod, J. (2000) *Factors Influencing the Educational Performance of Males and Females in School and their Initial Destinations after Leaving School.* Canberra: DEETYA.

Connell, R.W. (1987) *Gender and Power.* Cambridge: Polity Press.

Connell, R.W. (1995) *Masculinities.* Sydney: Allen and Unwin.

Cox, E. (1995) Boys and girls and the costs of gendered behaviour. Proceedings of the Promoting Gender Equity Conference, February 22–4. Canberra: ACT Department of Education and Training.

Davies, B. (1993) *Shards of Glass.* Sydney: Allen and Unwin.

Davies, B. (1995) What about the boys? The parable of the bear and the rabbit. *Interpretations*, 28 (2): 1–17.

Epstein, D. (1994) *Challenging Lesbian and Gay Inequalities in Education.* Buckingham and Philadelphia, PA: Open University Press.

Epstein, D., Elwood, J., Hey, V. and Maw, J. (eds) (1998) *Failing Boys?* Buckingham: Open University Press.

Fausto-Sterling, A. (2000) *Sexing the Body.* New York: Basic Books.

Frank, B. (1987) Hegemonic heterosexual masculinity. *Studies in Political Economy*, 24: 159–70.

Frank, B. (1993) Straight/strait jackets for masculinity: educating for real men. *Atlantis*, 18 (1 and 2): 47–59.

Gilbert, R. and Gilbert, P. (1998) *Masculinity Goes to School.* Sydney: Allen and Unwin.

Giroux, H.A. and McLaren, P. (eds) (1994) *Between Borders: Pedagogy and the Politics of Cultural Studies.* New York, NY: Routledge.

Jackson, D. and Salisbury, J. (1996) Why should secondary schools take working with boys seriously? *Gender and Education*, 8 (1): 103–15.

Kenway, J. (1997) Boys' education, masculinity and gender reform: some introductory remarks. *Curriculum Perspectives*, 17 (1): 57–60.

Kenway, J., Willis, S., Blackmore, J. and Rennie, L. (1997) *Answering Back.* Sydney: Allen and Unwin.

Kessler, S., Ashenden, D.J., Connell, R.W. and Dowsett, G.W. (1985) Gender relations in secondary schooling. *Sociology of Education*, 58: 34–48.

Lingard, B. and Douglas, P. (1999) *Men Engaging Feminisms: Profeminism, Backlashes and Schooling.* Buckingham: Open University Press.

Mac an Ghaill, M. (1994) *The Making of Men: Masculinities, Sexualities, and Schooling.* Buckingham: Open University Press.

Martino, W. and Pallotta-Chiarolli (in press) *So What's a Boy?* Buckingham: Open University Press.

Pallotta-Chiarolli, M. (1997) 'We want to address boys' education but . . .'. *Curriculum Perspectives*, 17 (1): 65–8.

Petersen, A. (2000) *Unmasking the Masculine: Men and Identity in a Sceptical Age.* London, Thousand Oaks, CA, New Dehli: Sage.

Skelton, C. (1996) Learning to be 'tough': the fostering of maleness in one primary school. *Gender and Education*, 8 (2): 185–97.

Skelton, C. (1998) Feminism and research into masculinities and schooling. *Gender and Education*, 10 (2): 217–27.

Steinberg, D.L., Epstein, D. and Johnson, R. (1997) *Border Patrols: Policing the Boundaries of Heterosexuality.* London: Cassell.

Walker, J.C. (1988) *Louts and Legends: Male Youth Culture in an Inner City School*. Sydney: Allen and Unwin.

Willis, P. (1977) *Learning to Labour*. Farnborough: Saxon House.

Yates, L. (1997) Gender equity and the boys debate: what sort of challenge is it? *British Journal of the Sociology of Education*, 18 (3): 337–47.

CHAPTER 1

'What about the boys?'
An overview of the debates

VICTORIA FOSTER, MICHAEL KIMMEL AND
CHRISTINE SKELTON[1]

Introduction

In this chapter we are concerned to provide an overview of the debates
'about the boys' in Australia, the United Kingdom and the United States.
The ways in which these debates have emerged in all three nations are
discussed at length to highlight the kind of polemic which continues to
inform the moral panic surrounding the plight of boys who have acquired
the status of the 'new disadvantaged' (see Epstein *et al.* 1998; Gilbert and
Gilbert 1998; Lingard and Douglas 1999). In fact, we highlight how the issue
has been portrayed in each context as the education crisis of the nineties
and how this problem has been attributed to the impact of feminism with
a number of writers, educationists and therapists directly attacking the
women's movement for the 'damage' it has supposedly done to boys! We
also draw attention to how a significant feature of these debates involves
reinscribing binary oppositions between, for example, boys/girls, femininity/
masculinity, etc. where girls' success is seen at the expense of boys (see
Kenway 1995; Yates 1997). Driving much of this rhetoric, which is espoused
by the popular media and men's movement advocates, is a fundamental
biological determinism and competing victims syndrome with boys' interests
being set against those of girls (Cox 1997). In this chapter we explore further
these kinds of problematics and highlight how a feminist backlash rhetoric
informs the moral panic suffusing the debates about boys' education in all
three countries.

Boys' underachievement in the UK

This moral panic has characterized much of the debates about boys' educational issues in the United Kingdom (UK). If articles in national newspapers are to be believed then 'boys' underachievement' began in the UK in 1995 and rapidly became a 'moral panic' (Epstein *et al.* 1998; Griffin 1998). For example, the main professional newspaper, the *Times Educational Supplement* (*TES*), carried headlines declaring that school work was 'Not for wimps' (6 October 1995) and later asking 'Where did we go wrong?' (*TES* 14 February 1997). Education correspondents for broadsheet newspapers similarly headlined articles which discussed 'The failing sex' (*Guardian,* Education Supplement, 12 March 1996) and called for schools to provide a 'Classroom rescue for Britain's lost boys' (*Independent*, 5 January 1998). That 'boys' underachievement' has or should become *the* gender issue for schools is evident in speeches given by government ministers. Since the comments of a Chief Inspector for Schools, Chris Woodhead, that 'the failure of boys and in particular white working class boys is one of the most disturbing problems we face within the whole education system' (*TES* 15 March 1996), education ministers have called for schools to 'challenge the laddish anti-learning culture which has been allowed to develop over recent years' (Stephen Byers, Standards Minister, 5 January 1998), noting that 'Many schools are already addressing the issue of boys' under-achievement successfully – but too many schools are not' (Morris 1996).

However, despite the media and government inference that boys' underachievement is a recent phenomenon here in the UK, problems of boys and schooling have long occupied a central place in studies of primary and secondary schools. Indeed, as far back as the seventeenth century, the English philosopher John Locke, among others, expressed a concern for boys' problems with language and literacy (Cohen 1998). More recently, literature on schooling written in the 1960s and early 1970s cautioned teachers against grouping boys according to academic ability as it resulted in less academic boys developing negative attitudes towards education and schools (Hargreaves 1967; Lacey 1970). There were also studies which showed how social class impacted upon boys' experiences of school (Parker 1974; Willis 1977; Robins and Cohen 1978), and where the effect of 'race' on education was under investigation the unwritten focus was on how the white, Eurocentric nature of the curriculum alienated and disadvantaged black and Asian boys (Wright 1986; Mirza 1992). Thus, the 'problem' of boys' underachievement was, in the 1960s and 1970s, conceived of in terms of inequalities of social class and/or 'race' rather than gender. In the 1990s the 'problem' of boys' underachievement is constructed as a consequence of 'boys being boys' resulting from the major changes to the educational system.

A series of Education Acts, passed under a Conservative government (1979–97), effectively shifted emphasis away from the idea of education as a means of promoting social democracy, where the eradication of inequalities was seen as necessary for the collective good, onto social diversity through promoting freedom of choice. This was achieved by moving the locus of power away from local education authorities (LEAs) to schools. The Education Act 1986 began this process by creating new governing bodies for schools. These new structures required fewer LEA representatives and more parents and people drawn from the local community, particularly those with knowledge and skills in the field of business. Greater powers were awarded to governing bodies in the Education Reform Act (ERA) 1988 when they, rather than LEAs, became responsible for school budgets. A funding formula was brought into operation whereby 80 per cent of each school's budget is determined by the number and age of the pupils (Whitty *et al.* 1998). In addition, the ERA allowed schools to adopt an open enrolment policy. Previously, schools were limited as to the number of pupils they could take and restricted to taking children from specific catchment areas, one of the reasons being to ensure other schools could remain open. The open enrolment principle meant that popular schools were allowed to admit as many pupils as they chose. Thus, the ERA set in place a market situation whereby 'educational institutions compete[d] with each other for finances and for consumers or customers as parents and/or students' (David 1995: 68).

However, this apparent move towards decentralization was counteracted by an increase of the central powers of the government. This came in the form of the introduction of the National Curriculum together with the implementation of complex assessment and reporting procedures. Pupils were to undertake national tests (known as Standard Assessment Tasks: SATs) at the ages of 7, 11 and 14. Schools were (and are) expected to ensure pupils achieve a particular 'level' by the time they reach these ages. In addition, schools were to be regularly and rigorously inspected. These inspections were central to the Education (Schools) Act 1992 which introduced national league tables. These tables ranked schools according to pupils' performance in the SATs and took no regard of the socio-economic context of individual schools.

Thus, the scene was set for the emergence of the 'boys' underachievement' debate. In order for schools to survive they had to attract 'clients' in the form of parents; they could only attract parents if they were able to demonstrate they provided and delivered a high standard of education. Schools were judged to be 'effective' by the national league tables according to their success in getting pupils to reach the requisite standards at ages 7, 11 and 14. Those schools which were 'effective' according to this criteria would thrive while the others would go to the wall. Despite the controversy raised by such naive and simplistic approaches to judging a school's 'effectiveness' (Ball 1994; Mortimore and Whitty 1997; Whitty *et al.* 1998) they have pushed schools into a position where, to survive, they need to address any areas which appear to have shortcomings. As places in the league tables were given according to examination performance then schools looked to their own results. It was in analysing the statistical results that the gender gap in performance across the majority of subjects, which had actually appeared in the 1980s but had gone relatively unremarked, became evident.

The complexity of boys' performance at school has been well rehearsed (Teese *et al.* 1995; Yates 1997; Murphy and Elwood 1998; Raphael Reed 1998; Arnot *et al.* 1999). We know that boys are well represented among the highest and also the lowest achievers. We know that the least differences in gender attainment occur between boys and girls from higher socio-economic groups and the most differences between those from lower socio-economic groups. We also know that inequalities generated by 'race' inequalities have apparently greater impact than those caused by gender (Gillborn 1997). These factors are not unique to the UK but have been identified elsewhere (see Lingard and Douglas 1999). The intention here is not to explore gender differences in academic achievement (for detailed analysis see Arnot *et al.* 1996), nor is it to explore fully the debates surrounding the simplistic framing of the 'boys' underachievement' debates in the UK (see Epstein *et al.* 1998). The following section summarizes the discourses surrounding the 'problem of boys' in order to consider what approaches are being taken.

'Failing boys'

In a recent collection of papers concerned with the 'problem of boys', the editors identify three dominant discourses evident in debates about boys and achievement; these are 'poor boys'; 'failing schools, failing boys' and 'boys will be boys' (Epstein *et al.* 1998). The 'poor boys' discourse has also been labelled as the 'lads' movement' (Kenway 1995). Here boys are positioned as 'victims', specifically of: single (fatherless) families; female-dominated primary schooling; and feminism, which has enabled girls' successes. This, as we will illustrate later, is also the case in Australia and the United States. As Epstein *et al.* (1998: 6–7) say:

> In the context of education and debates about boys' underachievement, the supporters of the 'Lads' Movement' develop a range of arguments which blame women for the failures of boys. If it is not women teachers, it is mothers; if not mothers, it is feminists; most often it is a combination.

The 'failing schools, failing boys' discourse emerges directly from the school effectiveness and school improvement movements. A 'failing school' is one which does not produce pupils with high levels of literacy and numeracy and above average passes in public examinations and/or does not achieve set standards laid down in external inspection procedures. These schools are seen as failing the boys (and presumably girls) who attend them. Unlike the 'poor boys' discourse it is rare for proponents of the 'failing schools' discourse to make overt and direct attacks on feminism.

Finally, the 'boys will be boys' discourse conceives of boys in conventional, stereotypical ways and attributes these traditional characteristics to 'natural differences' as a result of biology and psychology. This discourse has much in common with 'poor boys' in that boys have been made 'victims' because of feminist women's successes at promoting the female over men and maleness, thus challenging traditional ways of being a man. Epstein *et al.* (1998: 9) have pointed to the contradictory nature of the 'boys will be boys' debate:

> What is particularly interesting . . . is the way it manages, at one and the same time, to posit an unchanging and unchangeable 'boyness', which involves aggression, fighting and delayed (some might say indefinitely!) maturity and yet situates poor achievement at school as extrinsic to boys themselves).

In terms of the 'solutions' offered to tackle boys' underachievement the 'boys will be boys' and 'poor boys' discourses are similar.

The predominant approach to tackling boys' underachievement comes into what Lingard and Douglas (1999) have termed in the Australian context 'recuperative masculinity' strategies. Here the argument is that 'boys' specific needs are subsumed under the priority given to girls and minority concerns, leaving them in the role of villains who must change in order to alleviate the problems they cause' (Lingard and Douglas 1999: 133). An example of this approach can be seen in the following extract taken from a report on an action research-based partnership between a university education department and a local school into the factors influencing the motivation and performance of Year 8 (12–13 years) boys:

> . . . males are having to reconcile themselves to a reversal of roles. They face the loss of their traditional superiority . . . They have no formal 'men's liberation movement', no informal male equivalent of 'the sisterhood', to help them cope with their increasing loss of identity, their disaffection and their sense of hopelessness.
>
> (Bleach *et al.* 1996: 6)

Thus it can be seen that a basic premise of *recuperative* programmes is that boys and girls are different but should be treated equally.

Teachers wanting to find ways in which they might address boys' underachievement are most likely to come across strategies linked to the concept of 'recuperative masculinity'. For example, the *TES* constantly carries reports of schools' use of football as a means of stimulating boys' interest. The government too has looked to football as a strategy by sponsoring a scheme called 'Playing for Success' which links clubs in the Premier and first divisions with specially set up study centres. While some academics have argued that drawing on conventional masculine cultures such as violent, competitive sports to tackle boys' underachievement are counter-productive in that they entrench macho stereotypes (Epstein 1999; Francis 1999), others have commented that 'anything has to be worth a try' (Wragg 1999: 9).

Other solutions to addressing the problems boys may be experiencing can not only marginalize girls but also, occasionally, rehearse the gendered pedagogies and practices found to be operating in schools in the 1970s. For example, in the research report by Bleach *et al.* (1996) just mentioned, recommendations are made that subvert the findings of feminists which show that in the classroom girls' needs are often ignored. Girls often experience difficulties in mixed sex groups where boys are monopolizing equipment and the teacher's time, and demonstrating intimidatory or harassing behaviours (Clarricoates 1983; Jones 1985; Frith and Mahony 1994). However, these research findings have been disregarded in the recommendations by Bleach *et al.* (1996: 25):

> Various approaches are being explored . . . for encouraging . . . boys to maintain a positive attitude . . . These include . . . giving boys a high profile in showing visitors around or performing in public, pairing boys with girls in group work to expose them to the 'feminine' skills of language and reflection . . .

Similarly, it is proposed by supporters influenced by *recuperative* approaches that more men teachers be encouraged into teaching to provide boys with male role models. Feminists have questioned the simplicity of the assumption that more men teachers would eradicate the problems many boys experience in school (Skelton 1994; Pepperell 1998; Smedley 1998). Indeed, there is ample evidence in studies of schooling of men teachers who adopt particular 'macho' styles of interaction often associated with the 'lads' (see Willis 1977; Mac an Ghaill 1994; Connolly 1998). As Penn (1998: 246) argues, 'men do not necessarily modify their views on coming into a woman's profession; they bring their masculinity . . . with them'.

There is, as yet, little evidence of programmes for boys in schools influenced by *pro-feminist* approaches where boys' problems are located within a larger concern for social justice. The book by Salisbury and Jackson, *Challenging Macho Values* (1996), provided activities whereby teachers might work with boys to consider how they go about 'doing' masculinity. Similarly, Pickering (1997) offered schools and teachers various ways in which they could consider how masculinity was constructed within their own sites in order to identify the causes of the underachievement of the boys they taught.

Although a distinction is being drawn here between *recuperative* approaches and *pro-feminist* programmes, both tend to concentrate on interpersonal relationships. The reason for the focus on the 'personal' has been argued to be a result of pragmatism rather than ideology (Mills 1998), as opportunities for schools to deal with personal and social issues are dependent upon the spaces available between national curriculum subjects. At the same time, such distinctions are not part of the 'language' of the boys' underachievement debate. Indeed, differences between the various ways of considering and tackling 'boys' underachievement' have yet to be picked up by either the government or the media. The UK has yet to begin to address publicly *who* these 'failing boys' are and to see them in relation to girls who are also 'failing'.

The Australian case: presumptive equality

Similarly in Australia boys are being constructed as the 'new disadvantaged'. In fact, much of the rhetoric in the popular media in Australia about failing boys appears to be driven by a backlash mentality which is informed by the presumption that boys experience educational disadvantage in ways which are comparable to that of girls. The context of 'presumptive equality' has characterized the politicization of boys' education in Australia over the past five years or so, in a trend very similar to that experienced in the UK and described by Weiner *et al.* (1997: 1) and Arnot *et al.* (1999) as a 'moral panic' that boys are the new disadvantaged in schooling. What needs to be emphasized, however, is that the focus on 'failing boys' in Australia also emerged as a reaction against girls' apparent superior performance and is driven by a 'recuperative masculinity politics' grounded in discourses of presumptive equality (Foster 1996b).

We draw out further nuances and meanings in the term 'presumptive equality' as an explanatory framework for understanding contemporary trends in relation to issues of boys' education in Australia and show how these are working rhetorically together. The particular discourse of presumptive equality (Foster 1995) is founded on a model of gender as equivalence in which the asymmetry of gender relations is ignored. This obfuscation of the 'material pay-off' (Connell 1994: 4) which men and boys enjoy as a result of their dominant position in the gender order and the social and political reality of 'male advantage' (Eveline 1995, 1998) permits simplistic notions such as the suggestion that men are the new second sex to gain popular acceptance. On this model, complex philosophical accounts of women's secondary status such as that of de Beauvoir ([1949] 1972) herself (but see also Lloyd 1984; Pateman and Gross 1986; Code 1991; Gatens 1991, 1997; Luke and Gore 1992; Probyn 1993) are ignored and men's place in gender relations is seen as roughly equivalent to women's place, and of the same order of oppression.

Equal disadvantage, equal victims

Following from the equivalence model is the proposition that boys are as disadvantaged as girls, and now possibly more so. This is a seductive and emotive line which has appealed to some parents who are genuinely concerned about their sons' development. Despite boys' greater post-school rewards as a population and the higher resourcing of boys' education extensively documented in a succession of national and state reports and in the gender and education literature, it is now held that schooling disadvantages boys. Warren Johnson, the Executive Officer of the New South Wales Federation of Parents and Citizens Associations, wrote in *Education* (1994) that 'it is demonstrable that many boys are in states of educational, social and emotional distress and they are in genuine need of targeted resources'.

Johnson lists as evidence the already disproportionate resources going to boys, such as counselling and special placements, special classes for emotional and behaviour disturbance, intensive remedial classes. At present, several Sydney regions estimate that 90–95 per cent of these resources go to boys.

The construction of boys' advantage in education as disadvantage is a rhetorical twist which increasingly has been used to great effect. Much of this rhetoric originated with health workers, psychologists and pop education writers who argued spuriously that inadequacies in boys' schooling were the cause of what has become a familiar catalogue of problems: head injuries, suicides, male violence and so on. Learning difficulties were conflated with the social manifestations of the problems of masculinity, and these arguments were illogically applied to education in an effort to reframe what are primarily social problems as educational ones (for an excellent critique see Gilbert and Gilbert 1998).

Connell (1995: 208) argues that this process, which he calls 'masculinity therapy', relies on 'a redefinition of power by shifting from the public world to the inner world of emotion' and (p. 210) 'a preoccupation with emotional relationships, a speculative method and a satisfaction with snippets of evidence'. Gilbert (1998: 21) describes 'a conservative and potentially divisive men's movement, which rejected feminism and wanted boys' work to be seen as separate from the broader project of the democratic reform of schooling'.

Unsubstantiated and extreme claims of boys' disadvantage are commonplace, such as that of Brown, who teaches at a prestigious Sydney boys' independent school and who argued in the journal *Gifted* (1994) that we are creating a new 'underclass': gifted males! He urges that advocacy is needed for the white, male, Caucasian, non-migrant child. More common media representations are 'girls are outperforming boys'; 'girls are succeeding at the expense of boys'; 'boys are struggling'; 'boys are in deep trouble', and these have been taken up as conventional wisdom. Media reporting of the 1998 New South Wales Higher School Certificate (HSC) results frequently referred to girls' apparent success as 'dangerous'.

Girls' educational 'successes'

Australia is typical of most western countries, where girls are now achieving statistically slightly better average school-leaving results than boys, in turn occasioning a hostile populist 'backlash' against this success (Foster 1996b; 1998; Martino and Meyenn, Preface, this volume). For example, a recent international collection (Mackinnon *et al.* 1998) argues that education in the twenty-first century will be 'dangerous terrain' for women.

In New South Wales, Australia (the largest state), the debate has focused almost exclusively on Higher School Certificate results, in what Gilbert (1996: 8) refers to as 'a narrow reading of assessment figures'. Moreover, a rapidly developing academic literature is providing an analysis and critique of claims of male disadvantage (for example, Connell 1994; Foster 1995, 1996a, 1996b; Gilbert and Gilbert 1995; Yates 1996; Weiner *et al.* 1997). An entire 1995 issue of the Swedish journal, *Lararutbildning och Forskning i Umea* (*Teacher Education and Research in Umea*) was devoted to the subject and at least two international collections are planned or recently published (Mackinnon *et al.* 1998; this volume). This literature demonstrates that there is very little common ground between academic research and populist discussions of gender differences in schooling and its outcomes.

As Weiner *et al.* (1997: 1) note, in the new populist discourse male failure in education is posited as a corollary of female success. They comment, however, that 'although there is little evidence that girls' improvement in examinations has been at the expense of boys, the predominant gender discourse in the mid 1990s is that of *male underachievement*' (authors' emphasis).

Girls' and boys' different uses of schooling

While media statements such as 'girls are outperforming boys' have become commonplace in both Australia and the UK, they are inaccurate in several ways. First, they confuse performance, or measured achievement, with participation – that is the number and composition of students. Second, they ignore the question of the inequities in post-school rewards for girls for the same or better achievement at school. These claims are typically based on the outstanding achievements of a small, select group of girls, not represent-ative of the diverse female population, and ignore complex within-gender differences for both boys and girls. Most important, they obscure the crucial point that, to date, girls' school achievement has had no positive impact on post-school career prospects for them. The latter have in fact deteriorated (Daniel 1993; Korosi *et al.* 1993; DETYA 2000).

Furthermore, recent Australian research (for example, Teese *et al.* 1995; NSW Board of Studies 1996; Yates and Leder 1996: Lamb and McKenzie 1999; DETYA 2000; Foster 2000a) shows that gender differences have emerged in students' use of schooling as a credential, and in post-school rewards, where girls are faring worse than boys for the same or better achievement than them. The populist climate which sees boys as the new disadvantaged has obscured, first, the fact that there is no clear nexus between school achieve-ment and post-school pathways for girls in the way there is for boys, and second, the question of why these pathways remain so restricted and limiting for girls, including the highest achievers.

Origins of the discourse of male disadvantage: two rhetorical shifts

In Australia at least, there have been two interrelated shifts in the discourses of disadvantage relating to gender. The first is in the rhetoric alleging that boys are the new disadvantaged, as has already been discussed. It is interesting that some of the recently emerging academic literature on boys' education tends to decontextualize boys and men from their asymmetrical power relations with girls and women in society, and in education. For instance, in an entire 1998 issue of the journal *Change: Transformations in Education*, which was devoted to boys' education and published by the University of Sydney, discussion of girls' continuing inferior post-school outcomes was virtually non-existent, as was a consideration of the unchanging nature of the sexual division of labour in private domestic life (Wolcott and Glezer 1995; Bittman and Pixley 1997; Dempsey 1997).

The second shift is in the construction of girls themselves. In Australia, initial attempts to achieve greater educational equality for girls centred on positioning girls within a deficit framework, in which they were seen as lacking in relation to male norms of the educated person. Equity policies encouraged girls to measure up to those norms (Foster 1992). The following *Education and Training Strategy for Women* of the NSW Ministry of Education and Youth Affairs (1989) is an example of this deficit framework formulated as policy:

In schools, girls:

- have a low level of participation in technical and key science subjects and in highest level mathematics and science courses;
- consider a narrow range of options in making career choices;
- have lower levels of self-esteem.

It is clearly a major discursive shift from this earlier deficit framework to the current depiction of girls as actively succeeding, and even beating boys, in male educational terrain. It is significant that in Australia the most contested curriculum areas are the high-prestige male-dominated areas of mathematics and science. It was only in 1997 that in New South Wales for the first time a girl topped 4 Unit Mathematics, the most difficult level of study. Nevertheless, this was widely misconstrued in the media as girls collectively beating boys at maths and science, and over a longer period of time. Certainly a significant factor in the recent politicization of girls' school performance is the nature of the contested areas themselves and the casting of girls as interlopers and 'space invaders' (Foster 1996b; 1998) in high-status educational terrain assumed to be the natural preserve of males. One wonders about the news value of girls beating boys in life management, or child and family studies, or care, for example!

It is interesting that the 'What about the boys!' refrain is endemic in countries which have experienced quite different policy contexts. For instance, Mahony and Smedley (1998: 49) note significant differences between the British 'particularly hard version of economic rationalism' and the Australian policy framework which is to some degree underpinned by social justice and equity principles. The subtext of the refrain is that notions of educational equality for girls entail taking something very crucial away from boys: their supremacy as learners, as well as the caretaking resources of women and girls, to which boys are assumed to be entitled. By contrast, male educational interests had earlier been strongly supported by a construction which emphasized girls as lacking, rather than viewing boys themselves as being advantaged (Eveline 1995).

Moral and ethical issues for boys

There is a great deal of evidence that boys' curricular and life choices are severely circumscribed by dominant notions of masculinity, and the desire of many boys to eschew any association with the feminine or curriculum areas related to the private, domestic sphere (see for example, Collins *et al.* 1996; and DETYA 2000). Indeed, education can be seen to be concerned primarily with the initiation of young men as citizens into the 'productive' processes of society and its culture (Foster 1992: 58). In this context, women and girls are often cast in the role of caretakers of the learning environment (Foster 2000b) and of boys' needs, according to what Pateman (1988: 126) calls an unspoken 'sexual contract' whereby the functions of caring, nurturance and emotional support are seen as belonging to women. The ways in which both boys and girls live the curriculum, in its broadest sense, reinforce this sexual contract.

On the other hand, the tenor of the current debates about boys and their schooling is having serious consequences for girls' equal standing with boys as learner-citizens (Martino 1997; Foster 1997, 2000b; Arnot and Dillabough 2000). The very processes in schooling which aim to empower boys place girls in a contradictory and paradoxical relationship with the rhetoric of equal and democratic participation which characterizes much contemporary education discourse. An unspoken question is, what would happen to boys if girls do become boys' equals as learners and stop being their caretakers? Interestingly, during the current backlash period in Australia, there has been no acknowledgment that girls' equal or better achievement in male-dominated subjects would actually be beneficial for boys in that it would give them an opportunity to see girls in a new, healthier light as respected peers and equals. And how would both boys' and girls' development as learner-citizens be enhanced by a curriculum which foregrounded the values of caring in both public and private life?

These questions, however, are not being addressed in the current debates about the boys in England and Australia and have important implications for boys' social, intellectual and emotional development, and for their futures as citizens able to participate in equal social and personal relations with women. This educational problem can only be addressed by school programmes which encourage boys to broaden their curricular and life choices, and their hopes and dreams for fulfilling human relationships.

Boy trouble in the US

In the United States similar anti-feminist and backlash discourses also appear to drive debates about the troubles boys are experiencing. In fact, some would go so far as to claim that there is a virtual war against boys in America. Best-sellers' subtitles counsel us to 'protect' boys, to 'rescue' them. Moreover, these texts construct boys as failing at school, where their behaviour is increasingly seen as a problem. For instance, we read that boys are depressed, suicidal, emotionally shut down. Therapists advise anguished parents about boys' fragility, their hidden despondence and depression, and issue stern warnings about the dire consequences if these problems are not addressed. What is important to highlight is that these kinds of discourses are not dissimilar to those informing the feminist backlash rhetoric driving debates about the boys in Australia and the UK.

For example, in the United States some argue that elementary schools are 'feminizing' boys. Gurian (1998) claims that, with testosterone surging through their limbs, the requirement that boys sit still, raise their hands, and take naps leads to 'pathologizing what is simply normal for boys'. He states that boys are given the message that 'boyhood is defective'. Virtually all the boy advocates invoke the same statistics: boys are four times more likely to kill themselves than girls, they are four times more likely to be diagnosed as emotionally disturbed, six times more likely to be diagnosed with Attention Deficit Disorder and fifteen times more likely to be the victim of a violent crime. In fact, there has been an explosion of boy books, most by therapists who alternate between psychological analyses of boys' development and handy guides for raising good boys. In some senses, of course, the evidence is convincing that boys are in trouble – perhaps worse trouble than they have ever been. Yet most boy advocates misdiagnose the problem and thus offer the wrong course of treatment.

Boys should be boys

For some observers, boys will simply be boys – if only we would allow them. This means that grown-ups, and especially meddlesome women, have to get out of their way and stop criticizing them all the time. It is nature, not nurture, that supposedly propels boys towards loud rambustious play or sadistic experiments on insects. For example, therapist Michael Gurian (1996, 1998) adroitly points out the nearly unbearable pressures on young boys to conform to behaving in certain ways, to resort to violence to solve problems, to disrupt classroom decorum, to take risks – not because of peer culture, media violence, or parental influence, but because testosterone propels them towards aggression and violence. Feminists, Gurian argues, only make the problem worse, with an unyielding critique of the very masculinity that young boys are trying so desperately to prove.

The apologists' over-reliance on biology lead them to misread the evidence, to overstate the difference between the sexes and ignore the differences among boys and girls. We have already demonstrated the effects of such a position in the UK and Australia in terms of how 'failing boys' are constructed as the 'new disadvantaged'. It also leads writers like Gurian in the United States to celebrate masculinity as the simple product of that pubertal chemical elixir. Gurian (1998), for example, celebrates all masculine rites of passage 'like military boot camp, fraternity hazings, graduation day, and bar mitzvah' as 'essential parts of every boy's life' (p. 151). However, the reports of boys dying at the hands of other boys on their bar mitzvah are not mentioned. Furthermore, his claim that boys have a harder time in school than girls ignores all reliable evidence from, for example, Sadker and Sadker's (1994) *Failing at Fairness*. According to writers like Gurian, feminist emphases on gender discrimination, sexual harassment or date rape only humiliate boys and distract us from intervening constructively.

These misdiagnoses lead to some rather chilling remedies. Gurian (1998) suggests reviving corporal punishment, both at home and at school – but only when administered privately with cool indifference and never in the heat of adult anger. He calls it 'spanking responsibly', though school boards and child welfare agencies might call it child abuse (p. 175). Such overly simplistic explanations, which rely on a biologically deterministic argument, ignore the evidence that boys are not just boys everywhere and in the same way. Few European nations would boast of such violent, homophobic and misogynist adolescent males. This begs the question: if it is all so biological, why are Norwegian or French or Swiss boys so different?

Boyhood as therapeutic opportunity

Another group of therapists eschew testosterone-tinged testimonials, and treat masculinity as an ideology that needs to be challenged. Kindlon and Thompson (1999) write that peers present a young boy with a 'culture of cruelty' in which he is forced to deny emotional neediness, 'routinely disguise his feelings' and end up feeling emotionally isolated. Pollack (1998) calls it the 'boy code' and the 'mask of masculinity' – a kind of swaggering posture that boys embrace to hide their fears, suppress dependency and vulnerability, and present a stoic, impervious front.

Pollack's observations provide an important parallel to the work on girls. Gilligan's (1997) astonishing and often moving work on adolescent girls describes how these assertive, confident and proud young girls 'lose their voices' when they reach adolescence. At the same moment, boys become more confident, even beyond their abilities. Boys suddenly find their voices – as girls lose confidence, boys seem to gain it – but it is the inauthentic voice of bravado, of constant posturing, of foolish risk-taking and gratuitous violence. The boy code teaches them that they are supposed to be in power, and thus begin to act like it. In fact, recent research on the gender gap in school achievement illustrates that girls suppress ambition and boys inflate it. In other words, girls are more likely to undervalue their abilities, especially in the more traditionally 'masculine' educational arenas such as maths and science. Only the most able and most secure girls take such courses. Thus, their numbers tend to be few, and their grades high. Boys, however, possessed of this false voice of bravado (and many facing strong family pressure), are likely to *over-value* their abilities, to remain in programmes though they are less qualified and capable of succeeding.

This difference, and not some putative discrimination against boys, is the reason that girls' mean test scores in maths and science are now, on average, approaching that of boys. Too many boys who over-value their abilities remain in difficult maths and science courses longer than they should; they pull the boys' mean scores down. By contrast, few girls, whose abilities and self-esteem are sufficient to enable them to 'trespass' into a male domain, skew female data upwards. This is something that has been highlighted in the discussion about the dichotomy of 'failing boys' and 'successful girls' in the British and Australian contexts.

A parallel process is at work in the humanities and social sciences. Girls' mean test scores in English and foreign languages, for example, also outpace boys. But this is not the result of 'reverse discrimination,' but because the boys bump up against the norms of masculinity. Boys regard English as a 'feminine' subject. Research in Australia by Wayne Martino found that boys are uninterested in English because of what it might say about their (inauthentic) masculine pose. 'Reading is lame, sitting down and looking at words is pathetic', commented one boy. 'Most guys who like English are faggots', commented another. The traditional liberal arts curriculum is seen as feminizing; as Stimpson (1998) recently put it sarcastically, 'real men don't speak French'. Boys tend to hate English and foreign languages for the same reasons that girls love it. In English, they observe, there are no hard and fast rules, but rather one expresses one's opinion about the topic and everyone's opinion is equally valued. 'The answer can be a variety of things, you're never really wrong', observed one boy. 'It's not like maths and science where there is one set answer to everything' (see Martino 1997).

It is not the school experience that 'feminizes' boys, but rather the ideology of traditional masculinity that keeps boys from wanting to succeed. 'The work you do here is girls' work', one school boy recently commented to a researcher. 'It's not real work.' It's the ideology of traditional masculinity that inhibits boys' development as well as girls' development. Boys eschew school work for the anti-intellectual rough and tumble; girls' achievement is inhibited by the incessant teasing and harassment of those rough and tumble boys. Most therapeutic analyses, however, do not touch these questions; it is always fears suppressed, pain swallowed. Kindlon and Thompson (1999), for example, write that the 'culture of cruelty imposes a code of silence on boys, requiring them to suffer without speaking of it and to be silent witnesses to acts of cruelty to others' (p. 92). But where does it give them permission to become victimizers?

The complexities of the social experiences of boys and girls negotiating their way through adolescence and schooling, however, is largely ignored by these therapists who rely on their clinical practices for examples, but then generalize from their patients to *all* boys. And 'all' boys refers to middle-class, suburban, white, heterosexual boys. Cute blond boys stare at us from all the books' covers, while inside the authors ignore large numbers of boys whose pain and low self-esteem may have to do with insecurities and anxieties that are somewhat more concrete. Gurian's books disingenuously place one boy of colour on each cover, but no real discussion of race in the book. Similarly, Thompson and Kindlon generalize from their work at an elite prep school. This tendency to homogenize boys also extends to issues of sexuality. In much of the therapeutic literature there is a sense that all boys are white, middle-class and heterosexual. Most casually treat homosexuality, dropping in a brief mention, 'explaining' it as biological, and urging compassion and understanding before returning to the important stuff. Only Pollack devotes a sensitive and carefully thought-out chapter to homosexuality, dismissing biological claims and actually using the term 'homophobia'.

Confronting privilege requires different strategies for intervention. Not surprisingly, the most coherent programmes are offered not by therapists at all. No 'rescuing' or 'protecting' for British high school teachers Salisbury and Jackson (1996) – they want, as their title indicates, to 'challenge' traditional masculinity, to disrupt the facile 'boys will be boys' model, and to erode boys' sense of entitlement. And for community activist Paul Kivel (1999) (he co-founded the Oakland's Men's Project), raising boys to manhood means confronting racism, sexism, homophobia – both in our communities and in ourselves. Their books are loaded with hands-on practical advice to allow adolescents to raise issues, confront fears, overcome anxieties and allow teachers to dispel myths, encourage cooperation, and discourage violent solutions to perceived problems. The most valuable material helps boys deconstruct sexuality myths and challenge sexual harassment and violence. 'We believe that masculine violence is intentional, deliberate, and purposeful', claim Salisbury and Jackson. 'It comes from an attempt by men and boys to create and sustain a system of masculine power and control that benefits them every minute of the day' (p. 108). Both these books, in fact, are the only ones to recognize that not all boys are the same, and that one key to enabling boys to express a wider range of emotions is to challenge the power and privilege that is part of their cultural heritage.

The therapists know that being a boy can mean the isolation and chronic anxiety of having to prove your manhood every second. Boyhood is a constant, relentless testing of manhood. And it is also freedom from manhood's responsibilities, and can mean the exhilaration of physical challenge and athletic triumph, the blushing, tentative thrill of first sexual exploration, the carefree play. However, boyhood also means the entitlement to get your way, to be heard, the often invisible privileges that come from being a man, the ability to see your reflection (at least if you are also white and hetero-sexual) in virtually every television show, action-hero comic book and movie, and be seated at every board room in the nation. In short, boyhood is the entitlement to and the anticipation of power.

The 'other' boy crisis

Such an argument leads to the 'real' boy crisis in America – not the crisis of inverted proportions that claims boys are the new victims of a feminist-inspired agenda run amok. The real boy crisis usually goes by another name known as 'teen violence,' 'youth violence,' 'gang violence,' 'suburban viol-ence,' 'violence in the schools'. And girls are certainly not perpetuating such acts of violence. But imagine if all the killers in all the high school shootings in America – in Littleton, Pearl, Paducah, Springfield, and Jonesboro – were all black girls from poor families who lived instead in New Haven, Newark, or Providence. There would certainly be a national debate about inner-city poor black girls. The entire focus would be on race, class, and gender. The media would invent a new term for their behaviour, as with 'wilding'[2] a decade ago. We would hear about the culture of poverty; about how living in the city breeds crime and violence; about some putative natural tendency among blacks towards violence. Someone would even blame feminism for causing girls to become violent in vain imitation of boys. Yet the obvious fact that these school killers were all middle-class white boys seems to have escaped most people's attention.

The real boy crisis is a crisis of violence, about the cultural prescriptions that equate masculinity with the capacity for violence. This is supported by the following statistics:

- Men and boys are responsible for 95 per cent of all violent crimes in this country.
- Every day twelve boys and young men commit suicide – seven times the number of girls.
- Every day eighteen boys and young men die from homicide – ten times the number of girls.
- From an early age, boys learn that violence is not only an acceptable form of conflict resolution, but one that is admired.
- Four times more teenage boys than teenage girls think fighting is appro-priate when someone cuts into the front of a line.
- Half of all teenage boys get into a physical fight each year.

The belief that violence is manly is not a trait carried on any chromosome, not soldered into the wiring of the right or left hemisphere, not juiced by testosterone (it is still the case that half the boys do not fight, most do not carry weapons, and almost all do not kill: are they not boys?). Boys learn it.

Violence, Gilligan (1997) writes, 'has far more to do with the cultural construction of manhood than it does with the hormonal substrates of biology' (p. 223).

Feminism and the boy crisis

Feminism has been helpful in this sense because it has offered the most trenchant critique of that cultural construction. The women's movement accomplished, at least partly, two important goals. First, women challenged all forms of gender discrimination – against both women and girls. Through every portal once closed to women – every profession, including the science and medicine, the military and its training colleges, every college and university – women have marched, despite all the putative biological evidence that women could not accomplish this, or, if they could, that they should not want to do it. As a result, the women's movement offered to young women a set of new role models – strong, accomplished, assertive, competent, creative. More young girls idealize Mia Hamm these days than boys idolize Michael Jordan. Here boys have been left behind. Gone are the bastions of untrammelled masculinity, the Virginia Military Institutes and the fire departments, Princeton and Yale. Despite all the models that encourage girls to be strong and assertive, there are precious few that encourage boys (or men, for that matter) to be as compassionate as they are competent, as able to express emotions as they are to excel professionally. These days, it is far easier for a girl to be a tomboy than a boy to be a sissy.

Feminism has also changed the rules of conduct – in the workplace, where sexual harassment is no longer business as usual, on dates, where attempted date rape is no longer 'dating etiquette', and in schools, where both subtle and overt forms of discrimination against girls – from being shuffled off to home economics when they want to take physics, or excluded from military schools and gym classes, to anatomy lectures using pornographic slides have been successfully challenged. Moreover, there have also been legal cases that have confronted bullying, and sexual harassment by teachers and peers.

In addition, feminism has offered a blueprint for a new boyhood and masculinity based on a passion for justice, a love of equality, and expression of a fuller emotional palette. So it is not surprising that feminists will be blamed for male bashing. In fact, it would appear that the anti-feminist right wing are the real male bashers. When apologists like Michael Gurian – or, in Australia, Steve Biddulph – claim that boys will be boys, they are promoting a particular version of masculinity which is treated unproblematically as an effect of biological sex differences. In fact, over a decade ago, feminist critic Miedzian (1991) offered the only reasonable response to these insulting images of an unchangeable hard-wired violent manhood. Even if we assume that the propensity for violence is innate, the inevitable fruition of that prenatal testosterone cocktail, we still must decide whether to organize society so as to maximize boys' 'natural' predisposition towards violence, or to minimize it. Biology alone cannot answer that question, and claiming that boys will be boys only leads us to abandon our social and political responsibility.

Conclusion

In this chapter we have attempted to address some of the complexities and problems surrounding the ways in which boys' educational issues in Australia, the United States and the United Kingdom have been articulated. What we have emphasized is that boys have emerged as a target for specific prob-lematization by the popular media, certain educationists and men's move-ment advocates in terms which are governed by a particular feminist backlash rhetoric. In this sense, attention has been drawn to the fact that the problems boys are experiencing in schools and the wider society are not new (Cohen 1998). Moreover, in these times such problems are often understood to be attributed to the direct exclusionary effects of a feminist political agenda designed to promote the interests of girls. We believe that it is important for those involved in curriculum development, teaching and policy formulation in schools and education departments to gain a detailed understanding of the politicized nature of the ways in which these debates about the boys have been conducted and in so doing develop an informed perspective on how to address the issues facing boys and girls in school.

Notes

1 Each contributor submitted an account of the boys' education debate in his or her own country which was then worked into the chapter in its present form by the editors of the book. We would like to emphasize that no one author is responsible for the words of the other.
2 'Wilding' was a term that was invented by the media in the aftermath of the brutal assault and gang rape of a young white female investment banker by a group of young black and Latino males in Central Park, New York City. It referred to the way that these young minority youths were out of control, and enjoyed sexual and physical predation as sport or simply a way to pass the time.

References

Arnot, M. and Dillabough, J. (2000) *Challenging Democracy: Feminist Perspectives on the Education of Citizens.* London: Routledge.
Arnot, M., David, M. and Weiner, G. (1996) *Educational Reforms and Gender Equality in Schools.* Manchester: Equal Opportunities Commission.

Arnot, M., David, M. and Weiner, G. (1999) *Closing the Gender Gap: Postwar Education and Social Change.* London: Polity Press.

Ball, S. (1994) *Education Reform.* Buckingham: Open University Press.

Bittman, M. and Pixley, J. (1997) *The Double Life of the Family: Myth, Hope and Experience.* Sydney: Allen and Unwin.

Bleach, K., with Blagden, T., Ebbutt, D., Green, A. *et al.* (1996) *What Difference Does It Make? An Investigation of Factors Influencing the Motivation and Performance of Year 8 Boys in a West Midlands Comprehensive School.* Wolverhampton: University of Wolverhampton, Educational Research Unit.

Brown, M. (1994) Educational opportunities for gifted and talented boys. *Gifted.* NSW Association for Gifted and Talented Children, 3–4.

Change: Transformations in Education (1998) 1 (2) November. University of Sydney.

Clarricoates, K. (1983) Classroom interaction, in J. Whyld (ed.) *Sexism in the Secondary Curriculum.* London: Harper and Row.

Code, L. (1991) *Feminist Theory and the Construction of Knowledge.* Ithaca, NY: Cornell University Press.

Cohen, M. (1998) 'A habit of healthy idleness': boys' underachievement in historical perspective, in D. Epstein., J. Elwood, V. Hey and J. Maw (eds) *Failing Boys? Issues in Gender and Achievement.* Buckingham: Open University Press.

Collins, C., Batten, M., Ainley, J. and Getty, C. (1996) *Gender and School Education.* Canberra: Australian Council for Educational Research.

Connell, R.W. (1994) Knowing about masculinity, teaching boys and men: education implications of the new sociology of masculinity and the old sociology of schools. Paper for Pacific Sociological Association Conference, San Diego, April.

Connell, R.W. (1995) *Masculinities.* Sydney: Allen and Unwin.

Connolly, P. (1998) *Racism, Gender Identities and Young Children.* London: Routledge.

Cox, E. (1997) Boys and girls and the costs of gendered behaviour, in *Gender Equity: A Framework for Australian Schools.* Canberra: Department of Employment, Education, Training and Youth Affairs.

Daniel, A. (1993) The containment of women. *Connect!* 1 (2): 2–6.

David, M. (1995) The education policy context: the idea of 'parentocracy', 1976–1992, in L. Dawtrey, J. Holland and M. Hammer (eds) *Equality and Inequality in Education Policy.* Clevedon: Multilingual Matters.

de Beauvoir, S. ([1949] 1972) *The Second Sex.* Aylesbury: Penguin.

Dempsey, K. (1997) *Inequalities in Marriage: Australia and Beyond.* Melbourne: Oxford University Press.

DETYA (Department of Education, Training and Youth Affairs) (2000) *Factors Influencing Educational Performance of Males and Females in School and their Initial Destinations after Leaving School.* Canberra: DETYA.

Epstein, D. (1999) quoted in 'Football approach risks an own goal'. *Times Educational Supplement,* 4 June: 9.

Epstein, D., Elwood, J., Hey, V. and Maw, J. (eds) (1998) *Failing Boys? Issues in Gender and Achievement.* Buckingham: Open University Press.

Eveline, J. (1995) The (im)possible reversal: Advantage, education and the process of feminist theorising. *Lararutbildning och Forskning i Umea (Teacher Education and Research in Umea),* published by Umea University, Sweden. 2 (3/4): 29–46.

Eveline, J. (1998) 'Naming male advantage: a feminist theorist looks to the future', in A. Mackinnon, I. Elgqvist-Saltzman and A. Prentice (eds) *Education into the 21st Century: Dangerous Terrain for Women?* London: Falmer.

Foster, V. (1992) Different but equal? Dilemmas in the reform of girls' education. *Australian Journal of Education,* 36 (1): 53–67.

Foster, V. (1995) 'What about the boys!' Presumptive equality in the education of girls and boys. Published proceedings of the National Social Policy Conference, 'Social Policy and the Challenges of Social Change', University of New South Wales, Vol. 1, pp. 81–97.

Foster, V. (1996a) 'Whereas the People' and civics education: another case of 'add women and stir?' *Curriculum Perspectives,* published by Australian Curriculum Studies Association, Canberra. Special issue, 'Reconstructing civics education: *Whereas the People* as a prescription for the new civics', 16 (1): 52–6.

Foster, V. (1996b) Space invaders: desire and threat in the schooling of girls. *Discourse: Studies in the Cultural Politics of Education,* 17 (1): 43–63.

Foster, V. (1997) Feminist theory and the construction of citizenship education in the modern state, in K. Kennedy *Citizenship Education and the Modern State.* London: Falmer.

Foster, V. (1998) Education: a site of desire and threat for Australian girls, in I. Elgqvist-Saltzman, A. Prentice and A. Mackinnon, *Education into the 21st Century: Dangerous Terrain for Women?* London: Falmer.

Foster, V. (2000a) Gender, schooling achievement and post-school pathways: beyond statistics and populist discourse, in S. Dinham and C. Scott (eds) *Teaching in Context.* Canberra: Australian Council for Educational Research.

Foster, V. (2000b) Is female educational 'success' destabilising the male learner-citizen?, in M. Arnot and J. Dillabough (eds) *Challenging Democracy: Feminist Perspectives on the Education of Citizens.* London: Routledge.

Francis, B. (1999) quoted in 'Football approach risks an own goal'. *Times Educational Supplement,* 4 June: 9.

Frith, R. and Mahony, P. (1994) *Promoting Quality and Equality in Schools.* London: David Fulton.

Gatens, M. (1991) *Feminism and Philosophy: Perspectives on Difference and Equality.* Cambridge: Polity Press.

Gatens, M. (1997) *Imaginary Bodies: Ethics, Power and Corporeality.* Cambridge: Polity Press.

Gilbert, P. (1996) *Talking about Gender: Terminology Used in the Education of Girls Policy Area and Implications for Policy Priorities and Programs.* Canberra: Australian Government Printing Service.

Gilbert, P. (1998) Gender and schooling in new times: the challenge of boys and literacy. *Australian Educational Researcher,* 25 (1) April: 15–36.

Gilbert, R. and Gilbert, P. (1995) Technologies of schooling and the education of boys. Paper presented to the annual conference of the Australian Sociological Association, Newcastle, 4–8 December.

Gilbert, R. and Gilbert, P. (1998) *Masculinity Goes to School.* Sydney: Allen and Unwin.

Gillborn, D. (1997) Racism and reform: new ethnicities/old inequalities. *British Educational Research Journal,* 23 (3): 345–60.

Gilligan, J. (1997) *Violence.* New York, NY: Vintage.

Griffin, C. (1998) Representations of youth and the 'boys' underachievement' debate: just the same old stories? Paper presented to Gendering the Millennium Conference, University of Dundee, 11–13 September.

Gurian, M. (1996) *The Wonder of Boys.* New York, NY: Tarcher/Putnam.

Gurian, M. (1998) *A Fine Young Man.* New York, NY: Tarcher/Putnam.

Hargreaves, D.H. (1967) *Social Relations in a Secondary School*. London: Routledge and Kegan Paul.

Johnson, W. (1994) Initiatives for boys. *Education: Journal of the NSW Teachers' Federation*, September 24.

Jones, C. (1985) Sexual tyranny: male violence in a mixed secondary school, in G. Weiner (ed.) *Just a Bunch of Girls*. Milton Keynes: Open University Press.

Kenway, J. (1995) Masculinities in schools: under siege, on the defensive and under reconstruction?. *Discourse*, 16 (1): 59–79.

Kindlon, D. and Thompson, M. (1999) *Raising Cain: Protecting the Emotional Life of Boys*. New York, NY: Ballantine.

Kivel, P. (1999) *Boys Will be Men*. Philadelphia, PA: New Society Publishers.

Koerner, B. (1999) 'Where the boys aren't'. *US News and World Report*, February 8.

Korosi, G., Parkinson, G., Rimmer, R.J. and Rimmer, S.M. (1993) Rising inequality? Shifts in the distributions of earnings and incomes among young Australians. Draft paper prepared for the 1993 National Social Policy Conference, Rethinking the Fundamentals, University of New South Wales, July.

Lacey, C. (1970) *Hightown Grammar*. Manchester: Manchester University Press.

Lamb, S. and McKenzie, P. (1999) *Patterns of Success and Failure in the Transition from School to Work in Australia*. Canberra: Australian Council for Educational Research.

Lararutbildning och Forskning i Umea (Teacher Education and Research in Umea) (1995) 2 (3/4). Umea: University of Umea.

Lingard, B. and Douglas, P. (1999) *Men Engaging Feminisms*. Buckingham: Open University Press.

Lloyd, G. (1984) *The Man of Reason: 'Male' and 'Female' in Western Philosophy*. London: Methuen.

Luke, C. and Gore, J. (1992) *Feminisms and Critical Pedagogies*. New York, NY: Routledge.

Mac an Ghaill, M. (1994) *The Making of Men: Masculinities, Sexualities and Schooling*. Buckingham: Open University Press.

Mackinnon, A., Elgqvist-Saltzman, I. and Prentice, A. (1998) *Education into the 21st Century: Dangerous Terrain for Women?* London: Falmer.

Mahony, P. and Smedley, S. (1998) New times, old panics: the underachievement of boys. *Change: Transformations in Education*, Published the University of Sydney, 1 (2), November: 41–50.

Martino, W. (1997) Gendered learning practices: exploring the costs of hegemonic masculinity for girls and boys in schools, in *Gender Equity: A Framework for Australian Schools*. Canberra: Ministerial Council for Employment, Education, Training and Youth Affairs.

Miedzian, M. (1991) *Boys will be Boys: Breaking the Link Between Masculinity and Violence*. New York, NY: Doubleday.

Mills, M. (1998) Challenging violence in schools: disruptive moments in the educational politics of masculinity. Unpublished PhD thesis, University of Queensland.

Mirza, H. (1992) *Young, Female and Black*. London: Routledge.

Morris, E. (1996) *Boys Will Be Boys? Closing the Gender Gap*. Labour Party consultation paper.

Mortimore, P. and Whitty, G. (1997) *Can School Improvement Overcome the Effects of Disadvantage?* London: Institute of Education.

Murphy, P. and Elwood, J. (1998) Gendered learning outside and inside school: influences on achievement, in D. Epstein, J. Elwood, V. Hey and J. Maw (eds) *Failing Boys? Issues in Gender and Achievement*. Buckingham: Open University Press.

NSW Board of Studies (1996) *The Report of the Gender Project Steering Committee.* Sydney: NSW Board of Studies.

NSW Ministry of Education and Youth Affairs (1989) *Education and Training Strategy for Women.* Sydney: NSW Ministry of Education and Youth Affairs.

Parker, H.J. (1974) *View from the Boys.* Newton Abbot: David and Charles.

Pateman, C. (1988) *The Sexual Contract.* Cambridge: Polity Press.

Pateman, C. and Gross, E. (eds) (1986) *Feminist Challenges: Social and Political Theory.* Sydney: Allen and Unwin.

Penn, H. (1998) Summary: men as workers in services for young children, in C. Owen, C. Cameron and P. Moss (eds) *Men as Workers in Services for Young Children: Issues of a Mixed Gender Workforce,* Bedford Way Papers. London: Institute of Education, University of London.

Pickering, J. (1997) *Raising Boys' Achievement.* London: Network Educational Press.

Pollack, W. (1998) *Real Boys: Rescuing our Sons from the Myths of Boyhood.* New York, NY: Henry Holt.

Probyn, E. (1993) *Sexing the Self: Gendered Positions in Cultural Studies.* London: Routledge.

Raphael Reed, L. (1998) 'Zero tolerance': gender performance and school failure, in D. Epstein, J. Elwood, V. Hey and J. Maw (eds) *Failing Boys? Issues in Gender and Achievement.* Buckingham: Open University Press.

Robins, D. and Cohen, P. (1978) *Knuckle-Sandwich: Growing Up in the Working-Class City.* Harmondsworth: Penguin.

Sadker, D. and Sadker, M. (1994) *Failing at Fairness.* New York: Simon and Schuster.

Salisbury, J. and Jackson, D. (1996) *Challenging Macho Values.* London: Falmer.

Skelton, C. (1994) Sex, male teachers and young children. *Gender and Education,* 6 (1): 87–93.

Smedley, S. (1998) Men working with young children: a natural development? in C. Owen, C. Cameron and P. Moss (eds) *Men as Workers in Services for Young Children: Issues of a Mixed Gender Workforce,* Bedford Way Papers. London: Institute of Education, University of London.

Stimpson, C. (1998) *New York Times,* April 13: A-22.

Teese, R., Davies, M., Charlton, M. and Polesel, J. (1995) *Who Wins at School? Boys and Girls in Australian Secondary Education.* Melbourne: University of Melbourne, Department of Education Policy and Management.

Weiner, G., Arnot, M. and David, M. (1997) Is the future female? Female success, male disadvantage and changing gender patterns in education, in A.H. Halsey, P. Brown and H. Lauder, *Education, Economy, Culture and Society.* Oxford University Press.

Whitty, G., Power, S. and Halpin, D. (1998) *Devolution and Choice in Education.* Buckingham: Open University Press.

Willis, P. (1977) *Learning to Labour.* Aldershot: Saxon House.

Wolcott, I. and Glezer, H. (1995) *Work and Family Life: Achieving Integration.* Melbourne: Australian Institute of Family Studies.

Wragg, T.E. (1999) quoted in 'Football approach risks an own goal'. *Times Educational Supplement,* 4 June: 9.

Wright, C. (1986) School process – an ethnographic study, in S. Eggleston, D. Dunn and M. Anjali (eds) *Education for Some: The Educational and Vocational Experiences of 15–18 Year Old Members of Minority Ethnic Groups.* Stoke-on-Trent: Trentham Books.

Yates, L. (1996) 'Understanding the boys' issues: What sort of challenge is it? Paper presented to the American Educational Research Association Annual Conference, Symposium on 'Masculinities and Schooling', New York, April.

Yates, L. (1997) Gender equity and the boys debate: what sort of challenge is it? *British Journal of the Sociology of Education*, 18 (3): 337–47.

Yates, L. and Leder, G. (1996) *The Student Pathways Project: A Review and Overview of National Databases*. Report to the Gender Equity Task Force of the Ministerial Council on Education, Employment, Training and Youth Affairs, Melbourne, La Trobe University.

CHAPTER 2

The significance of teaching English boys: exploring social change, modern schooling and the making of masculinities

CHRIS HAYWOOD AND MÁIRTÍN MAC AN GHAILL

Introduction

Most of the vast literature that has been generated about 'failing boys' – and the associated moral panic accompanying this discourse – is not engaging with contemporary theory on masculinities and sexualities. As a consequence, there is an under-conceptualized understanding of key interrelated elements in discussions about the significance of teaching boys: that of social and cultural transformations, modern schooling, and the sex gender system. Therefore, in this chapter, we suggest that these elements are of central significance in making sense of teaching boys as a social practice. In fact, one of the main arguments in this chapter is that schools are complicit in the production and regulation of young male heterosexualities and, in this sense, are crucial sites where boys learn important lessons about acceptable lifestyles and normalized masculinities. The problem is that an understanding of the production of heterosexual subjectivities has not always been situated within a broader framework that takes account of rapid, socio-cultural and economic changes. More specifically, in an educational context we examine how a politically defined and state-sponsored cultural force of entrepreneurialism has been significant in remasculinizing and resexualizing schooling practices. At the same time, these contextual changes highlight the need for sociologists of education to reconsider critically how we might explore the sex/gender dynamics of boys' and teachers' lives at school.

Social/cultural transformations: the crisis of modern schooling

Much analysis on 'failing boys' is taking place in a socio-economic vacuum. In response important historical questions need to be addressed about why these issues are developing a high political profile. Currently, we are living through a time of rapid global socio-economic and cultural changes in a period of late capitalism (Harvey 1989; Giddens 1990; Jameson 1991). These changes, such as deindustrialization, feminization of labour markets and the diversification of family forms, are contesting and fragmenting traditional lifestyles. Alongside this, education as a postwar representation of the modernist project, involving comprehensive reorganization, child-centred pedagogy, and an anti-oppressive curriculum, underpinned by a belief in universalism, collectivism, humanism, rational progression and social justice, is being destabilized by this emerging socio-economic uncertainty. For example, fundamental changes in the relationship between the reward structures of the school and the labour market has led to great confusion among large sectors of female and male students concerning the purpose of school in preparing them for occupational and social destinies. However, education continues to be a social and cultural refuge for the projection and temporary resolution of English social anxieties, as media representations of school standards are portrayed as national exemplars of social, moral and economic standards. At the same time, schools are actively involved in the production of these anxieties. Current controversies around the absence of male teachers in primary schools, working-class boys' under-achievement and middle-class boys' disaffection are shifting concern away from social minorities to social majorities, with the implication that we are no longer sure about the purpose of education in late modernity (Epstein *et al.* 1998).

The remasculinization of public sector work

Over the last two decades we have witnessed a radical restructuring of English state schooling. This restructuring was located within the more fundamental socio-political changes following the breakdown of the postwar educational settlement, with its main tenet that the role of education was of central strategic importance to the development of economic growth, equality of opportunity and social justice. Schools have been fundamentally restratified with the accompanying privatization, commercialization and commodification of institutions located within competitive local markets. This New Right agenda served to marginalize the quest for social justice and in the process the 'social subject' tended to be discarded. This means that a New Right agenda diminished the significance of categories such as 'gender', 'race/ethnicity' or 'sexuality' and reconstructed 'social' practices within a neo-liberal political framework. As a result, attempts were made to reconfigure the labour process of teaching solely as an economic practice. It was against this background that studies of schooling and masculinities started to be produced, albeit in a rather sketchy and indirect way. The election of a 'New Labour' government has not fundamentally challenged this conservative agenda.

Most importantly this institutional restructuring has involved the re-masculinization of primary and secondary schooling. At a time of rapid change, teachers are currently constructing their work identities within the context of selecting and combining strategic responses to contradictory work-place demands. However, teacher 'choices' cannot be understood in terms of any simple commercial metaphors. In other words, they do not take place in a socio-historical vacuum. Dominant state and occupational discourses cir-cumscribe the 'gendering' and 'regendering' of these different work practices which have resulted in increased complexities and contradictions. A highly salient feature is the promotion of new gender-specific hierarchies of domi-nation and subordination. There is a long history of female teachers identi-fying discriminatory sex role allocation of male teachers to positions of authority and management. More recently, this has been displaced by a growing concern with the remasculinization of the whole workplace. Metcalf (1985: 11) has provided the political and ideological background to this shift from the 'soft' welfare state to the 'harder' new realism of market economics. He writes:

> In the popularization of a monetarist economic policy . . . care has been taken to present these strategies as being proper to the competitive instincts of red-blooded American and British males. The call goes out to kill off all lame ducks, to forswear compassion. It is asserted that in the market place only the fittest should survive, and that a hard, lean industrial sector is necessary. Appeals to machismo and to disdain soft emotions are quite naked, as politicians of the radical right pour scorn on the need to care for the less fortunate, on the whole idea of the welfare state.

Connell (1989: 191) has argued that the institutionalized structure of schooling is central to the production of masculine subjectivities:

> Broadly, the strongest effects of schooling on the construction of mascu-linity are the indirect effects of schooling, of streaming and failure, authority pattern, the academic curriculum, and definitions of knowledge – rather than the direct effects of equity programmes or courses dealing with gender.

At present in English schools the combined effects of the changing labour process of teaching and the emergence of an entrepreneurial curriculum has meant that the restructuring of teaching can be understood as a direct state attempt to remasculinize schooling. The cumulative effect of the restructured authority system with accompanying intensified surveillance, disciplinary codes, curriculum and testing stratification technologies, subject allocation and knowledge selection is serving to demarcate a range of 'new' hierarchically ordered masculinities.

Remasculinizing teacher hierarchies/identities

There are many aspects of modern schooling that could be drawn upon to illustrate the under-conceptualization of boys that is embedded in the 'failing boys' discourse. We, however, are concerned to focus upon the impact of broader social and cultural changes on issues of teaching. We also want to continue the theme that social transformations at institutional levels are simultaneously mediating transformations of social practices. In a study of an English secondary school, Mac an Ghaill (1994) identified three teacher occupational types: the Professionals, the Old Collectivists and the New Entrepreneurs. These constituted the teachers' cultures, which served to shape a range of contradictory and fractured masculine identities that the teachers inhabited. The Professionals represented a group of teachers who supported streaming and subject-based learning, were in favour of norm reference assessment but were opposed to equal opportunity interventions. The Old Collectivists, who embodied an older style of public sector masculinity, identified with themes of collectivism, egalitarianism and meritocracy. The influence of both of these groups on schooling administration and organization was in the descendancy, with the New Entrepreneurs in the ascendancy as the emerging dominant mode of modern masculinity. The New Entrepreneurs were the 'ideal teachers', whose masculinity was developed within the political nexus of managerialism, vocationalism and commercialization, with its values of rationalism, possessive individualism and instrumentalism. This approach to the curriculum and pedagogy was indicative of a broader political renaming of professional teaching. The New Entrepreneurs advocated a *new* professionalism where education initiatives are primarily concerned with the quantitative 'masculine' world of the technology of change rather than the qualitative world of values. Their managerialist approach produced a positivist-based, technicist response that was overly preoccupied with the 'how' rather than the 'why' of curriculum change. The establishment of this entrepreneurial curriculum involved the reworking of conventional 'masculine' commercial and industrial images, in the process of aligning schools with commerce and industry. The school principal as an institutional moral gatekeeper sponsored and promoted a hybrid form of 'new' masculinity, whose main contradictory themes included bureaucratic centralization of control, rationality, overt forms of career ambition, collegiality and delegation. They could be located within the projected post-Fordist era with its emphasis on small-scale, flat hierarchies and flexible team work, within a differentiated market place in which new school systems are helping to shape new teaching cultures. This new professionalism is interrelated to a new 'masculine' authoritarianism, in which overt forms of technologies of power are being displaced by 'modern' forms of technical bureaucratic knowledge. They are developed in the high-tech offices of modern administration, with their dominant discursive themes of managerial efficiency and economic rationality. Johnson (1991: 94), writing in the early 1990s, has captured this modern public sector masculinity. He notes that:

> This is the public (and inner?) narrative of conventional masculinity. It is the story of the classic middle-class career, of the buccaneering entrepreneur, of the hero of the Falklands 'task force' (before he is struck down). It is the story of 'man's mastery over nature'. Here science and techno-social interventions subordinate a complex natural-social reality ('Nature'), with which women and black people are often aligned.

In order to understand more fully the specific sexual/gender dynamics of teaching in English schools, it is necessary to examine the interrelationship between broader themes, such as dominant conceptions of power, authority, management and emotional commitment. A legacy of the restructuring of state schooling in the 1990s is the masculinization of the administrative functions that have come to predominate school life. High status has been ascribed to the 'hard masculine' functions of the accountant, the Key Stage tester, the curriculum coordinator, and the Information and Communications Technology expert. At the same time, female teachers are associated with and directed into the 'soft feminine' functions of profiling and counselling. In short, the remasculinization of teaching is being played out within conventional cultural forms of splitting the rational and the emotional. Seidler (1989: 286) locates the association of authority and masculinity within the Enlightenment tradition, in which reason is defined in opposition to nature, that is our emotions, feelings and desires. He argues that: 'in traditional masculinity terms we can only strive for independence through releasing ourselves from all the forms of dependency'. This makes it difficult for men to acknowledge their emotions and needs without feeling that their masculinity is somehow brought into question (Middleton 1992). Connell (1985: 153) writes of the apparent incompatibility between the conventional positioning of femininity and the disciplinary role of the teacher. He argues that: 'it is a tension about gender itself. Authority, in our society, is felt to be masculine; to assert it is to undermine one's femininity, in other people's eyes and in one's own . . .'. Connel (1985: 155) adds that teaching, which is often seen as a 'soft' job, is not however unambiguously masculine, because it involves emotional manipulation and caring for children, which are traditionally defined in England as women's work. Classroom life is not predisposed to accommodate such emotional ambiguity, that challenges the gender-ascribed 'masculine' function of disciplining and the 'feminine' function of caring/nurturing, with their attendant juxtaposed connotations of physical strength and emotional vulnerability.

Teacher practices: towards a resexualizing

The debate around failing boys has brought into sharper focus this confusion surrounding the purpose of contemporary schooling. Situated within this confusion, we have argued that a remasculinization of schooling is taking place. At a local level, we have argued that this is constituted by various discourses and that a notion of entrepreneuralism signifying a new professionalism has become an ascendant set of values in the modern schooling of boys. At the same time, post-structuralist analysis provides a multidimensional understanding of power that encompasses a range of modalities. In this way, the remasculinization of schooling has profound effects upon the categories of adult/child relationship through which many schooling practices are lived out. Schools shaped by a broader cultural imagination operate as containers, with cultural signs, values, memories, myths and traditions existing as dimensions of Englishness within Britishness, cultural community and identity (Smith 1994).

Mills (1996: 318) argues in his study of a secondary school in Australia: 'The primary effect of the 'professionalism' discourse is that it shapes administrative actions, which reinforce boundaries between the categories of teacher–student to create the perception of consensus.' The impact of 'new professionalism' (outlined above) on teaching in English schools is not predictable. However, emerging from the remasculization of schools is the potential reconstruction of the relationship between teachers and students. Gewirtz (1997) has argued that, due to longer classes, increased paperwork and an emphasis on performance rather than process, the social relations between teacher and pupils have been reshaped. As indicated above, schooling is being reconstructed with values of managerialism, vocationalism and commercialization taking the ascendancy in the educational arena. As a consequence, Gewirtz maintains that such shifts cultivate less sociability between teacher and pupils. There is evidence to suggest that the increasing impact of new professionalism in English schools is reconstituting the categories of teachers/students. Contemporary teaching appears more formalized, dissolving the intimacy and complexity of teacher/student relationships. It could be argued that a move towards a more post-welfarist organization creates contradictions and tensions in modern schooling as welfarism and entrepreneurialism elide.

Central to the remasculinization of teaching is a refocusing on the meaning of childhood. As Franklin (1995: 9) has pointed out: 'Definitions of a "child" and "children" entail more than a specification of an age of majority; they articulate society's values and attitudes towards children.' Knowledge in the ascendant rationalist economy of education has become a cherished commodity and 'clients' (parents) shop around, by way of league tables, for the 'best deal'. Children are conceptualized as value-added knowledge containers. However, the discursive traces of a postwar modern welfarist project continue to have significance in schooling policy. Gillis (1974) has argued

that childhood is a relatively modern construction and our present understanding derives from the ascendancy of welfare institutions in our society.
Historically, the active management of national moral decay has shifted
from understanding children as innately sinful, requiring harsh physical
punishment and excessive regulation, to a notion of innocence and vulnerability (Silin 1995). There has been a move from religious notions of childhood to a more romantic conception that defines boys' identities as morally
contingent; undecided, unshaped and mutable. Alongside a Piagetian notion
of child development, many postwar policy responses to educational reform
have been informed by a welfarist conception of childhood. Other contributors to this book have outlined that a dominant policy response to the problem of 'failing boys' has been to suggest practical interventions designed
to effect recuperation of boys' masculinity (see Chapter I). Echoing earlier
feminist anti-sexist frameworks, such responses assume that masculinity
can be simply written on to the bodies of boys so that if they are exposed
to certain kinds of (more or less) masculinity they will become 'properly'
socialized boys.

English contemporary accounts of masculinity and boyhood tend to leave
out issues of sexuality. Where it does appear, it is 'added on' as part of a
panacea of analytic tools including gender, 'race'/ethnicity, class and age.
However, the recent emergence of a discourse of child abuse (Davies 1993)
alongside the implementation of Section 28 and the homosexual age of
consent in the early 1990s has in part regenerated the ambivalence surrounding teaching boys.[1] Safety and protection are key themes of these
debates and sex education has become a contested site as different moral
alliances seek to define appropriate knowledge and its acceptable transmission (Johnson 1996). As a result teaching practice has come into sharper
critical focus with a range of publicly documented incidents problematizing
professional conduct in schools. More recently, the reintroduction of the
debate over the repeal of Section 28 combined with a moral panic around
teenage pregnancy and sexually transmitted infections has publicly connected
issues of gender with issues of sexuality. In these debates not only are boys
discursively constructed as 'desexualized', but adult masculine sexuality is
inserted into the debate embodied by perverts, strangers, homosexuals and
child abusers.

It can be argued that the policy responses to the 'failing boys', with their
emphasis on social justice and welfarism, not only exist in direct tension
with the remasculinization of schools, but transgress broader social boundaries of the sexual and the non-sexual. The assumption behind a welfarist
concern for boyhood is premised upon a need for care and a need for
intimacy. The dangers of teacher intimacy has been well documented by the
English teaching unions, highlighting teacher vulnerability in issues of child
sex allegations. Alongside this, not only has (men's) professional distance as
a teaching style and emotional practice been heavily policed and regulated,
but language is also an area that requires regulation. For instance, training

manuals aimed at primary schools produced by the Royal College of Nursing were withdrawn because of their 'explicit terminology' (see also Lees 1994). It could be argued that it is a tough masculinity that characterizes the new professionalism, that displaces the 'feminized' and seeks to regulate the caring curriculum. It is in the interconnection of masculinity and sexuality that particular forms of heterosexuality emerge.

Conventional understandings of a masculine sexuality as voracious and biologically determined continue to underpin both heterosexuality and homosexuality in English society. It appears that in the context of schooling, men and sexuality are in conceptual tension. This is illustrated by a court case featured in the national media. They report on a teacher with eighteen years' experience, Mr Baxter, who was claiming damages after his school accused him of serious misconduct. In response to the stealing of a boy's bicycle and the boy being approached by a stranger, Mr Baxter warned a class of 8-year-olds of the possibility of sexual assault. He apparently used inappropriate words to warn pupils that strangers could touch their genitals. The headmaster, backed by the governors, charged Mr Baxter with professional misconduct. As Judith Butler (1997) suggests, language is metynomic. This means that spoken or written words constitute the very actions that they intend to describe. So in the case above, talking about sexuality became sexuality in itself. Words do not merely describe; they are figured as performing what they describe, not only in that they constitute the speaker as sexual, but that they constitute the speech as sexual conduct. The move away from a welfarist teaching ethic complements a broader escalation of social and cultural anxieties around sexuality itself. Men teaching about sexual issues to boys capture these anxieties.

Rethinking the sex/gender system and schooling

During the 1980s and 1990s, research in education opened up the discussion of masculinity and sought to understand it by grounding it in the different social contexts (Connell 1987, 1995; Mac an Ghaill 1994). These studies indicated that the social, ethnic, class and sexual specificities of male identities within local sites influence the range of masculinities that are inhabited. As Connell (1992: 736) claims: 'Different masculinities are constituted in relation to other masculinities and to femininities through the structure of gender relations.' From this perspective, masculinities should be conceptualized in terms of *relationships*. Moving away from the singular 'role' based on gender, masculinities need to be conceptualized in relation to their class, sexual and ethnic locations (Thorne 1993). This has led to the theorizing of masculinity in terms of multiple masculinities (Brittan 1989). Masculinities do not have a one-dimensional identity; rather they embody multiple dimensions. For example, there are white working-class gay masculinities alongside

Asian middle-class heterosexualities. An important development in the theorization of masculinities and schooling is to see that these social locations create the conditions for relations of power. There are different masculinities with differential access to power, practices of power and effects of power.

In placing a multidimensional view of power at the centre of analysis of male students' identity formation, it is important to comprehend fully the complexity of its dynamic within different institutional sites. The conceptual difficulties involved in moving beyond earlier monocausal explanations, that employed 'simple' models of power, are highlighted in an attempt to hold on to the tension between social reproductionist and post-structuralist accounts of male students' identity formation. Post-structuralist theories have been important in moving beyond role model, social reproduction and resistance theories that often assume that young men and women are unitary, rational subjects occupying predictable power positions. The suggestion that there is a range of subject positions that may be occupied within different contradictory discourses is useful; it helps in understanding the local cultural contextual specificity in the production and reproduction of young men's schooling formations (Henriques *et al.* 1984; Walkerdine 1990). On the other hand, the development of male student identities takes place within the continuing materially structured asymmetrical relations of power that constitute the state's hegemonic class divisions and gender/heterosexual arrangements (Walby 1991; Mac an Ghaill 1996).

In emphasizing the need for an inclusive account of multiple forms of social power, we are particularly focusing upon three aspects of post-structuralist theorizing: namely the imbrication of gender and sexuality in the search for 'real' boyness; multiplicity and the making of sexual subjectivity; and finally, inversions and the disruption of the sexual normative.

The search for 'real' boyness

In earlier work we have tried to clarify some of the connections between schooling and 'proper' gender designations (Haywood and Mac an Ghaill 1995). Using an ethnographic methodology, we aimed to analyse some of the ways in which inhabiting particular forms of heterosexual masculinity enables male students to negotiate wider gender relations and the formal/informal culture of schooling. However, it does not immediately explain why these 'proper' forms of masculinity are heterosexual. A question arises: what is it about occupying 'proper' forms of masculinity that almost inevitably implies a heterosexual identity? The answer to this seems to lie in the fact that, in mainstream contemporary Anglo-American cultures at least, heterosexuality and gender are profoundly imbricated. For example, Judith Butler (1993) argues that gender is routinely spoken through a 'heterosexual matrix' in which heterosexuality is presupposed in the expression 'real' forms of masculinity or femininity. Thus she writes (1993: 238):

Although forms of sexuality do not unilaterally determine gender, a non-causal and non-reductive connection between sexuality and gender is nevertheless crucial to maintain. Precisely because homophobia often operates through the attribution of a damaged, failed, or otherwise abject gender to homosexuals, that is, calling gay men 'feminine' or calling lesbians 'masculine', and because the homophobic terror over performing homosexual acts, where it exists, is often also a terror over losing proper gender ('no longer being a real or proper man' or 'no longer being a real or proper woman'), it seems crucial to retain a theoretical apparatus that will account for how sexuality is regulated through the policing and the shaming of gender.

Eve Kosofsky Sedgwick's (1991) work on changes in Anglo-American male–male relations has begun to fill in some of the historical background to this imbrication of gender and sexuality. She argues that the current exclusion of male–male erotic contact from 'proper' forms of masculinity has its origins in an eighteenth-century shift from the religious to the secular discursive construction of sexuality, and that an important consequence of this 'endemic and ineradicable state of homosexual panic' has been the fact that homophobia is used to police the boundaries of acceptable heterosexual male behaviour and identity as well as more overtly (and often violently) being used to police homosexual behaviour and identity. Hence, in structuring the attributes of 'real' boyness, the various forms of masculinity that are hegemonic in English schools can all be argued to be crucially involved in policing the boundaries of heterosexuality as much as the boundaries of 'proper' masculinity.

As research on masculinities develops, international continuities are emerging. For instance, Martino (1999) has highlighted in the Australian context that to be a 'real' boy in schools is to be in opposition to the feminine and to 'feminized' versions of masculinity. At an institutional level, boys' identities are formed in relation to the formal curriculum and the categories it makes available, including the academic/vocational, arts/science, and the academic/ sporting polarities. For example, the 'hard' scientific version of cleverness that is validated in school exists in opposition to supposedly 'soft' subjects like art, music and literature, which are seen as easy options, as essentially frivolous, or somehow lacking in due rigour and seriousness. They are, in effect, girlish subjects not for 'real' boys. Similarly to be 'bad at games' can be read as a cultural index, implying a suspect lack of manly vigour and hinted-at effeminacy, while to be uninterested in the core aspects of 'laddishness' (in particular school opposition, a certain level of working-class credibility, football and the 'pub') is to be a 'bit of a poof'.

This is illustrated within the specificities of an English context by Redman and Mac an Ghaill's (1996) article, 'Schooling sexualities: heterosexual masculinities, schooling and the unconscious', in which they discuss an English student's experiences (Peter) of 'becoming heterosexual' in an all-boys grammar school in the late 1970s and early 1980s. Using an (auto)biographical methodology, they explore the meaning of Peter's investment in a particular form of heterosexual masculinity, what they called 'muscular intellectualness'. We argued that Peter's fascination with the muscular intellectualness he identified in his teacher Mr Lefevre could be understood in terms of the access it promised to give him to the entitlements of conventional masculinity. The world of ideas and knowledge that Mr Lefevre seemed to inhabit no longer seemed effeminately middle-class and thus the object of ridicule or embarrassment, but powerfully middle-class, a source of personal strength and a means to exercise control over others. Thus, as a source of 'real' masculinity, muscular intellectualness 'defeminized' academic work in the humanities and refused the label 'bit of a poof'.

Boyhood sexuality speaks ethnicity, speaks class

As we have argued in this chapter, it is important to conceptualize subjectivity as a process of becoming, characterized by fluidity, oppositions and alliances between particular narrative positions that speak identities (see Davies 1993). This allows a simultaneous relationship between analytic concepts such as age, race/ethnicity, gender, sexuality and class, suggesting that in order to understand identities in educational sites, researchers and teachers need to examine the simultaneous articulations of a dispersed and localized shifting nexus of social power. It is in this sense that we need to understand how sexual identities are simultaneously racialized and gendered.

In early research conducted by one of us with ethnic minority male students an issue emerged that illustrated how one category fails to capture the complexity of boys' social and cultural practices. The two main ethnic groups involved were Asian (Indian, Pakistani and Bangladeshi young men) and African Caribbeans. At the time (the mid-1980s) there was a racist practice called 'paki-bashing', which involved white boys physically and verbally attacking Asian students. A research question emerged: why was there no African Caribbean-bashing? The research framed social behaviour exclusively in terms of racial interaction and hence could not resolve this absence in these terms.

It became apparent that racial politics was simultaneously a sexual and gender politics and the research began to highlight how in the white imagination Asian boys were constructed as a weak masculinity, in relation to the tough masculinity of the African Caribbean boys. The usefulness of exploring school boyhoods as cultural differences, spoken through each other, began to link 'paki-bashing' with 'poofter-bashing', that is physical and verbal attacks by straight people on gays – another soft masculinity, so that to be a 'paki' is to be a 'poof' is to be a 'non-proper' boy. The notion of multiplicity offers a frame for making some sense of the way boys

were policing themselves, particularly within informal peer group cultures/
subcultures.

Inversions and the disruption of the sexual normative

Another aspect of post-structuralism that is helpful in rethinking boyhood
has been to invert predictable logocentric assumptions that surround the
formation of gender/sexual identities that appear in earlier feminist forms
of analysis. Skeggs (1991) in her paper 'Challenging masculinity and using
sexuality' provides a clear illustration of the explanatory power of this
theoretical position. Earlier feminist approaches to the formation of identity
in educational arenas have positioned females as both subordinated females
and students. Skeggs's work on females within a further education college
suggests that being female students did not necessitate a double oppression.
Rather, the females in her study were able to contest the dominant institutional gender/sexual hierarchies. For example, the females would openly
challenge the teachers' sexuality. In doing so, they repositioned themselves
with an active positive female sexuality and simultaneously challenged the
implicit student position as being the object of teaching. Importantly, Skeggs
argues that such displays of power by the young females constituted resistance.
As resistance, she suggests that the discursive space won by the females, in
contesting the dominant gender/sexual categories, were not momentary dis-
ruptions to an all-encompassing dominant gender/sexual discourse. Rather,
the repositioning by the females was an effective means of maintaining and
defending their own identities.

Similar work we have undertaken with black and Asian gays and lesbians
has highlighted their contradictory position within educational arenas that
actively proscribe sexuality. As a consequence, the gay students articulated
the isolation, confusion, marginalization and alienation they experienced in
a secondary school that privileged a naturalized heterosexuality. However,
this account became more complex because their dissonant institutional
location also contained a positive and creative experience. In particular, the
gay and lesbian students had an insight into the contradictory constitution
of a naturalized heterosexuality that was structured through ambivalent
misogyny and homophobia. In this way, gay and lesbian students were able
to occupy positions of power that allowed the contestation and inversion of
heterosexual power. As Matthew, a young gay man illustrates:

> The RE teacher said one day in class that teenagers go through a homo-
> sexual phase just like earlier on they go through an 'anti-girls' phase . . . I
> told him, I did not think that boys go through phases. I said that if boys
> go through an 'anti-girl' phase, it was a long phase because men were
> abusing women all of their lives . . . The teacher went mad. It was gays
> that were supposed to be the problem and I turned it round to show the
> way that it really is . . .

Conclusion

In this chapter we have covered a broad range of issues that connects with the teaching of boys. The focus has been on drawing links between socio-cultural transformations in modern schooling and the need for a conceptual framework that is sensitive to complex sex/gender dynamics. One of the reasons for covering schooling and masculinities in this broader scope is to contribute to the sharpening of critical questions and practice that focus on masculinity issues and teaching boys in schools. Post-structuralist theory, with its focus on examining social relations in terms of fragmentation and discontinuities, has much to offer in developing an understanding of the significance of teaching boys within a globalized context of late capitalism. It is a sociological and a post-structuralist necessity to see such practices as part of the social, cultural and historical webs of meaning and action in which the formation of masculinities and the teaching of boys are implicated.

Acknowledgements

We would like thank Monica Rudberg, the staff and the students for their productive discussions in and out of the seminars on 'Boyhood: the social construction of gender and sexuality' at the Centre of Gender and Women's Studies at Oslo University, Norway, on 11–13 May, 2000.

Note

1 Clause 28 of the Local Government Bill (later Section 28 of the Local Government Act 1988) states that a local authority shall not 'promote the teaching in any maintained school of the acceptance of homosexuality as a pretended family relationship'.

References

Brittan, A. (1989) *Masculinity and Power*. Oxford: Blackwell.
Butler, J.P. (1993) *Bodies that Matter: On the Discursive Limits of 'Sex'*. London: Routledge.
Butler, J.P. (1997) *Excitable Speech: The Politics of the Performative*. London: Routledge.
Connell, R.W. (1985) *Teachers' Work*. London: Allen and Unwin.
Connell, R.W. (1987) *Gender and Power*. Cambridge: Polity Press.
Connell, R.W. (1989) Cool guys, swots and wimps: the interplay of masculinity and education. *Oxford Review of Education*, 15 (3): 291–303.
Connell, R.W. (1992) A very straight gay: masculinity, homosexual experience and the dynamics of gender. *American Sociological Review*, 57 (6): 735–51.
Connell, R.W. (1995) *Masculinities*. Cambridge: Polity.
Davies, B. (1993) *Shards of Glass: Children, Reading and Writing beyond Gendered Identities*. Sydney: Allen and Unwin.

Epstein, D., Elwood, J., Hey, V. and Maw, J. (eds) (1998) *Failing Boys? Issues in Gender and Achievement*. Buckingham: Open University Press.

Franklin, B. (1995) *The Handbook of Children's Rights: Comparative Policy and Practice*. London: Routledge.

Gewirtz, S. (1997) Post-welfarism and the reconstruction of teachers' work in the UK. *Journal of Education Policy*, 12 (4): 217–31.

Giddens, A. (1990) *The Consequences of Modernity*. Oxford: Polity.

Gillis, J.R. (1974) *Youth and History: Tradition and Change in European Age Relations 1770 – present*. London: Academic Press.

Harvey, D. (1989) *The Conditions of Post-Modernity*. Oxford: Blackwell.

Haywood, C. and Mac an Ghaill, M. (1995) The sexual politics of the curriculum: contesting values. *International Studies in Sociology of Education*. 5 (2): 221–36.

Henriques, J., Hollway, W., Urwin, C., Venn, C. and Walkerdine, V. (1984) *Changing the Subject: Psychology, Social Regulation and Subjectivity*. London: Methuen.

Jameson, F. (1991) *Postmodernism or the Cultural Logic of Late Capitalism*. London: Verso.

Johnson, R. (1991) My New Right education, in University of Birmingham, Dept of Cultural Studies, Education Group II (eds) *Education Limited: Schooling, Training and the New Right in England Since 1979*. Winchester, MA: Unwin Hyman.

Johnson, R. (1996) Sexual dissonances: or the 'impossibility' of sexuality education, in M.J. Kehily, C. Haywood and M. Mac an Ghaill (eds) *Curriculum Studies*, 4 (2): 163–89.

Lees, S. (1994) Talking about sex in sex education. *Gender and Education*, 6 (4): 281–91.

Mac an Ghaill, M. (1994) *The Making of Men: Masculinities, Sexualities and Schooling*. Buckingham: Open University Press.

Mac an Ghaill, M. (1996) (ed.) *Understanding Masculinities*. Buckingham: Open University Press.

Martino, W. (1999) 'Cool boys', 'party animals', 'squids' and 'poofters': interrogating the dynamics and politics of adolescent masculinities in school. *British Journal of Sociology of Education*, 20 (2): 239–63.

Metcalf, A. (1985) Introduction, in A. Metcalf and M. Humphries (eds) *The Sexuality of Men*. London: Pluto Press.

Middleton, P. (1992) *The Inward Gaze: Masculinity and Subjectivity in Modern Culture*. London: Routledge.

Mills, M. (1996) Homophobia kills: disruptive moments in the educational politics of legitimation. *British Journal of Sociology of Education*, 17: 315–26.

Redman, P. and Mac an Ghaill, M. (1996) Schooling sexualities: heterosexual masculinities, schooling, and the unconscious. *Discourse*, 17 (2): 243–56.

Sedgwick, E.K. (1991) *Epistemology of the Closet*. London: Harvester Wheatsheaf.

Seidler, V.J. (1989) *Rediscovering Masculinity: Reason, Language and Sexuality*. London: Routledge.

Silin, J.G. (1995) *Sex, Death, and the Education of Children: Our Passion for Ignorance in the Age of AIDS*. New York, NY: Teachers College Press.

Skeggs, B. (1991) Challenging masculinity and using sexuality. *British Journal of Sociology of Education*, 12: 127–40.

Smith, A.M. (1994) *New Right Discourse on Race and Sexuality: Britain, 1968–1990*. Cambridge: Cambridge University Press.

Thorne, B. (1993) *Gender Play: Girls and Boys in School*. Buckingham: Open University Press.

Walby, S. (1991) *Theorizing Patriarchy*. London: Basil Blackwell.

Walkerdine, V. (1990) *Schoolgirl Fictions*. London and New York, NY: Verso.

CHAPTER 3

Rethinking masculinities: new ideas for schooling boys

MICHAEL C. REICHERT

Introduction

Around the world, there are concerns about boys' educational achievement, their health, their relationships with each other – to the point that a collection such as this book seems warranted. Where before such dimensions of boys' experience resisted scrutiny, schools today grope through the darkness of hopelessly inadequate theory to recalculate their curricula for boys. As Connell observed (1996: 207):

> It is clear from the responses to current debates about boys that many teachers and parents see these issues as urgent. Schools are launching 'Programs for Boys' whether researchers and policy makers give them guidance or not.

Such new concern about boys, however, does not assure improvement in their lives. Lavish attention has not historically produced boys who are better off. Lefkowitz's (1997) chronicle of the most popular and darling boys in a New Jersey town's high school, who mistook the town's indulgence towards them as permission to abuse and rape, reminds us that attention alone does not necessarily free boys for healthier or more just lives.

In fact, the obscuring myths of biological determinism on the one hand, and of corrupting privilege on the other, have kept us from appreciating the degree to which boys' lives develop within institutional structures that are carefully, if often unconsciously, arranged to produce particular outcomes. From conception on, male children are embraced and enfolded in an unremitting system of allure, control and punishment, in which certain ideas have blanketed and suppressed all alternatives (Miedzian 1991; Silverstein

1994; Pollack 1998). The point of this curriculum is the production of men prepared to uphold traditional identities and systems of relations (for example Heward 1988). No price seems too high to ensure its success.

However, at a boys' day school in south eastern Pennsylvania, historic commitment to boys was leveraged following an enrolment crisis into a strategic decision to become 'both a laboratory for providing the best practices for the education of boys and a beacon whose leadership in teaching them will be a model for other schools' (The Haverford School 1994). The Trustees and administrators of the school created an 'On Behalf of Boys' project, designed to serve as a centre for research, discussion, self-reflection and advocacy. A psychologist serving at the school at the time, I was asked to direct this effort. Inviting national scholars on to a Research Advisory Board, conducting a survey of the past thirty years' graduates (Addelston 1995), holding symposia for parents on raising sons and encouraging teachers' inquiry into the effectiveness of the tacit curriculum were some of our early moves. Spotty, fraught with contention, resistance, projection and misunderstanding, the school's pursuit of this mission nonetheless permitted experiments for rethinking masculinities.

This chapter chronicles the story of the early years of this programme, during which boys outlined their co-construction of identities and positions as men and the school endeavoured to respond with new initiatives intended to support their imaginations and lives. The first section analyses the story told by one young man, the consummate 'winner' and a 'lifer' at the school, of his travels from age 5 to age 18 through the highly evolved, carefully patrolled and deeply affecting programme for boys. The second section expands the focus, taking into account the relations boys construct among themselves, viewing the school less as an agent and more as a 'site of gender production' (Connell 1996) which facilitates certain types of interactions among boys. The final section recounts the efforts of the school to respond to insights derived from this ear to boys' stories, to create opportunities for them to imagine new destinies.

A boy and his school: where the hallways lead

I met in 1994–95 for a series of interviews with a graduate of the school. This young man, whom we may call Ed, then a junior at a highly selective Eastern US university, had been a 'lifer' (attending from kindergarten through to 12th grade) at the school. He had been a success from most viewpoints – an awarded student and athlete, popular and well-respected – and seemed a good starting point for our inquiry into the school's man-making. At the outset, Ed outlined certain features of the school's design which had influenced his thinking about himself as a boy. These 'masculinizing practices' (Connell 1996), as well as their purpose, were vivid features of the school in his memory:

There was a definite point from 3rd grade to 4th grade where at 3rd, and all before 3rd grade, you had all woman teachers, sort of mother figures almost. And that's very much what they were. They were very kind to you and everything, you know, like they did your homework with you, they explained it very nicely and concretely. They treated you like children. And then 4th grade came, where you had all male teachers. From that point on it was all male teachers.

The message to him conveyed by these school practices was neither subtle nor solicitous. The idea that boys simply must manage an abrupt transition from childhood to boyhood was infused into all aspects of school design and structure:

There was even a separate hallway. But the 3rd, 2nd and 1st hallway went north–south and the 4th, 5th and 6th went east–west. There was this sharp corner, you turned this corner and there you were. And everything was bigger, brighter and stronger. You know, more pressure. It was all, sort of, denoted by this all-male environment, where it had been a male–female environment before.

The school's physical design, its teacher assignments and its vision of the purpose of boys' lives were all premised on ideas about difference and dissociation: that males are distinguished from females, that the way to manhood involves a repudiation of the 'other' and a willingness to assume male duties, constraints and prerogatives:

But it was at this point where we were expected to grow up just a little bit. We sort of moved away from being mothered to being taught and being pushed along these paths. That's the point where we were expected to start taking notes in class, to understand everything without being shown it every single time, pulled through every single time.

In Ed's story, we hear of early childhood encounters with a ubiquitous and powerful prescription for manhood. As Martino (1999) found in his study of adolescent boys in an Australian school, separating boys from the feminine is often a powerful feature in the design of a school, signalling a series of distinctions and obligations about the trajectories boys are expected to follow. This prescription is often taught to boys in many ways, on many levels, in an emotionally compelling discourse about manhood and valour. In an address delivered to students at Ed's school by a popular teacher, lessons about boys' lot were persuasively argued:

Perhaps more than any other human endeavour, trying to learn something teaches the hard but precious lesson that nothing of value in this life can be ours without hard work – with the sole exception, perhaps, of our mothers' love. Real learning is a difficult business, and if the life of the mind is increasingly rewarding and fulfilling, it is also always taxing, enervating, and just plain hard. It is also usually lonely.

Innocent, trusting and dutiful boys, led to manhood; social spaces filled with custom, design and practice: these were basic ingredients in the formation of male identities remembered by Ed. School cultures invent, develop and fine-tune such recipes in their work of channelling children's choices, striving to make the dominant conception of possibility – 'hegemonic masculinity', as Donaldson (1993) defined it – a matter of 'common sense'. The point seems to be an overdetermined social practice within the school which compels and dominates imagination. As Dale explained (1982: 157):

> Hegemony is not so much about winning approval for the status quo, winning consent for it or even acceptance of it. Rather what seems to be involved is the prevention of rejection, opposition or alternatives to the status quo through denying the use of the school for such purposes.

Thus, we found many other ingredients to the recipe for helping boys to manhood at this historic school, each contributing to the goal of occupying the minds and hearts of those in the community. Role modelling, for example, was an idea used to explain the gendered division of labour among faculty. Ed spoke of the arrival on centre stage, upon the departure of the 'mother figure' female teacher, of the male role model teacher: 'the intellectual giants of the community. People who were very intelligent, very involved, very assertive and strong':

> We were the ones who were being told all this whole way that the greatest people in the community were the assertive, strong people, confident people. And when you've got this leader in the room who sort of keeps you in control, it helps you. Everybody recognizes that the teacher in the front is the one who's supposed to have the power and control, that he's the aggressive person, he's the person in control at the time.

Such ideals of manhood not only point the way forward. They also suggest what a man should not be, what failure would involve, what alternative views of manhood boys should eschew. Donaldson characterized this curriculum, found at Ed's school and many others, when he wrote of hegemonic masculinity: 'It is exclusive, anxiety provoking, internally and hierarchically differentiated, brutal and violent' (1993: 646). Boys are assiduously instructed not just in what to emulate but also in what to avoid. Ed remembered an experience which taught him lessons about the intersection of power and identity:

> Chemistry I didn't learn a single thing. The teacher was like a joke. We ruled on him all the time. We set fire to things, burned stuff, chairs, people's prescription medicine, smoke would be everywhere and we'd have to clear out the class for a day, people were getting sick. He just had no control whatsoever because he wasn't the assertive type, he wasn't the, you know, hammer everything down and make sure he's in control. We immediately took control.

Through the domination of such normative ideals and their embeddedness within practices, structures and roles, schools manage to direct and limit boys' sense of what will be okay and what not. Ed characterized the ideal in this way:

> It was all about how the outward self creates an image onto the inward self which is one, almost, of superiority. The clothes – the tie, the jacket – are all part of this grand idealized picture of the intellectual, competent, aggressive male. You know, the high-powered Wall Street accountant, in his power tie and all that jazz. It was all about creating that image and being part of that image, building that image for yourself and building those characteristics for yourself.

In the same way, sports were prominent in the life of Ed's school. And, again, Ed appreciated their contribution to the construction of the finished product, the 'Haverford Man':

> Athletics, just like every other activity, was a way of finding something you were good at and excelling at it. And using that to build confidence for yourself and build this feeling that you can rule the world if you want, you can do anything you want to, you are good and you are able, you can do it. Part of this whole abstract male thing is being good, being good at something or other, excelling at it. Being superior at it. And what Haverford tries very hard at, is excellence. Sort of strives for this model of excellence, which includes all of these things, which includes athleticism and artistic talent, intellectualism, music. And people who excel are all held up on these pedestals as great people, as who you want to strive to be.

The school's lavish attention to its masculinizing ideals, as we have said, directed attention away from as much as toward. Ed spoke about the pressures for conformity implicit in this curriculum, his realization that well before he could imagine being a man himself he sensed a controlling destiny held for him:

> When you are 12, 13, 14 years old, masculinity is not something you can begin to comprehend or know what it is. You're just trying to go through school, essentially trying to fit in with everybody else, the whole idea.

In the face of this destiny and its sanctions, like many boys Ed opted to play it safe, accommodating himself to the preferred ways for comporting and expressing himself:

> Getting along in the world is not hard. There's a couple of rules you've got to follow. It's not hard to follow the rules, you know, to fill the roles. Roles and expectations are something we fill out every day, regardless of whether we believe them or not, unthinkingly, you know.

And while the rules and roles were quite clear to him, the ease with which he handled them and managed their cost was far more uncertain:

> You know, you've got to be good at sports, you know, strong, blah, blah, know a lot of girls, you have to be kissing a couple, and all that. Even after all that, even after I became good at sports and started kissing girls, I was still very insecure. Like I was scared, very scared, about everything. I didn't really know what was going on, what I should be doing, what was expected, how aggressive you should be, how hard you should work, who you should be talking to, even.

Pressured, bewildered and desperate, boys like Ed absorb the lessons implied in the structures and curriculum of their schools, families and communities. Sometimes their choices reflect a noble effort to be themselves, to determine despite their destinies what they want their lives to mean. More commonly, however, young boys like Ed simply strive to 'fit in' and, thereby, avoid the punishing sanctions meted out to those boys who cannot. If education at its best is about the 'formation of capacities for practice' (Connell 1995: 239), the constraints which are imposed upon boys within traditional curricula such as Ed described surely limit their adaptability for modern life.

The part played by peers

Boys' relationships with each other are also organized by this curriculum. Observed frequently to be exclusive, harsh and crude, boys' peer relations are seldom acknowledged as reflections of the deep man-making structures they are contained and encouraged by. Under the noses of adults who lament their punishing harshness, boys enact relationships with each other which begin as Ed recalled:

> There were always alliances and lines that little kids form. And that becomes evident in, like gym class, when people pick teams and during recess when you set up teams for – we played some crazy games, jailbreak, that was the name of one game where we all set up teams and people were, like, 'OK, you're a fast runner, you're on our team', or 'You can dodge like anything.' There were all these alliances being formed all the way through which are relatively still true today.

In the context of a school culture which defines manhood as being about production and prowess and which offers vivid examples of what should be as well as what should not, boys discover that they are measured, sorted and played against each other. Being valued in school depends upon running fast, acting cool, being good at things as well as not being unathletic, uncool, inept: boys quickly learn the behaviours and the attitudes which will earn them rewards (and spare them the negative sanctions) of the curriculum. As

Martino (1999: 248) put it, boys are 'incited to adopt certain practices of masculinity and to display themselves as particular kinds of boys'.

In addition to life history interviews with Ed, we conducted a series of group interviews with adolescent boys (Reichert 2000). These interviews revealed the organization of boys' peer relationships within the priorities and values of the school's curriculum. We heard, for example, a great deal about boys' efforts to master their public face so as to fit in. One boy, a Jewish student at a time when the school was predominantly Christian, expressed a key theme, echoed by most boys in the group interviews: 'You've got to leave some things at home to make it here. If you come to this school and bring the baggage of your background, you'll likely meet with more failure than success.' This young man explained how it had been that, absent from the school for several days, none of his friends or teachers had known that he and his family were at home celebrating the High Holidays. He simply believed that there was nothing to be gained by displaying his religious commitments publicly. For boys in all the groups we interviewed, there was a marked observance of distinct borders between personal life and public persona. Matters such as these, the Jewish boy explained, matters of family or culture or of the heart, matters of difference, had no place in the social life of the school.

In the context of an institutional curriculum which promotes a specific, purposeful identity, boys enact social relations rigidly, separating those dimensions of experience, family and self which offer no public advantage from those which might gain them position. They travel together through the gender landscape described by Ed, somehow reckoning with this abiding logic: they are in school to develop certain habits of work, style and attitude, symbols of a hegemonic masculine identity. And they enact these distinctions both within and between themselves.

We interviewed groups of boys who were distinguished from each other by wealth and economic privilege: 'lifers', whose families had the means to enable them, from kindergarten, to take up the elite education offered by the school; 'recruits', presumed to be on scholarship to fill out athletic teams in the ninth year. We observed broad efforts to mark differences, especially in terms of conflicting concepts of masculinity. Lifers evidenced a smug certainty about the absolute value of their approach to work, achievement and morality, condemning 'those kids from poor backgrounds who make little effort': 'They're angry tough guys with different morals and no regard for the rules. With their spitballs, snowballs, food fights, they intend to be malicious.' On the other side, recruits were quite conscious of being different from lifers: 'We feel like Blacks must feel walking through a White neighbourhood.' And as they reflected on their differences generally, these recruits had their own reactions to differences in masculinity:

> In grade school, we all had a sissy in our class and we were the majority. Here it's just the reverse. The sissies are in the majority.

Never seen anybody run away from a fight before.

We've been brought up not to rat on each other; they're brought up to kiss ass and tell on others.

The kids I hang out with don't act like and aren't like the kids here. They dress different, look different, talk different.

When I came here someone gave a talk and I couldn't understand half the words. If I ever used a big word with my friends, they'd get right on me. You can't sound smart.

Among these groups of boys, rival postures of manhood developed in relation to the institution's masculinity curriculum. Lifers conformed to the school's values for hard work and were rewarded with status in the school's hierarchy: they won the prizes at Honors Day and graduation, achieved entrance into the Ivy League colleges. Recruits struggled for a footing in a social practice which discounted and derogated them. The results of the competition for recognition and attention between groups of boys were not seen as arbitrary or deliberate by lifers; they were, in fact, loudly and frequently reified as moral and absolute. But, to the eyes of the recruits, this practice of rewarding those most successful at posing as the 'Haverford Man' was quite obviously prejudiced. They felt both excluded and generally alienated by the whole deal:

> I think one problem with this school is that it gives a lot of academic awards and prizes to the kids who excel at the academics, you know, because the way the kids are getting real high SAT grades and stuff like that. When I think there should be more emphasis on kids who put a lot more effort, you know, and do within the best of their ability. Not the highest level the school has, like getting 95s and 99s, but if the kid's highest potential is an 85, an 80, a 75, give him that kind of award: 'You did a good job', 'You got through'.

Set against lifers in the contest for recognition and institutional attention, recruits found their choices for position polarized. One option was to conform, even to beat the more privileged at their own game. For example, one young man we spoke with, a recruit to the school in ninth grade, had been voted 'Key Man' by his teachers and classmates. While he relished his victory over a prototypical lifer rival for this honour, he regretted what it had cost him in his relationships with other recruits:

> I came in as a freshman from a school that was 100 per cent different into a school of basically really privileged kids. I was a financial aid student so that first year was really difficult. I was labeled a 'recruit' mainly because I was coming in to make the basketball team better. I started getting good grades early on and no one else did and when that happened I was sort of ostracized from all the kids who were also labelled 'recruits'.

But in the context of the school's peer relations hierarchy, the choice seemed to be either to win or to lose. He explained the meaning of being represented as a 'recruit':

> It's that kind of feeling that people expected you to fail. At one of my Mom's parent conferences with one of my teachers, I was doing really well in my classes freshman year and the guy, it came out like halfway through the conference that I wasn't a Haverford student my whole life and he goes, like, 'Wow, I can't believe that your son comes from some other . . .', I don't remember the quotation but it was like he was astonished that someone who was doing well came from another background.

Propelled by determination and resentment, carrying his family's hopes and ambitions, this student went on to win on all levels, climaxing at graduation with the school's ultimate honour, the Key Man award. Yet all the while, he explained, he felt 'that when I won, half the people there would have been just as unhappy that I won as the people who were happy'.

For other recruits, perhaps those who had less sense of competitive possibility, the other choice was an oppositional identity, in which their outgroup status crystallized as unalterably distinguished from lifers: 'I don't want to talk with my hands, look like a fag – guys flicking their hair out of their eyes. Never saw weird haircuts like this. I want to have money but I don't want to act like them.' For these young men, the traditional practices of gay bashing and homophobia were weapons deployed to gain some advantage in a competition for centrality and the meaning of difference.

Group relations for boys, as the contest between recruits and lifers illustrated, are driven, teased and shaped by the logic of masculinity politics. From the school's masculinizing practices – dress codes, teacher models, athletics, even space design – boys learn the ideals and parameters for being male. In their relations with each other, they reenact these lessons, responding to the recognitional structures of the school as they vie among themselves for centrality, validation and reward. Their competitions seize upon differences of all kinds – size, colour, ability, religion, family background – to provide an edge, whatever might provide a boost over the top of the other boys scrambling for survival. What is assumed – or taken for granted – by this deliberate and cherished system for reproducing identities is that, in their scramble over the top of each other for advantage, somehow good men survive.

Programmes for boys: addressing gender equity

It is important to highlight that despite these institutionalized regimes of masculinity, at this boys' school, The Haverford School, there was also a commitment to exploring new ideas for schooling boys. While many teachers find themselves unconsciously playing a collusive role in the reproductive work of the school, there are many others – 'transformative intellectuals', as Giroux (1997) referred to them – consciously yearning to break free, to follow the minds and imaginations of the children they serve for new ways of being male. As the work of The Haverford School's research progressed, new ideas were hatched and new programmes and practices tried out. It is worth outlining some of these, if only to describe the arc of imagination inspired by the project's invitation.

Gender awareness programmes were developed and tried out with boys from The Haverford School and girls from two neighbouring girls' schools. The aim was to help boys, on the basis of their close relationships with friends and intimates, understand the force of gender relations (Connell 1996; McLean 1996). A series of opportunities for boys and girls to inform each other about the experience of being male and being female began in 1995. The first programme, which students called the 'Gender Awareness Workshop', included 80 young men and women in a six-hour series of discussions and exercises which aimed, as a male member of the planning group wrote in his school's newspaper, 'to look at the role gender plays in dating, sex, friendships, families and education, with a particular emphasis on the stereotypes society has developed for each gender' (Levinson 1995).

There was much anticipation and trepidation about the day; boys came fearful of 'male-bashing' while girls came expecting to have to fight for a voice. The same male student explained the hope of the planning group: 'We are all single-sex schools and felt it was important to be exposed to the opposite sex in an open discussion, to clear up misconceptions about the other gender, to learn the other's viewpoints, how they think' (Levinson 1995). Largely student-driven, the workshops evolved to include dialogues, skits, exercises, talks by male and female facilitators and opportunities for the boys and girls to listen closely to each other. Perhaps most thrilling to the participants was the consciousness which emerged from each other's stories and from the collective effort to 'name the plot' of their communities' and schools' gender regimes (Denborough 1996).

In the closing circle of the first workshop both boys and girls expressed the satisfaction that they had joined hands to resist gender's limitations. One powerful outcome for the workshop was an organized effort by boys to challenge sexist comments and assumptions at their school more vigorously. Several students addressed themselves even to teachers in a commitment to the spirit of the workshops. One boy made the following comment: 'Never before has an effort been made to integrate the Haverford community with the neighbouring girls' schools in an organized manner to study the effects of sexism, and the day was a complete success' (Levinson 1995).

Emotional literacy and peer support

Several years ago, in response to a suicide note, Ed's school initiated a peer counselling programme for its upper schoolers, hoping that students themselves could provide a front line of support and assistance to each other. Behind the programme's creation was also an unspoken hope for a sanctuary within the larger school masculinity regime in which safety and connection could be promoted. Under the tyranny of masculinity politics which encouraged dissociation of personal from public and boys to humiliate and hurt each other, a programme of mutual support and personal expression offered a determinedly alternative opportunity.

In its initial phases, the meetings of students struggled with the sarcastic and combative postures boys had adopted in school. But encouraged by the young adult leader, himself a graduate of the school, they managed to relate to each other in more respectful and supportive ways, quickly creating a social space for the personal, eventually telling each other about their families and loves, fears and struggles. From their first meeting together, this alternative community mattered as much to the programme's participants as any of the skills or counselling experiences. As the leader wrote:

> By caring about the welfare of the entire group as well as each individual, and more importantly by fully opening up and showing their own personal struggles, this group of young men have built the safety and trust of the group to a high level and have inspired newer members.
>
> (Gallagher 1998: 11)

Overall, the boys in the group agreed. As one reported:

> There are certain things I need to be able to say, simply to get hard feelings off my chest. If I don't let them out in a constructive format like Peer Counseling, I end up carrying them around and feeling bad or blowing up at somebody, and I hate that. When I get a chance to vent, I can be me again, it's as simple as that.
>
> (Gallagher 1998: 11).

From these glimpses of alternative ways of relating to each other, boys developed perspective about the arbitrary nature of their school's culture and their own ability to influence outcomes in it. Another boy, quoted in the same report, said:

> Not only do I feel good when I get a chance to emote, I feel good and useful when I can help someone else express their feelings. I get the sense of the group having a larger purpose that is inclusive of, yet larger than, the individual.
>
> (Gallagher 1998: 11)

Within the context of the group's norms for honesty and voice, the young men in the group spoke to each other about many of the dimensions of their experience which were banished from the public life of the school. For example, they addressed difficult cultural and racial issues. An Asian student, for example, was able to relate for the group the stereotypes and misunderstanding about Asians he encountered, sufficiently motivated following this step to initiate the school's first Asian Cultures Club. Recruits in the group came to rely on the community of the group to challenge the lifer/recruit oppositions which dominated school life. Within the context of their new relationships, these boys established new social practices which naturally spilled over into the larger school community, upsetting the personal and social silences of the school.

Teacher critique

Among many teachers there abides a fear that schooling can devolve into 'a technology of power, language and practice that . . . offer human beings particular views of themselves and the world' (Giroux 1997: 226). Many teachers reject the role of mere technicians; they prefer an active role in partnership with their students. Where encouraged to lead, teachers often resist pressures to conform and can actually be counted on to challenge traditional practices which may not fit with their students' needs. The teacher researcher movement in schools has been one mechanism schools find to mobilize their faculties' passions for justice (Lytle and Cochran-Smith 1990, 1992).

An opportunity for teacher leadership developed at The Haverford School in response to the lifer/recruit tension. In response to incidents in which this tension erupted into public conflict, a group of teachers and administrators created a 'Diversity Research' project, charging themselves with generating an understanding of the roots of the tension. Groups of students, present and past, were interviewed in focus groups. The results were reported in written form and an oral presentation was made to school Trustees and fellow faculty. As the different focus groups were interviewed, faculty researchers discovered that among all the groups interviewed, the group of African American boys was singularly quiet. In the words of their report:

> Of all the groups with which the task force met, the African American students seemed least spontaneous. They were generally quiet, mannered, studied, careful and cautious. There was a pronounced lack of emotional expression in their responses. It seemed their reluctance to talk stemmed from the fact that the business of conforming, assimilating and fitting in is so demanding, it's hard to relax and break loose from.
>
> (Bergh *et al.* 1994: 3)

These males, in particular, seemed to the teachers to be in an extreme position in the gender politics of the school. Unable to hide, these boys kept their difference to themselves, huddling with each other at lunch tables or in hallways, passing through the school day rather unobtrusively. Through their interviews with various groups of boys – lifers, students of colour, recruits – the teachers became convinced that this school's culture for dealing with difference adversely affected all the boys at the school. What flared between the lifers and the recruits silenced the African American students and caused religious minorities to dissociate their personal lives from their public participation.

Discovering this unhappy dynamic in boys' relationships to the school, it was quite natural that teachers followed the discoveries from their research with action. They imposed on the administration, other faculty and trustees to intervene and, as a result of their persistent advocacy, the school began aggressively to pursue faculty of colour, pursuing a 'critical mass' of numbers, images and opportunities for its students of colour (Slaughter and Johnson 1988). New outreach was made to families. New programmes were introduced to facilitate the adjustment of all students socially and academically to the school, including a 'bridge' programme for recruits. As these results witnessed, in supporting teachers to critique and to imagine, the school unleashed a reliable resource for reform. The clear view of the professionals who have dedicated their lives to their students has helped refine its programme in myriad ways.

Conclusion

The strength of the investment institutions make in their masculinity curricula cannot be overestimated. We discovered that efforts to advocate for boys in a manner which transcends the 'recuperative masculinity' approaches, described in the introductory chapter to this volume, aroused a hornets' nest of reaction and mobilized a school system well able to defend its investment. Powerfully threatened by programmes which seek to dislodge the unexamined predominance of particular masculinity practices and discourses, forces of resistance surrounding the dominant masculinity play to fears, promote distortions and fantasies, and make quite personal attacks (Sokolove 1997). Our experience taught us how precious and central these masculinity regimes can be to the schools historically created to reproduce them (Cookson and Persell 1985). Our experience, in fact, suggests that a veritable fetish for the production of certain types and identities of boys develops in schools. As Fine found in her study of public schools in New York City, the production of privilege tends to be surrounded by 'echoed beliefs' and 'entrenched behaviors and resource allocations' most closely resembling the fervor of fetishism (1991: 184). The posture and rhetoric of those defending tradition mimics the zealotry of worship.

Ultimately, few of the programmes initiated by this new boys' project at The Haverford School survived the various conscious and unconscious strategies for resistance mounted in response to their introduction. In these times of 'turbo capitalism' (Luttwack 1999) and greater than ever winner-take-all economic rules (Frank and Cook 1995), there seems to be even more incentive for families and schools to rely on tried and true strategies for producing winners. The programmes described here, as well as others, were not obviously opposed. They were, more simply, regarded as irrelevant or, even more commonly, appreciated but not embraced by a school staff struggling mightily to keep pace with the runaway careerism of students and families.

Still, the school accomplished something for its effort. Boys' lives at The Haverford School are not the same as before. There is a new sensitivity, inarticulate and often unaware, on the part of those connected to the school and a new hope on the part of the boys themselves. The simple existence of such a deliberate effort perhaps signalled a legitimate challenge to ideas which had held sway for generations before. Perhaps it is as Bhabha suggested, that those challenging a school's gender practice aim 'not to deny or disavow masculinity, but to disturb its manifest destiny' (1995: 57). Or, as Greene suggests, we offer hope not so much by our successes as by our reach: 'People trying to be more fully human must not only engage in critical thinking but must be able to imagine something coming out of their hopes; their silence must be overcome by their search' (1995: 20).

References

Addelston, J. (1995) *Exploring Masculinities: Gender Enactments in Preparatory High Schools.* Unpublished dissertation, City University of New York, New York.

Bhabha, H.K. (1995) Are you a man or a mouse?, in M. Berger, B. Wallis and S. Watson (eds) *Constructing Masculinity.* New York, NY: Routledge.

Connell, R.W. (1996) Teaching the boys: new research on masculinity and gender strategies for schools. *Teachers' College Record,* 98 (2): 206–35.

Cookson, P.W. and Persell, C.H. (1985) *Preparing for Power.* New York, NY: Basic Books.

Denborough, D. (1996) Step by step: developing respectful and effective ways of working with young males to reduce violence, in C. McLean, M. Carey and C. White (eds), *Men's Ways of Being.* Boulder, CO: Westview Press.

Donaldson, M. (1993) What is hegemonic masculinity? *Theory and Society,* 22: 643–57.

Fine, M. (1991) *Framing Dropouts.* Albany, NY: State University of NY Press.

Frank, R.H. and Cook, P.J. (1995) *The Winner-Take-All Society.* New York, NY: Free Press.

Giroux, H.A. (1997) *Pedagogy and the Politics of Hope.* Boulder, CO: Westview Press.

Greene, M. (1995) *Releasing the Imagination.* San Francisco, CA: Jossey Bass.

Hawley, R. (1991) About boys' schools: a progressive case for an ancient form. *Teachers' College Record,* 92 (3): 433–44.

Heward, C. (1988) *Making a Man of Him: Parents and their Sons' Education at an English Public School 1929–50.* London: Routledge.

Lefkowitz, B. (1997) *Our Guys.* Berkeley, CA: University of California Press.

Levinson, M. (1995) Gender issues workshop: a first for the Main Line. *The Index,* March, The Haverford School.

Luttwack, E. (1999) *Turbo-capitalism.* New York, NY: HarperCollins Publishers.

Lytle, S.L. and Cochran-Smith, M. (1990) Learning from teacher research: a working typology. *Teachers' College Record,* 72: 83–103.

Lytle, S.L. and Cochran-Smith, M. (1992) Teacher research as a way of knowing. *Harvard Educational Review,* 62 (Winter): 447–74.

McLean, C. (1996) Boys and education in Australia, in C. McLean, M. Carey and C. White (eds) *Men's Ways of Being*. Boulder, CO: Westview Press.

Martino, W. (1999) 'Cool boys', 'party animals', 'squids' and 'poofters': interrogating the dynamics and politics of adolescent masculinities in school. *British Journal of Sociology of Education*, 20 (2): 239–63.

Miedzian, M. (1991) *Boys Will Be Boys*. New York, NY: Anchor Books.

Pollack, W. (1998) *Real Boys*. New York, NY: Random House.

Reichert, M.C. (2000) Disturbances of difference: lessons from a boys' school, in M. Fine and L. Weis (eds) *Construction Sites: Excavating Gender, Race and Class Among Urban Youth*. New York, NY: Teachers College Press.

Silverstein, O. (1994) *The Courage to Raise Good Men*. New York, NY: Viking.

Slaughter, D.T. and Johnson, D.J. (1988) Introduction and overview, in D.T. Slaughter and D.J. Johnson (eds) *Visible Now*. New York, NY: Greenwood Press.

Sokolove, M.Y. (1997) What men are made of: helping boys find new paths to manhood. *Philadelphia Inquirer Magazine*, June 8, 12–30.

The Haverford School (1994) *Executive Summary of the Draft Strategic Plan*. Haverford, PA: The Haverford School.

CHAPTER 4

Pushing it to the max: interrogating the risky business of being a boy

MARTIN MILLS

Introduction

There is a need to take the issue of boys and schooling seriously. Unfortunately though, many of the arguments for doing this have, as the introductions to this book indicate, been grounded in a backlash, or anti-feminist, politics. These 'what about the boys?' rumblings have served to overstate the achievements of feminist struggles in education, and have consequently worked to roll back some of the gains for girls in schools while further entrenching boys as the privileged sex within schools (Hayes 1998). However, the debate about boys has also opened up some opportunities for work in schools which problematizes what it means to be a normal or proper boy (Lingard 1998). The seizing of these opportunities need not be done from an anti-feminist perspective. For as Jane Kenway (1996: 447) has stated: 'Most feminists want boys and men to change so that they cause less trouble for girls and women and themselves, so the sexes can live alongside each other in a safe, secure, stable, respectful, harmonious way and in relationships of mutual life-enhancing respect.'

Several years ago I used to run programmes for boys in schools which were constructed with such an intention (see Mills 1998, 2000, 2001 for discussion of such programmes). Many of the activities I conducted with the boys in these groups revolved around discussing notions of 'gender construction' and 'gender policing'. One such activity entailed exploring the lives of a hypothetical female and a hypothetical male through the use of birthday cards. We would discuss a range of cards, bought at a local department store, which these hypothetical people could have received at various stages in their lives. One birthday card for a 14-year-old boy always served as a useful discussion starter for talking about masculinity and risk taking. It had a picture of a group of four boys on motorcycles leaping through the air on a dirt trail. The inside of the card read 'Push it to the max and have some fun!'

In many ways the sentiments expressed through this card serve as an indicator of the ways in which 'normal' boys are supposed to live out their lives. That is, they are expected to attempt to maximize their fun by engaging in dangerous activities. Among many of the current crop of writers on boys' issues there is a tendency to focus on the harm that boys do to themselves, and occasionally others, through such behaviours (Biddulph 1997; Gurian 1999; Kindlon and Thompson 1999; Pollack 1999). This is work well worth doing. Many boys do themselves and others great harm in attempting to demonstrate their manhood. However, what many of these writers do not acknowledge is that these behaviours also work to maintain an unjust gender system which operates in the favour of the social group of boys and men. Indeed, some even appear to suggest that these behaviours work in the favour of girls and women (see for example Farrell 1993). Nor do many of them acknowledge the extent to which these behaviours maintain existing relations of power based upon issues of class and race/ethnicity. This chapter, while considering the harms boys do to themselves and others, also looks at some of the ways in which class and race/ethnicity issues infuse boys' risk-taking behaviours, and how these behaviours impact upon the maintenance of existing gender relations. I conclude with some suggestions as to how the notion of risk taking may be taken up in non-normalized ways in order to challenge dominant relations of power. Throughout the chapter I will draw on interview data collected from some boys who had participated in gender and violence programmes implemented in two Australian state high schools.

The effects of risk taking

There are several things worth noting in relation to the birthday card exhorting 14-year-old males to 'live life to the max': the boys are in a group; the riding of motorcycles by boys of this age is illegal; the activity is noisy and dirty; it is an outside activity; and it is physically dangerous. These are all important points in relation to normalized risk-taking practices and their association with masculinity. There are a number of popular texts on boys which suggest such behaviours as those depicted in the card are part and parcel of growing up as a boy, and that boys will be boys because of hormones or the wirings of their brains. Hence, in order to protect boys, and presumably others, from 'boysie' behaviours, such things as male mentors and the re-structuring of schooling to meet boys' needs are suggested. For example, Biddulph (1997: 20–1) makes the following claim:

> In our society all we offer the mid-teens is 'more of the same': more school, more of the routines of home. But the adolescent is hungry for

something more. He is hormonally and physically ready to break out into an adult role, but we want him to wait another five or six years! It's little wonder that problems arise.

What's needed is something that will engage the spirit of a boy – pull him headlong into some creative effort or passion that gives his life wings. All the things that parents have nightmares about (adolescent risk-taking, alcohol, drugs and criminal activity) happen because we do not find channels for young men's desire for glory and heroic roles.

These claims about boys' desires deny the ways in which desires and fears are socially constructed. There is little which is natural about boys' risk-taking adventures. For many boys, riding loud motorcycles and driving noisy cars are ways of asserting their claims to valorized forms of masculinities and distancing themselves from girls and women. As one grade nine boy, John,[1] told me:

John: . . . anyone can, you know, drive a car, but like men have the more hotted up type car . . . The more beefy car.

Martin: Why?

John: I don't know – it shows their muscles or something.

There is a social aspect to this, someone needs to see them 'showing their muscles'. Hence, the fact that the boys in the card are in a group is significant. Boys have often told me about boys' greater willingness to engage in particular forms of masculinized behaviour when in the presence of 'mates' (this is of course usually said in relation to 'other' boys). For example, in a discussion about boys and fighting, one Grade 11 boy commented that

. . . usually the ones that have their groups, they feel tougher and they go around, you know, boxing heads more, but when they're by themselves they don't say nothing. They don't want to get their heads punched in. They only do it when they're in a group.

While 'boxing heads' is most likely to be a safer practice when surrounded by one's 'group', there is also no point in engaging in such risky activities unless others know about it. As Salisbury and Jackson (1996: 219) note: '. . . manly acts of living on the edge can't just be done in isolation. They need the confirmation and approval of the male peer group.' By engaging in dangerous activities in front of other boys, such boys are able to establish their credentials within a hierarchy of masculinities, or what Bob Connell (1995) refers to as the social organization of masculinity.

The extent to which a boy can demonstrate to his peers, and others, his willingness to engage in risky behaviours is significant in his placing within this hierarchy. For example, Raphaela Best, in her fieldwork in an American primary school, notes how a teacher worried about a dangerous game a couple of boys were playing was met with the following comment by one of the boys: 'It's like my granddaddy says, "If a boy doesn't have a couple of scars, he'll never be a man"' (see also Skelton 1996; Danby and Baker 1998). Hence, the eagerness with which a boy is prepared to accept a dare or a challenge becomes the litmus test by which masculinities can be measured against each other and by which they can be contrasted with femininities. This can have dangerous consequences for both the boys accepting such challenges and for others who may be unwilling participants in the scenarios which develop around risk-taking behaviours. As Salisbury and Jackson (1996: 219) note:

> 'Real lads' are deliberately careless about their lives. Through their risky bravado they attempt to distance themselves from the world of femininity/domesticity/caring. They often welcome dangerous actions where they can get a buzz out of displaying just how wild and hard they are . . . That's why a wide range of games and activities that manufacture excitement – from cheeking the teacher in front of your mates through to biking and joy riding as well as excessive drinking, smoking and taking drugs – are important in enabling boys to identify themselves as part of the club of 'real lads'.

The importance of the male peer group was also captured nicely in Joyce Canaan's (1996) study of a group of working-class men. She notes in relation to these men that:

> They performed outrageous acts with friends, in which they demonstrated bodily might or acted violently towards a subordinate. Thus, individual acts of hardness took place amongst peers who drank and laughed at individual and collective acts of strength, power and daring. Peers competed to see who had most and least self-control – that is, who could drink most and take it manfully, and who could push the bounds of self-control by performing outrageous acts in the group context.
>
> (Canaan 1996: 119)

Outrageous acts can take many forms. For instance, the serial rapes by members of the group known as the 'posse' in the US (Faludi 1999), violence performed by some soccer supporters, and gang wars between rival motorcycle groups all represent outrageous acts of risk taking. The actions of the 'posse' had devastating consequences for many of the young women they came in contact with. However, as with the other two examples, such actions are often constructed as 'risk taking' due to the danger, for the boys or men performing the acts, of retribution if prosecuted. In the last two instances there is also the physical danger present for all the boys and men concerned. By engaging in these sorts of activities boys and men prove their superiority over women and also over other men. For instance, in relation to the 'posse' and their boasts about how many girls they had had sex with, they were demonstrating not only their ability to 'conquer' girls but also their superiority over 'normal' boys.

These are, of course, extreme examples. However, there are a multitude of other ways in which boys engage in risk taking to demonstrate their dominance over girls and other boys. The schoolyard fight, the sexual harassment of girls, riding motorbikes illegally, playing contact sports such as rugby league, or accepting dares are all forms of risk taking which have the potential to result in harm to oneself or another, and which serve to demonstrate some boys' supremacy over other boys and over girls in general. And they all take place where others can judge the success or failure of the performance.

The extent to which many boys associate risk taking with becoming a man is apparent in a series of comments made about one 16-year-old boy, Ian, in one Queensland state high school. Ian's name came up several times in interviews about the types of boys who were often the subject of teasing within this particular school. Ian was identified as someone who was picked on a lot because 'he's naturally quiet . . . He's just real weird sometimes.' One boy commented how Ian was often the butt of homophobic humour:

I've called my mates poofters and that. You know it doesn't mean nothing. It doesn't mean that they are a poofter . . . it's just a joke . . . Like that Ian he gets a bit of flak. Because he just does things that everybody else (boys?) doesn't do and they just make fun of him.

During an interview with Ian, when he was questioned about homophobia in the school, he stated: 'That's what is happening to me. What I'm getting teased about. I'm not gay.' Indeed, Ian made a point of stating how much he disliked homosexuals. Soon after this point Ian began to cry in the interview. For him the teasing was far more than 'just a joke' as suggested by the boy above. Interestingly, while not surprisingly, when questioned about what he would like to do after leaving school Ian said he would like to be 'A police, fireman something like that. Some job with action instead of a boring job . . . You risk your life to try and save people and stuff like that.' Throughout his schooling life Ian has been having his masculinity questioned in most hurtful ways. His occupational aspirations are perhaps shaped by his desire finally to shake off the labels he has acquired through the schooling process: that is, by becoming a 'real man' who is prepared to risk his life in demonstrations of masculine prowess. Homophobia, along with misogyny, thus work to police dominant constructions of masculinity. As a Grade 9 boy commented:

. . . in our society you like, you gotta be, for men, you gotta be, like you gotta be like you can't be like a little queer. Like a little shy you know like a little softie sort of thing. You can't be like that. Or people start sussing you out, 'Ahh, shit, this fella looks a bit suss. Stay away from him.'

This group pressure and the consequences for boys and others is sometimes recognized within the popular literature on boys (Gurian 1999; Pollack 1999). This is important. There is plenty of evidence to suggest that many young men can do themselves a great deal of harm in their attempts to prove their manhood. For instance, there are statistics which indicate that young boys and men are more likely than young women or girls to die from road accidents, commit suicide, experience criminal violence, engage in criminal activities or be suspended or expelled from school (see for example Gilbert and Gilbert 1998). However, as Gilbert and Gilbert argue, this is just one side of the story. The focus that many men have on this angle of the risk-taking story enables them to tap into what Eva Cox (1996) has referred to as 'a competing victim syndrome'. This syndrome serves to construct boys and men as being equally oppressed (and sometimes more so) by the current gender system and to deny the extent to which these practices benefit boys and men as a group, and some boys and men in particular. This is stated well by Chris McLean (1996: 25, original emphasis):

> . . . it is meaningless to argue that men are oppressed on the grounds of gender. As I have already said, it is perfectly legitimate to argue that men *suffer* as a result of conforming to gender stereotypes, as long as it is also recognised that this suffering contributes to the maintenance of systems that actually oppress others.

The ways in which this suffering contributes to the maintenance of oppressive systems is complex. The effect of associating risk taking as part of a boy's development into manhood is to demonstrate that boys have had a better training than girls in how to hold their nerve in stressful situations and, hence, that men are more suited to certain occupations than are women. These are often the occupations which are most privileged or are those which demonstrate men's supposed superiority over women. For instance, risk taking is often associated with the skills necessary for participation in the financial and commercial worlds; with being able to make decisions about dangerous and life-threatening situations, such as those expected from people in emergency services; and also with being able to perform in a multitude of high-pressure systems such as politics, medicine and the law. However, there is a sleight of hand going on here.

The men in these occupations have seldom engaged in any activities through their boyhood and adolescence, beyond perhaps schoolboy football (from which they often gain a significant amount of mileage), which have posed any threat to them personally. The homogenization of men in this instance serves to unite all men as 'risk takers'. Who pays the cost here? Clearly all women do. But so do many of the boys and men who have taken the risks, quite often unsuccessfully, in the name of 'masculinity'. They pay it on behalf of all men.

However, it is only certain boys and men who tend to pay these costs, and they usually come from marginalized backgrounds. For instance, there are class and race/ethnicity dynamics associated with boys' risk taking. Clearly, it is particular kinds of boys who are more likely to end up as traffic accident statistics, in prison, as victims and perpetrators of violent incidents and as participants in dangerous sports. Such boys tend to come from low socio-economic and/or marginalized racial/ethnic backgrounds. Hence, as a number of those writing in the field of boys' education have suggested, questions such as 'Which boys are we talking about here?' need to be asked (see for example Gilbert and Gilbert 1998; Lingard and Douglas 1999). For instance, in Australia, Gardiner (1997: 54) notes how in 1993–4 the arrest rate in Victoria for 14 to 16-year-old Aboriginal boys was about six times higher than for non-Aboriginal males. In the US, Sadker and Sadker (1994: 222) report on statistics which indicate that one in every six African American males is arrested by the time they turn 19, and how, for example, in the state of Milwaukee 94 per cent of all expelled students are African American boys. Similar stories can be told about the UK (Gillborn 1997; Sewell 1997, 1998; Wright *et al.* 1998).

There is also a clear class element to normalized risk-taking activities. When Jackson and Salisbury refer to 'real lads' there is a sense that they are not meaning upper middle-class boys, and the men in Canaan's study who demonstrate the excesses of masculinity are working-class. This is a common pattern. In Connell's (1995) study of masculinities, the men who engage in hypermasculine behaviours demonstrate a number of signifiers of working-class masculinities. For instance, motorbikes and the riding of them, often associated with a rebellious working-class masculinity,[2] are a key feature of the gender identity of the working-class men who demonstrated some of the most frightening aspects of masculinity. This comes through in one man's response to a question about becoming involved in fights. He states that he doesn't become involved in many fights because very few people (men?) have the 'guts to stand up' to him and his biking friends because of the 'way we look and the fact that we have got earrings and tattoos, we ride bikes. That's enough to scare the shit out of most people' (Connell 1995: 107). The same man when describing his job aspirations in the computer industry notes that he is only likely to follow this particular career path if he is not dead by the age of 40. When asked what he might be dead from, he responds: 'I don't know. But well, live fast and die young sort of thing . . . I love my bikes. I'll be on my bike till the day I die. I'll die on my bike' (Connell 1995: 117).

It is perhaps no surprise that it is boys and men from working-class and marginalized racial/ethnic backgrounds who are most likely to be hurt or have their lives ruined by engaging in risk-taking activities. For many boys and men, these forms of masculinity are among the few ways in which they can exert some form of power within a world in which they have very little influence. For as Connell (1989: 298) states, in relation to the white middle-aged men who form the powerful elite in western societies, for example politicians, generals, bankers, company directors and media owners: 'A man who can command this power has no need of riding leathers and engine noise to assert masculinity. His masculinity is asserted and amplified on an immensely greater scale by the society itself.' This is of course too simplistic an argument in itself for explaining why it is that disproportionate numbers of boys from marginalized backgrounds engage in physically risky behaviours. There are significant pressures upon such boys to do so which are often grounded in racist presumptions about Black masculinities. For instance, as Wright *et al.* (1998: 85) state in relation to the school exclusion of Black male students in the UK:

> Though clearly there are problems with the ways in which some forms of Black male behaviour act to reinforce stereotypes of Black masculinity, it is not a construct which consists solely of Black male attempts to gain the privileges of hegemonic (White) masculinities. To suggest that Black identities are constructed out of negativity because they have failed to achieve Whiteness renders meaningless the attempts of young male excludes to challenge the differential treatment to which they are subjected, generating the differential damaging stereotypes of Black male pupils as threatening, overtly stylistic and confrontational.

There is a paradoxical process at play here. On the one hand the high-risk behaviours of such boys are used to highlight the superiority of males over females. An example of how this works came through in a discussion about sport I had with one grade 11 boy: 'I think oh if people want equal rights then it should be equal rights in the sporting field, but then physical features aren't the same and stuff like that.' Here, the behaviours of 'sportsmen' become associated with the qualities of *all* men and are used to justify particular forms of gender discrimination. However, there is a flipside to individualized demonstrations of men's supposed superiority over women. In concord with the homogenization of men is a 'differencing' process which focuses on the class and race/ethnicity of boys and men who engage in risk-taking activities. The fact that it is boys from particular backgrounds who take risk taking 'too far' serves to identify boys from these backgrounds as 'primitive', 'barbaric', 'prone to excess' and so on. For instance, in Australia the over-involvement of particular social groupings of men in high-risk sports, such as boxing, reinforces dominant images of working-class and/or Aboriginal men as being more aggressive and violent than white middle-class 'civilized' men. The ways in which such activities serve the interests of privileged men is captured well by Messner (1990: 103) in his studies on masculinities and violent sports:

> For middle class men, the tough guys of the culture industry – the Rambos, the Ronnie Lotts who are fearsome 'hitters,' who play 'hurt' – are the heroes who prove that men, 'we', are superior to women. At the same time, these heroes play the role of the primitive other, against whom higher status men define themselves as modern and civilised.

The racism and classism of essentialist associations of violence with working-class men and men from marginalized racial/ethnic backgrounds is played out in many areas of society. For instance, in the UK, as Wright *et al.* (1998) argue, racialized constructions of Black masculinities serve to homogenize Black boys in ways which contribute significantly to their disproportionate representation in statistics on school exclusions and suspensions (see also Mac an Ghaill 1994; Gardiner 1997; Gillborn 1997; Sewell 1997; Sewell 1998). As such 'suspendable' behaviours become associated with class or racial/ethnic factors embodied within the individual, and the structural nature of violence perpetuated through institutional practices which maintain dominant gender, racial/ethnic and class relations goes unquestioned, thus, the performance by certain boys of normalized risk-taking practices does not necessarily lead to long-term privileges for those boys. These performances are often more important for the collective benefit of men, and in particular for the benefit of already privileged men who usually do not take the physical risks associated with such performances.

Rearticulating risk taking

Like many positive human behaviours, such as courage and determination, risk taking has been colonized by boys and men, and shaped in such a way as to maintain the privileges of boys and men within current gender relations. However, 'risk taking' can be read differently and with very different effects. For instance, the dominant ways in which risk taking is currently taken up by boys leads to behaviours which are often more about conforming and taking the safer option in relation to gender behaviours than about accepting a challenge to disrupt existing relations of power. 'Risk taking', though, can also be read as processes which challenge the existing order, and also as practices which can be performed equally well by both girls and boys. A case in point would be where students refuse to perform those behaviours commonly associated with their sex. A significant objective for those in schools concerned about the ways in which boys hurt themselves and others will thus be to engage boys (and men) in practices which reconstruct their notions of what constitutes risk taking and to recognize that risk taking is not their (our) property. This is not going to be easy.

Boys have an investment in maintaining the existing construction of risk taking. As mentioned throughout this chapter, it shores up their privileged positioning within existing gendered relations of power. Consequently, in order to challenge these behaviours, boys and men will need to engage in a risk taking of a different sort. As Salisbury and Jackson (1996: 222) have argued: '(Boys) need to learn how to open up more about themselves and take the occasional risk of being vulnerable in groups rather than keeping their guards up.' However, the risks associated with opposing or rejecting normalized risk-taking practices often entail greater dangers for boys (and girls) than performing normalized behaviours. Consequently, some of the greatest risk taking that a boy is likely to engage in at school is to resist dominant masculinizing practices. In such instances it is unlikely that a boy will receive much credit for 'bravery'; instead he is likely to be punished by his peers in ways which seek to strip him of the mantle of masculinity. For as Chris McLean (1996: 17) observes:

> Male camaraderie or 'mateship' is founded on sharing the rituals of masculine identity. The exclusion of women is an integral aspect, and many of these rituals turn out to be destructive or oppressive. Binge drinking, gambling and violent sports are obvious examples. Men become close through the experiences of battle, through conquering the wilderness, hunting, and even through the ritual of pack rape. This kind of male friendship, however, is extremely fragile. If unspoken limits are transgressed or rules broken, then the full fury of male condemnation rapidly descends upon the head of the guilty party.

Transgressing these unspoken limits is often likely to attract homophobic and misogynist abuse. Homophobia and misogyny are two of the most important policing mechanisms of dominant masculinities. Boys in schools regularly comment on the extent to which their fears of being labelled as 'gay' or a 'girl' work to ensure that they do not demonstrate a disloyalty to the rules of masculinity (see for example Martino 1999; Mills 1999). For instance, in discussions about boys sharing their feelings with other boys I have often been met with comments which are used as ways of explaining why boys do not do this. They have included such things as: 'They'd probably be called a wuss or a gaybo.' This creates a number of tasks for those working within schools who are concerned about the dangers which normalized risk takings pose to boys and others, and about the ways in which schools are complicit in perpetuating a gender order that works in the long-term interests of white middle-class men.

One such task is the emasculation of current constructions of risk taking. This might involve explorations of women's engagement in high-risk activities such as the suffragette movement; the anti-slave movement in the US; the women's peace movement in Australia (Pine Gap) and in the UK (Greenham Common); and also of course less sensationalized forms of risk taking such as childbirth. It could also include providing girls with opportunities in schools to be involved in risk-taking activities that encourage them to step out of traditional gender roles. The purpose of such activities should be twofold. On the one hand girls need to be provided with opportunities to access the beneficial aspects of risk taking (and hence be able to legitimate their access to many of a society's most privileged occupations) without having to take up particular masculinized constructions of risk taking. On the other hand, boys need to be provided with alternative ways of constructing risk taking as a positive attribute which need not lead to the harm of oneself or others.

This latter aspect of the emasculation of risk taking will also entail an examination of the pressures which encourage boys to engage in physically high-risk behaviours in order to conform to dominant representations of masculinity. This examination needs to take place at all levels of schooling:

for instance, within the curriculum, forms of pedagogy, behaviours of male teachers, discipline structures and the forms of extra-curricular activities valued and promoted within the school. Ways in which misogyny and homophobia are utilized within each of these areas of schooling to push boys towards engaging in normalized risk-taking ventures need to be confronted. In addition there should also be a consideration of the ways in which students (and teachers) from working-class and marginalized race/ethnic backgrounds are being constructed within schools. Thinking about issues of gender also involves thinking about matters of class and race/ethnicity.

There are a number of useful resources available to teachers in schools which provide useful starting points for beginning such work. These include Salisbury and Jackson's (1996) *Challenging Macho Values*; the *No Fear* kits produced in Australia by the Curriculum and Gender Equity Policy Unit (1995); David Denborough's (1996) programme, 'Step by step: developing respectful and effective ways of working with young men to reduce violence'; and Brook Friedman's (1995) *Boys-Talk: A Program for Young Men about Masculinity, Non-violence and Relationships*. These approaches to boys' education are based upon the premise that there are multiple masculinities; that these masculinities are positioned against each other within various relations of power; that boys/men are not discriminated against as boys/men; and that gender justice requires that boys' and men's complicity in the oppression of girls and women be treated as a social justice issue. However, these are just starting points. Schools will need to develop their own approaches to these issues, and these approaches will have to go beyond one-off 'quick fix' programmes and consider whole-school approaches to change.

The positive aspects of risk taking as a means of engaging with the school curriculum also need to be promoted within schools as a valued practice for boys *and* girls. This can involve the creation of socially supportive school environments which encourage students to take risks in the classroom. It can also involve them in engaging in practices which challenge dominant gender stereotypes by, for example, girls taking manual arts or boys taking early childhood studies in the senior years of schooling. However, adults in schools need to be aware of the dangers which face girls and boys who take risks by refusing to conform to dominant gender constructions. Students should not be encouraged to take such dangerous risks without the presence of adequate structures which serve to protect those who engage in this form of risk taking. Such structures should work to normalize a new form of risk taking which, as its basis, seeks to challenge existing gender relations.

The reduction of normalized risk-taking activities, and the concomitant dangers that they represent, will thus require the reconstructions of dominant representations of masculinity. Boys need to be made aware of alternative forms of masculinity which are neither dangerous to themselves or others. They will also need to be made aware of the fact that the risks of taking up these alternative performances of masculinity are worth it. For as Sadker and Sadker (1994: 220) have commented: 'When risk taking, violence and sexual aggression are out of control and caring and nurturance are repressed, a distorted profile emerges, one that is detrimental to the good of society and to the healthy development of men.' Thus boys should be encouraged to see that 'Pushing it to the max' does not necessarily involve danger, but rather enjoying a well-rounded life based upon mutually supportive and cooperative relationships in a world which is free from misogyny and homophobia.

Notes

1 All names used here are pseudonyms.
2 This is often romanticized by white, middle-aged, middle-class men who can afford expensive motorbikes.

References

Biddulph, S. (1997) *Raising Boys.* Sydney: Finch.
Canaan, J. (1996) 'One thing leads to another': drinking, fighting and working-class masculinities, in M. Mac an Ghaill (ed.) *Understanding Masculinities: Social Relations and Cultural Arenas.* Buckingham: Open University Press.
Connell, R. (1989) Cool guys, swots and wimps: the interplay of masculinity and education. *Oxford Review of Education,* 15 (3): 291–303.
Connell, R. (1995) *Masculinities.* St Leonards: Allen and Unwin.
Cox, E. (1996) *Leading Women: Tactics for Making the Difference.* Sydney: Random House.
Curriculum and Gender Equity Policy Unit (1995) *No Fear Kit.* Canberra: Commonwealth Department of Employment, Education and Training.
Danby, S. and Baker, C. (1998) How to be masculine in the block area. *Childhood: A Global Journal of Child Research,* 5 (2): 151–75.
Denborough, D. (1996) Step by step: developing respectful and effective ways of working with young men to reduce violence, in C. McLean, M. Carey and C. White, (eds) *Men's Ways of Being.* Boulder, CO: Westview Press.
Faludi, S. (1999) *Stiffed: The Betrayal of Modern Man.* London: Chatto and Windus.
Farrell, W. (1993) *The Myth of Male Power: Why Men are the Disposable Sex.* New York, NY: Simon and Schuster.
Friedman, B. (1995) *Boys-Talk: A Program for Young Men about Masculinity, Non-Violence and Relationships.* Adelaide: Men Against Sexual Assault.
Gardiner, G. (1997) Aboriginal boys' business: a study of indigenous youth in Victoria in relation to educational participation and contact with the juvenile justice system. *Journal of Intercultural Studies,* 18 (1): 49–61.
Gilbert, R. and Gilbert, P. (1998) *Masculinity Goes to School.* St. Leonards: Allen and Unwin.
Gillborn, D. (1997) Young, black and failed by school: the market, education reform and Black students. *International Journal of Inclusive Education,* 1 (1): 65–87.
Gurian, M. (1999) *A Fine Young Man: What Parents, Mentors, and Educators can Do to Shape Adolescent Boys into Exceptional Men.* New York, NY: Jeremy P. Tarcher/Putnam.

Hayes, D. (1998) The displacement of girls as the 'educationally disadvantaged' subject: a genealogical tale. *Change: Transformations in Education*, 1 (2): 7–15.

Kenway, J. (1996) Reasserting masculinity in Australian schools. *Women's Studies International Forum*, 19 (4): 447–66.

Kindlon, D. and Thompson, M. (1999) *Raising Cain: Protecting the Emotional Life of Boys*. London: Michael Joseph.

Lingard, B. (1998) Contextualising and utilising the 'What about the boys?' discourse in education. *Change: Transformations in Education* 1 (2): 16–30.

Lingard, B. and Douglas, P. (1999) *Men Engaging Feminisms: Pro-Feminism, Backlashes and Schooling*. Buckingham: Open University Press.

McLean, C. (1996) Boys and education in Australia, in C. McLean, M. Carey and C. White (eds) *Men's Ways of Being*. Boulder, CO: Westview Press.

Martino, W. (1999) 'Cool boys', 'party animals', 'squids' and 'poofters': interrogating the dynamics and politics of adolescent masculinities in school. *British Journal of Sociology of Education*, 20 (2): 239–63.

Messner, M. (1990) Masculinities and athletic careers: bonding and status differences, in M. Messner and D. Sabo (eds) *Sport, Men and the Gender Order: Critical Feminist Perspectives*. Champaign: Human Kinetics Books.

Mills, M. (1998) The human relationships education curriculum and gender and violence programs. *Change: Transformations in Education*, 1 (2): 68–81.

Mills, M. (2000) Issues in implementing boys' programmes in schools: male teachers and empowerment. *Gender and Education*, 12 (2): 221–38.

Mills, M. (2000) *Challenging Violence in Schools: An Issue of Masculinities*. Buckingham: Open University Press.

Pollack, W. (1999) *Real Boys: Rescuing our Sons from the Myths of Boyhood*. New York, NY: Henry Holt.

Sadker, M. and Sadker, D. (1994) *Failing at Fairness: How our Schools Cheat Girls*. New York, NY: Touchstone.

Salisbury, J. and Jackson, D. (1996) *Challenging Macho Values: Practical Ways of Working with Adolescent Boys*. London: Falmer.

Sewell, T. (1997) *Black Masculinities and Schooling: How Black Boys Survive Modern Schooling*. Stoke-on-Trent: Trentham Books.

Sewell, T. (1998) Loose cannons: exploding the myth of the 'black macho' lad, in D. Epstein, J. Elwood, V. Hey and J. Maw (eds) *Failing Boys? Issues in Gender and Achievement*. Buckingham: Open University Press.

Skelton, C. (1996) Learning to be 'tough': the fostering of maleness in one primary school. *Gender and Education*, 3 (2): 185–97.

Wright, C. *et al.* (1998) Masculinized discourses within education and the construction of Black male identities amongst African Caribbean youth. *British Journal of Sociology of Education*, 19 (1): 75–87.

CHAPTER 5

Challenging boys: addressing issues of masculinity within a gender equity framework

LORI BECKETT

Introduction

Teaching boys presents a particular challenge. Any teacher will confirm that the effort required is demanding. From a young age, through the primary school years to high school and beyond, boys present some difficult challenges. These can range from what to do about their approach to schooling and attitude to education, to devising ways to improve their participation, performance and learning outcomes. In this chapter, therefore, I am concerned to explore what a gender equity approach to dealing with boys and addressing masculinities might entail. Within such a framework the focus is not so much on boys *per se*, but on the 'gender system' (Connell 1996) which limits and constrains both genders in different but significant ways. In this sense, I draw attention to the local site of the classroom and school where boys are constrained and compromised by dominant versions of masculinity.

This sort of recognition begins the task of exploring possible pedagogical strategies that might be useful in challenging boys to reconsider the effects of dominant versions of masculinity in their lives at school. It shows that the social construction of gender (Gender Equity Taskforce 1997) is an important consideration in developing curriculum and managing student behaviour. This is because the ways in which many boys construct their gendered identities impacts significantly on their participation and engagement with school, both in terms of their performance and in the way they behave and relate to others (see Willis 1977; Walker 1988; Mac an Ghaill 1994; Gilbert and Gilbert 1998). The effects can be far reaching because boys' ways of acting out masculinity and what it means to be a proper or a 'cool' boy have consequences, not only for the boys themselves, but for everyone else at school. Boys' participation, performance and learning outcomes can suffer, but they can also disrupt the learning and working environment of the classroom and school, which impacts negatively on other students' learning, school work and social standing (see Mahony 1985; Collins *et al.* 1996). It is in this sense that dominant constructions of masculinity need to be considered as an educational issue.

Privileged boys

I draw on research with three boys at a selective high school for academically gifted students to explore how dominant constructions of masculinity impacted on their lives at school and to illustrate the need to address such issues within a gender equity framework. I will describe their educational biographies, outline briefly their experiences of underperformance and non-participation and discuss the concerns within the context of a wider debate about boys' education. It is apparent that gender equity issues need to be addressed with boys, given that their masculinities are mostly taken for granted or perhaps just seen as a natural consequence of their biological make-up. Two of the boys, for example, who identify as heterosexual, subscribe to a particular version of masculinity which features as an unproblematized construction in terms of its impact on their lives at school. The third boy, however, who identifies as gay, is more aware of the social construction of masculinity, but throughout his education, apparently, he had not been encouraged to reflect on links between gender identity, power and social relations at school.

The task of articulating challenging pedagogies or strategies for teaching boys, therefore, is based on the understanding that gender is a consideration that should be taken seriously, and it suggests that boys need to learn about different ways of being boys and young men. This is not a concern with healing the damage through the mythopoeic masculinity therapy described by Connell (1995), although I describe responsive teaching programmes geared towards boys as future workers, citizens, partners and parents. Rather it is a concern that masculinity, the meanings of manhood, and gender relations are primary considerations. In short, there is both an acknowledgment of, and a challenge to, the masculinist way society and schools are organized, and the ways we all contribute to it by our individual decisions and actions. Thus, it is not my intention to construct the three privileged boys I refer to in this chapter as the 'new disadvantaged', or to constitute them as the 'new victims'. These views are peddled by those who are intent on promoting anti-feminist notions of educational and social reform (for a critical discussion of these concerns see Cox 1995; Kenway *et al.* 1997; Mills and Lingard 1997; Lingard and Douglas 1999).

My research takes a cue from the New South Wales (NSW) gender equity strategy, *Girls and Boys at School*, which is based on principles of equity, and which is intended to achieve improved educational outcomes for both girls and boys. It defines gender as the social arrangements made to deal with sex differences and recognizes a complex set of social and historical factors that influence the ways in which women and girls, men and boys experience and express their femininities and masculinities. *Girls and Boys at School* also recognizes that current beliefs about feminine and masculine behaviour shape the differences in girls' and boys' educational and social outcomes. It admits that these differences contribute to reproducing unequal power relationships between men and women, and that gender interacts with other social indicators like ethnicity, Aboriginality, socio-economic status, sexuality and disability, which can be linked to patterns of participation in education and post-school destinations (see Department of School Education 1996).

I used *Girls and Boys at School* to frame my interview questions. I wanted to investigate the boys' beliefs about masculine behaviours, their expectations of educational and social outcomes, and the way these beliefs about gender are linked to patterns of boys' participation and performance and, in the case of senior students, their post-school outcomes. I also wanted to investigate the boys' views about gender equity. These insights should shed light on the limitations of the populist debates about girls' and boys' educational experiences, particularly the cry that 'girls are outperforming boys'. The media focus on girls' higher average matriculation performances, girls' higher retention rates, and the decline of boys' average matriculation scores fuels teachers' and parents' anxieties and fears as well as public disquiet about girls' and boys' education as illustrated in the introductory chapter to this volume. Thus, my case story work with these three boys is intended to provide a more insightful understanding of teaching boys and the way gender equity work can help improve the lot of teachers and boys in schools.

'Schooling didn't put me off; it was just the good times that turned me on!'

This section describes the educational biographies of two boys, Caleb and Joel, who attend a selective high school in New South Wales. I am concerned to explore these boys' experience of schooling and education and to examine their understandings of gender and gender relations. Like most selective high schools, there appeared to be a preoccupation with student achievement and a focus on developing a culture which emphasized learning outcomes (Lingard and Douglas 1999).

Caleb was 17 years old when he failed to achieve a high enough score to enter university. Expecting to do so much better and with a university education in mind, he was shattered by his results. He had completed Years 11 and 12 at the selective high school, and received exceptionally good assessment reports throughout his last two years. He had been dux of his primary school, talented in music, dance and drama, and devoted to sport.

The reasons for his poor performance were clear when Caleb and his parents did a 'post-mortem' on his results. Caleb's dad pinpointed poor study skills, too much wasted 'free' time, 'the social scene', and a rebelliousness when it came to school rules and school uniform. They had argued about Caleb's hyped up music and hours on the telephone. Earlier in his schooling Caleb had been a high achiever, but he became a youth obsessed with manliness, basketball, showmanship and girlfriends, all to the detriment of his school work. His mother had recalled how he had wanted to pursue a vocational education course and drama but his father had insisted on Physics, Chemistry, Maths, Computer Studies, Business Studies and English. Caleb felt that he was out of his depth, and considered that 'mucking around', missing classes, body building, playing sport, and spending time with his mates was the more enjoyable thing to do:

LB: What was it about schooling that put you off?

Caleb: Schooling didn't put me off; it was just the good times that turned me on. I enjoyed school. I looked forward to getting up each morning to go to school.

LB: For the social reasons.

Caleb: Yeah, unfortunately for the social reasons.

Caleb appeared to be more concerned to enact a desirable cool masculinity which is based on a denigration of the educational values of schooling related to an investment in mental labour (see Willis 1977; Martino 1999a). He was more concerned to have 'a good time' with his friends at school instead of concentrating on his studies. In fact, he could be described as a young man who experienced failure in part as a consequence of his struggle with issues of gender identity and his subject choices, that is, his 'masculinist' subject choices in a gendered curriculum. As Teese *et al.* (1995) put it, subject choice and success are embedded in broader discursive constructions of masculinity and femininity. This is substantiated when he talks about his involvement in the curriculum:

LB: Let's talk about your subject choices.

Caleb: I reckon I would have done a lot better if I had chosen the subjects I really enjoyed. When my subject choices had to be picked, my parents picked them all for me. I didn't really get to pick my own subjects. Every time I'd say this, I'd get 'no'. They said you have to leave your options open for university.

LB: That must be linked to your parents' vision of what they wanted as a career for you. What did they have in mind? Was it Mum and Dad, or was it Dad?

Caleb: Mostly Dad. Mum was more 'let him do want he wants. Let him decide what he wants.' Dad was more like 'no he can't'.

As Mills and Lingard (1997) have noted, it is the construction of hegemonic masculinity which limits choices for many boys. In Caleb's case, it was such a form of masculinity that impacted on his performance, so it is important to highlight the constraints of dominant versions of masculinity with a view to working with boys like him. The intention is not to preserve Caleb's middle-class privilege but to highlight how dominant versions of masculinity can also limit and constrain middle-class boys. In this sense, it is important to emphasize that the focus on boys I am advocating is not driven by a competing victim rhetoric based on the concern that girls are outperforming boys. Some boys like some girls do not do well at school because of the impact of dominant versions of masculinity and femininity on their lives. This draws attention to the plight of different and diverse boys and groups of boys, and recognizes that middle-class boys as a group fare well at school. However, boys like Caleb cannot go unremarked.

> *LB:*   You were just saying what happened at school, for the girls and
> for the boys.
> *Caleb:* The girls were a lot more neat and tidy at school. All the girls
> came wearing blazers and long skirts, ties and polished shoes. For
> the boys, there were more earrings, more radical haircuts, baggy
> jeans. It was more of a social event than going to school. School
> was playing basketball, hanging out, watching TV in the library,
> and going into town. Chuck the occasional period of maths in
> here and there.

Here Caleb highlights the different norms governing boys' and girls' social practices and hence fashioning of identity at school. He seems to be highlighting how even middle-class boys are caught up in normalizing practices through which they strive to enact a 'cool' masculinity. This raises questions about the need to re-examine the relationship between social class and schooling and the interaction of gender and class. Again, as Mills and Lingard (1997) noted, a positive outcome would be a refocusing on the complex relationships between social class and schooling, and on the ways gender intersects with social class in different ways in relation to the lived experiences and the outcomes from schooling (see Weiner 1998). In this sense, it is important to avoid seeing resistance to the formalized aims of schooling as confined to working-class boys but still to acknowledge the differential power relations for different groups of boys on the basis of socio-economic standing (Willis 1977).

Skaties, schooling and dominant masculinity

The ways in which dominant versions of masculinity limit and constrain boys are also apparent in Joel's story. Joel is a 16-year-old boy who had both good and bad experiences at the selective high school. He remained for four years from Years 7 to 10, performing well and enjoying school at first, but falling into what he called a gradual decline. Joel was gifted in mathematics and electronics, but he did not succeed in such a competitive environment. He was bored with the subjects that were of no interest to him, and became mischievous, getting into trouble and ultimately accepting the label 'trouble maker'. Joel joined his mates with skateboards in a 'skaties' group, donned trench-coats, caused some disruption in class, truanted and, in receipt of a reasonable amount of pocket money, experimented with soft drugs.

Joel felt the teachers were out to get him, and on one occasion he got caught making an implement to smoke cannabis out of an orange drink bottle. As a consequence, he spent five days at school with nothing to do in an interview room adjacent to the Deputy Principal's office on an 'in-school suspension', known by the boys as solitary confinement. He said it did not deter him from misbehaviour, but convinced him that none of the teachers cared about his education. He got to the point of non-participation and non-cooperation before leaving the school on request, to avoid expulsion. Joel did not attain his School Certificate[1] at the level he was capable of achieving. He has since enrolled in a local comprehensive school, and he says he has 'turned over a new leaf'. He wanted to try the Year 11 mid-year and yearly exams and consider doing the Higher School Certificate or an apprenticeship in the navy or airforce. Joel is set on making electronics his career:

LB: What field do you want to work in?
Joel: Electrical engineering.
LB: So university qualifications . . .
Joel: No, TAFE qualifications.
LB: What work can you do . . .
Joel: I can work in communications, either working on high-tech equipment or repairing it.

Joel could be described as an 'oppositional boy', that is, a boy whose educational performance was affected by his behaviour, a boy no doubt included in the data on learning difficulties, behavioural support, truancy, vandalism, suspension and exclusion (see Collins *et al.* 1996).[2] It is true that Joel earned the label 'trouble maker'. He said he let off fire crackers in the school, and he admitted he stole chemicals from the science laboratory with the intention of making explosives. It is accurate to say Joel was not engaged in, nor was he engaged by, the education being provided. By his own admission he contributed to his failure at the selective high school:

LB: So you have mentioned wagging. Was this something you did?
Joel: Yes, all the time. Like at the end of Year 10, the Board of Education [*sic*] wouldn't allow us to do our Year 11 subjects, so every single day for every single lesson, we did revision. So I wagged. There was no point. I wasn't learning anything.
LB: What did you do?
Joel: I went into town; out to the skate board ramp. Just hung out.

Joel, like Caleb, is a middle-class boy whose gender also impacted on his performance. Where Caleb was set up for failure, Joel drew some strength and dignity from a dominant construction of masculinity. Finding himself in a competitive environment that did not accommodate him, Joel resorted to acting out a particular version of masculinity in the form of misbehaviour as a way to give himself some power and comfort:

LB: So where did you come undone? Where and when, or was it a gradual decline?

Joel: It was a gradual decline.

LB: Can you describe it?

Joel: I don't know.

LB: Was it getting kicked out of class?

Joel: No, not really. It was more mischief, like the explosives.

LB: What prompted you to do that?

Joel: I was bored. I was with my mates.

These two case stories of Caleb and Joel are instructive. They illuminate not only the influences on the boys to express and experience their masculinity, but also their beliefs about masculine behaviour, which shape their participation, performance and learning outcomes. This is not confined to the boys themselves. In Caleb's case, he and his mates were absorbed in the transition from youth to manhood, and his parents, or more accurately his father, subscribed to a particular view of what boys and young men need to do in terms of subject choices. This is in keeping with the gender and class patterns of privileged families described by Connell *et al.* (1985), where it is the men who are more involved with decisions about choice of schools, subject choices, career paths and discipline. This is also in line with the masculinist priorities embedded in the curriculum, or, as Collins *et al.* (1996) described it, the way boys are caught in a narrower stereotype of what is appropriate for them. In Joel's case, he was typecast as a behaviour problem, as if the responsibility was his and his alone. However, a closer examination suggests the masculinizing practices of the school (Connell 1996) and the policing practices of the teachers (Lingard and Douglas 1999) need to be called in to question.

It is important to reiterate that these boys should not be described as disadvantaged nor constituted as the new victims in need of mythopoeic masculinity therapy. Together with the third boy, Michael, they are privileged. They are white middle-class boys who benefit from schooling and education to the point where they are better educated and more articulate than most of their peers, and they rarely experience exclusion especially given their success in gaining entry to the selective high school. The boys are well suited intellectually to what Connell *et al.* (1985) called the competitive academic curriculum, which is tailored to the needs of middle Australia. The boys are expected to do well in the school, particularly as it is supposed to promote a culture of successful learning and cater for its clientele's cultural capital.

In what follows, I will describe Michael's educational biography and the ways in which his subordinated homosexual masculinity has impacted on his participation and performance.

Sexuality and marginalized masculinities

Michael is a boy of 15 who identifies as gay, and who is out to his immediate family and close friends. He has come out over the last twelve months, first with two girls, then one by one with the boys and other girls in his group at school. Michael has not told his teachers, and he is sure none of the other students in the school know about his gay identity. His greatest concern is the prejudice and discrimination, and the threat of violence which goes hand in hand with what he calls emotional stability.

Michael: I can understand why my parents are ... um ... worried ... er ...

LB: about the threat of violence?

Michael: Yes, with the threat of violence and it's like they rely on me to do something about it. I can deal with the bashing, but I can't deal with the decision to bash me.

LB: Talk to me about the fear of homosexuality; the way it affects you.

Michael: ... um ... your ability to learn, like your ability to be school captain, doesn't change because of your sexuality. Sure your emotional stability is affected because you're always being discriminated against, constantly being discriminated against because of your homosexuality. That might affect your learning, just like it was for women in the earlier part of this century because they were always doubted; much like racism I guess.

LB: Any wonder your parents are worried.

Michael: My parents are always worried. They always tell me to watch out. There's people out there who don't care. They'll bash you up. They'll ... they'll ... they'll kill me. I don't know. Will they kill me? What will they do?

As I mentioned earlier, Michael is a privileged boy, but only in terms of his family's social background and his attendance at a selective high school. Because of his homosexuality, he is also a marginalized boy who knows that being gay does not measure up to the dominant constructions that define what it means to be a 'normal' or proper boy at his school.

LB: What about in the school?

Michael: There's a big group of boys and the only thing I ever hear is them calling people poofters and faggots. They use it as a put down. They think homosexuality is unnatural, but it's as natural as anything. They call anyone they don't like gay.

That Michael chose to stagger his 'coming out' indicates he knew his particular form of masculinity was not valued, and that he had to carefully consider and test his friends' homophobia as well as their acceptance. In this relatively safe space, Michael can practise his marginalized masculinity and exercise his right to be treated equally. Michael can also negotiate the other boys' fears and attempts to define their heterosexual masculinity. With one exception, the boys together with the girls in his group take seriously the idea of a just adolescent society:

LB: Why is it that your group of friends are accepting of you?
Michael: . . . I don't know . . . they like me . . . I don't know . . . I think
          my friends accept me because it's the thing to do . . . we don't
          really talk about it, but we stick up for people's rights . . . it
          would be unfair . . . it is just mean to discriminate . . .

The one boy, Jeremy, who has difficulty in coming to terms with Michael's sexuality also struggles with his own heterosexual masculinity and essentialist notions of gender. As Mills and Lingard (1997) claim, to speak of the 'true' natures of men and women, the masculine equates with activeness, assertiveness, aggressiveness, and the feminine with passivity. It follows that men who do not act the 'warrior' and who are soft and gentle are not real men. It is these essential binaries that work against those who seek to subvert the 'true nature' of men, that is, feminists and gay males.

Not that Michael sets out to aggravate boys like Jeremy, though Michael does present a challenge to heterosexual masculinity. In response, Jeremy avoids Michael and refuses to sit with him in the class and in the playground. In doing so, Jeremy unknowingly valorizes particular masculinist qualities and builds a hierarchical relationship between the boys' masculinities (see Connell, 1995; Kimmel, 1996; Clark, n.d.). This has consequences for Michael, who experiences bouts of insecurity and anxiety, and who acts out irritability and anger. It should come as no surprise that Michael chooses to remain closeted from teachers and other students, which typifies gay boys' and young men's experiences of non-hegemonic masculinity and 'othering', especially when they are accompanied by threats of verbal and physical harassment and violence.

LB: Tell me about the other boys at school.
Michael: One group is all guys. That's the 'skatie' group. They swear.
          They do the tough guy walk. They are the ones who muck up,
          seriously muck up and get kicked out. They are always talking
          about who they bashed, what they've done. They are always
          making flatulent noises. I just wish they'd go away.

It is these concerns about gender that impact on Michael's participation and performance, which ultimately affect his learning outcomes. In fact, Michael's learning outcomes are at times in jeopardy:

Michael: If they knew I was gay, I would be bagged out and shoved around. I have got so much to worry about, I don't want to think about it.

Clearly, this is only the beginning of the analysis of these three boys' schooling experiences and their education, which needs rigorous investigation by all concerned. Gender offers some explanation as to why the boys, who are in a socially and educationally advantaged position, seemed least able to attend to their schooling and education in the most productive way. The interviews suggested that they were willing to do so, but of concern are the ways they encountered the construction of gender, that is, dominant constructions of masculinity at the selective high school, and acted out their identity to the detriment of their schooling.[3]

It should be noted that the three boys concerned are not wedded to the ideas of dominant macho versions of masculinity. As Caleb put it, he thinks everything is changing. He wants to be not so much macho but a more considerate and caring sort of person. Joel was quick to say he did not believe in hitting women. He thought he should behave diplomatically, like his parents, and treat women equally and with respect. Michael was more sensitive to masculinity and was familiar with the term.

LB: Talk to me about masculinity. What is that for you?

Michael: It's about being masculine. It's maleness. Like people try to prove their masculinity. Like the boys who play football, and get a girl and get laid. It's like they prove their sex. (My friends) don't try to be this type of masculinity. There's different kinds. There's charming and sophisticated and gym-fit. That's me I guess. That's what I'd like to be. Like my friends. They play handball, and they read books, and use computers, and play computer games . . .

This speaks to the fluidity and changing character of masculinity (Kimmel 1996; Mills and Lingard 1997; Clark n.d.), which is critical to understanding the work that needs to be done with the boys. That said, the question must be asked, Why did the boys, each finding themselves in differing circumstances, behave in the ways they did? In answering the question, it must be acknowledged that the boys do not blindly follow their nascent sense of social justice, countering inequality. There are other influences, including youth culture and the mass media in terms of music, films and sport. The boys are active participants in constructing their own identity and social relations, and they know the benefits of the patriarchal dividend (Connell 1995). Of course it would be instructive to interview the boys further, as well as their teachers and parents, to get a more rounded perspective on what happens at school.

The boys' stories provide some direction for doing gender equity work and challenging dominant relations and inequalities. This requires challenging pedagogies. I turn to this in the final part of the chapter. As the name implies, the pedagogies or strategies for teaching and learning are intended to challenge boys' ideas about masculinity.

Challenging pedagogies

Taking up this challenge means that teachers engage a theory of gender as it relates to the practice of teaching boys.[4] This is the theory of practice mentioned at the beginning of the chapter. It begins with a consideration of some basic pedagogical questions.[5] How do boys and young men define gender? What factors contribute to their sense of boyhood and manhood? How do they experience and express masculinity? What are their current beliefs about masculine behaviours? In what ways do these shape learning? What are the educational and social outcomes for different boys and groups of boys? How might these differences be described? What sort of social relations do they act out? How do they understand gender equity? As we ponder answers, one step is crucial. We must consider gender to be an educational issue and build it into existing teaching programmes across the key learning areas in order to attend to boys' personal and social development as future workers, citizens, partners and parents.[6] This means that teachers and boys, in conjunction with parents and others, begin to define the kind of young men they want the boys to become. They begin to articulate the kinds of knowledge, attitudes and skills they envisage the boys will need when they leave school to fulfil such roles.[7]

It is crucial for the boys to see the folly of believing there is only one form of masculinity which is narrow, rigid and inflexible.[8] As Lingard and Douglas (1999) claim, there is a need for the boys to be valued and affirmed as boys, but in concert with this it is also necessary to broaden the acceptable range of masculine expression available to boys. This needs to be underlined because it means teaching boys about gender in general and masculinities in particular, which requires an understanding of gender as a social construction. After Gould (1985), teaching about and to boys and young men means engaging them in the same way girls and young women have been engaged in studying women.[9] This means teaching them not only about men but also what it means to be a man and engaging them in a self-critical commentary.

For Caleb, as for Joel and Michael, there is a need to grapple with, contest and question their common-sense assumptions about being men and in the process begin to dismantle the 'masculine mystique' and learn how they have become masculinized (Salisbury and Jackson 1996). In other words, they need to learn about the masculinist ways in which society and schools are organized. This includes adolescent society and schoolboy customs like acting manly, conforming to a group identity, needing to belong, pressuring peers, putting down boys who are different, scapegoating, denigrating girls and anything regarded as feminine, and deriding any form of intellectualism and academic achievement.[10]

For Caleb, this also includes an understanding of his subject choices and the fact that a dominant construction of masculinity tied him not only to a narrow range of subjects but to a gender-divided social world.[11] As Kenway *et al.* (1997) argue, gender is deeply and often unconsciously ingrained in people's psyches and behaviour and inscribed in school cultures and education systems. It is important for Caleb and boys like him to learn about the gender order with its public and private spheres, power imbalances and inequities. It is crucial they know about the binaries that keep women and girls tied to the private domestic sphere, and men and boys positioned in the more privileged public sphere.

I suggested earlier that Caleb's subject choices were in line with the traditions of the competitive academic curriculum and influenced by the school's culture of success. Salisbury and Jackson (1996) counselled that some boys find it difficult in a climate that overemphasizes winning and success, because they often have to prove they are somebody special as a way of covering up and countering a fear of helplessness and impotence. Seidler (1991) argued that many boys live out the dilemma between being exceptional and being worthless. This helps explain Caleb's remake from a high achiever to a youth obsessed with a particular version of masculinity.

This also helps to explain Joel's non-participation and underperformance. In the wake of his disinterest and gradual decline at school, his misbehaviour came to be a way of proving his masculinity. Similarly, his experimentation with soft drugs and association with other youths in trench coats came to be a way of proving a more extreme version of masculinity, characterized not only by risky bravado but confirmation and approval by the male peer group. In their view, the male peer group valuation has more status than teachers and parents, especially when there is little respect across the age groups. As Salisbury and Jackson (1996) pointed out, this proving of masculinity is a central part of becoming a 'real lad', where 'real lads' are deliberately careless about their lives.

In Michael's experience, the test of 'real lad' status and dominant masculinity is homophobia, where the fear of homosexuality has a negative impact on boys' sense of self and their social relations with other boys and men but also girls and women. This includes heterosexual boys who are quick to distance themselves from anything considered feminine and unwilling to express their emotions, much less demonstrate intimacy. Gilbert and Gilbert (1998) pointed out that projects to counter homophobia need to do some gender equity work with and for the minority boys, not just the mainstream who are taught to be more tolerant of such differences.

In these ways, Caleb, Joel and Michael can explore the taken for granted about being boys and young men, especially the expectations of what is required to be men who are privileged and powerful. Most of all, the boys need to understand that their own masculinity is a peculiarity and there are debilitating effects of hegemonic masculinity not only on women and girls, but also on men and boys, especially those who do not conform to dominant norms governing what it means to be a proper boy. This adds to their developing understanding of social justice.

We should not be surprised to learn that there is a long way to go with this sort of gender equity work, as the boys in my case stories made abundantly clear:

LB: Talk to me about what it means to be a man, a young man.
Joel: I don't know . . . a broad chest . . . I don't know . . . to be able to drive.
LB: What is your understanding of gender equity?
Caleb: I don't understand what gender equity is, one hundred per cent. The way it sounds is the way males and females are treated against one another, like in comparison. That would be my understanding. I have never actually listened to, read or talked about gender equity. I probably have, but I haven't known I have talked about it really.

This is significant because it highlights the need for teachers explicitly to address issues of gender and how they impact on both girls' and boys' lives at school.

Conclusion

This chapter has highlighted the importance of addressing masculinities within a gender equity framework that is committed to exploring the ways in which hegemonic heterosexual masculinity impacts on boys and their experiences of schooling. In this sense attention has been drawn to the challenge of teaching boys, which I argue must involve assisting them to interrogate the role that dominant constructions of masculinity play in their lives at school and in the wider society. Such a pedagogical practice involves creating spaces for students to discuss gender issues in their classrooms. The research has shown that boys are willing to participate in these kinds of discussions and are concerned to interrogate the limits of existing gender regimes. As one of the boys stated when asked about what could be done to change the gender status quo:

Michael: Education would be the best thing, just like that guy who had a dream . . . Martin Luther King. He said a man would be judged not by the colour of his skin. Well, my version is that a man will be judged not by his sexuality, nor by his wealth, but by the contents of his mind.

And so the realization of this dream must involve a whole-school commitment to addressing – with students, teachers and parents – the effects of dominant constructions of masculinity. This chapter represents a small step in assisting teachers to undertake this important kind of gender work.

Notes

1 The School Certificate is awarded at the end of Year 10 by the Board of Studies on the provision that students satisfy the requirements of an external examination in English, maths and science, and internal assessments in all subjects across the Key Learning Areas. This includes students' application to work.

2 This description of Joel is different to Kenway's (1996) idea of 'oppositional boys', who construct themselves as victims in response to feminist reforms in schools, arguing that such programmes blame and punish boys and fail to address their concerns, prompting them to be resentful and angry.

3 There was a word of caution about identity politics from Mills and Lingard (1997) who, after Connell (1995), were hesitant about the claims for recognition and redress being made by marginalized groups. They argued that any concern with boys must acknowledge the patriarchal dividend or the benefits accrued to men and boys and counter the inequalities inherent in contemporary patriarchy.

4 Boulden and Parker (1998) ran numerous professional development sessions for teachers in Queensland schools. They came to the conclusion that the best approach to gender equity work is to provide teachers with the opportunities to consider gender as it works in the lives of students, rather than to view the issues as problems which have to be managed and contained. This sits well with Salisbury and Jackson (1996), especially Chapter 11, 'How boys become "real lads": life stories about the making of boys'.

5 These pedagogical questions, like my interview questions, are derived from the NSW gender equity strategy, *Girls and Boys at School*.

6 See Clark's (1996) paper, 'Gender as an educational issue', which builds an argument that schools must respond to their mandate to equip young people with the skills, understandings and values to participate as active, informed and competent adults in work, home and civic life.

7 These ideas are adapted from M.F.D. Young (1999), especially Chapter 7, 'Integrating personal and social development into the 14–19 curriculum'.

8 See Martino (1999a, b) and Gilbert and Gilbert (1998).

9 This is not confined to boys' education as a mirror image of girls' education. As Gilbert and Gilbert (1998) noted, the appropriation of early girls' education work on access and equity and the effort to have women's knowledge and experiences valued is worth investigating, but there are some differences to the boys' agenda. Where gender work for boys and girls aligns, however, is through more recent reforms that focus on different and diverse experiences of masculinity and femininity and understanding the social and cultural construction of gender, gender relations, and gendered subjectivities and personalities.

10 Thanks to Alan Scully in the Faculty of Education, University of Technology Sydney (UTS) for sharing his stories of boyhood and the culture of dominant masculinity in schools.

11 See Clark's (1995) *The Gender Divide*.

References

Boulden, K. and Parker, M. (1998) Where the boys are. *Redress. Journal of the Australian Women Educators*, 7 (2): 5–9.

Clark, M. (1995) *The Great Divide: Gender in the Primary School*. Melbourne: Curriculum, Corporation.

Clark, M. (1996) Gender as an educational issue. Unpublished paper included in the *Gender Equity Resource Kit*. Sydney: Department of School Education.

Collins, C. Batten, M., Ainley, J. and Getty, C. (1996) *Gender and School Education*. Melbourne: Australian Council for Educational Research.

Connell, R.W. (1995) *Masculinities*. Sydney: Allen and Unwin.

Connell, R.W. (1996) Teaching the boys: new research on masculinity and gender strategies for schools. *Teachers' College Record*, 98 (2): 206–35.

Connell, R.W., Ashenden, D.J., Kessler, S. and Dowsett, G. (1985) *Making the Difference*. Sydney: Allen and Unwin.

Cox, E. (1995) Boys and girls and the costs of gendered behaviour. Transcribed address in Gender Equity Taskforce (eds) *Proceedings of the Promoting Gender Equity Conference*. Canberra: Ministerial Council for Education, Employment, Training and Youth Affairs.

Department of School Education (1996) *Girls and Boys at School. Gender Equity Strategy, 1996–2001*. Sydney: Department of School Education.

Gender Equity Taskforce (1997) *Gender Equity: A Framework for Australian Schools*. Canberra: Ministerial Council for Education, Employment, Training and Youth Affairs.

Gilbert, R. and Gilbert, P. (1998) *Masculinity Goes to School*. Sydney: Allen and Unwin.

Gould, M. (1985) Teaching about men and masculinity. Method and meaning. *Teaching Sociology*, 12 (4): 285–98.

Kenway, J. (1996) Reasserting masculinity in Australian schools. *Women's Studies International Forum*, 19 (4); 447–66.

Kenway, J., Willis, S., Blackmore, J. and Rennie, L. (1997) *Answering Back. Girls, Boys and Feminism in Schools*. Sydney: Allen and Unwin.

Kimmel, M. (1996) *Manhood in America: A Cultural History*. New York: The Free Press.

Lingard, B. and Douglas, P. (1999) *Men Engaging Feminisms*. Buckingham: Open University Press.

Mac an Ghaill, M. (1994) *The Making of Men: Masculinities, Sexualities and Schooling*. Buckingham: Open University Press.

Mahony, P. (1985) *Schools for the Boys? Co-education Reassessed*. London: Hutchinson.

Martino, W. (1999a) 'Cool boys', 'party animals', 'squids' and 'poofters': interrogating the dynamics and politics of adolescent masculinities in school. *British Journal of Sociology of Education*, 20 (2): 239–63.

Martino, W. (1999b) Disruptive moments in the education of boys: debating populist discourses on boys, schooling and masculinities. *Discourse: Studies in the Cultural Politics of Education*, 20 (2): 289–94.

Mills, M. and Lingard, B. (1997) Masculinity politics, myths and boys' schooling: a review essay. *British Journal of Educational Studies*, 45 (3): 276–92.

Salisbury, J. and Jackson, D. (1996) *Challenging Macho Values. Practical Ways of Working with Adolescent Boys*. London: Falmer.

Seidler, V. (1991) *Recreating Sexual Politics: Men, Feminism and Politics*. London: Routledge.

Teese, R., Davies, M., Charlton, M. and Polesel, J. (1995) *Who Wins at School? Boys and Girls in Australian Secondary Education*. Melbourne: University of Melbourne Department of Education Policy and Management.

Walker, J. (1988) *Louts and Legends: Male Youth Culture in an Inner City School*. Sydney: Allen and Unwin.

Weiner, G. (1998) New era or old times: class, gender and education. *International Journal of Inclusive Education*, 2 (3): 189–207.

Willis, P. (1977) *Learning to Labour: How Working Class Kids Get Working Class Jobs*. Aldershot: Saxon House.

Young, M.F.D. (1999) *The Curriculum of the Future: From the New 'Sociology of Education' to a Critical Theory of Learning*. London: Falmer.

CHAPTER 6

'Powerful people aren't usually real kind, friendly, open people!' Boys interrogating masculinities at school[1]

WAYNE MARTINO

Introduction

In this chapter I draw on research with two adolescent boys to highlight what I consider to be the implications for encouraging boys to interrogate masculinities in schools. While the focus is only on two boys, this work is part of a broader project involving interviews conducted with over 150 boys from diverse backgrounds and locations in Australia (see Martino and Pallotta-Chiarolli in press). One of my aims is to try to access for teachers some of the ways in which these boys interrogate issues of masculinities in their own lives. I have chosen these interviews because they are fairly representative of the willingness of many boys to respond to the questions about masculinities that were posed to them in the research. In fact, many boys we interviewed were willing to discuss these issues, but claimed that no opportunity in schools had been provided for them to do so! Hence, in light of what these two boys have to say about practices of masculinity in their own lives, I look at what the pedagogical possibilities might be for working with adolescent boys in schools (see Salisbury and Jackson 1996; Gilbert and Gilbert 1998; Mills 1998; Reichert, this volume).

This focus on interrogating masculinities is important, particularly in light of the 'competing victim' rhetoric that informs many of the debates surrounding boys' education in Australia, the United Kingdom and United States (see Chapter 1, this volume; Epstein *et al.* 1998; Arndt 2000; Capp 2000; Hoff Sommers 2000). Boys' interests are often set against those of girls and such perspectives are driven by a feminist backlash rhetoric (see Kenway, 1995; Yates, 1997; Lingard and Douglas, 1999). As Foster, Kimmell and Skelton have illustrated only too well in the introductory chapter to this book, the rhetoric about 'boys as victims' has a seductive but dangerous influence in its capacity to reinforce the very versions of masculinity that need to be challenged in schools. This is why it is crucial to explore ways of working with boys in schools to encourage them to interrogate how they perform and define their masculinities.

'Guys who are real masculine don't like talking [about their emotions]!'

In this section I focus on one student's awareness and interrogation of how boys learn to relate and regulate themselves. Bruce, a Year 11 student aged 16, highlights that there is a requirement for boys not to express their emotions when relating to their peers. He claims that this is because girls are 'more in touch of their emotions':

> Girls are kind of more open. I guess if guys all kind of opened up to one another, it sounds strange, they might find out that they're all really the same and that they could accept one another. Say, I open up my emotions to people and some guys, still they'll reject you . . . females can get in touch with their emotions and they're not afraid to talk about them, while a lot of guys are. So you talk to these guys who are real masculine and don't like talking about it when they're with their friends who make fun of women and treat them as objects, but when they're by themselves, they start to open up as well and you see the real them and they talk about what they like and how they feel about certain things and they're alright . . . They're by themselves so they don't have to prove themselves to anyone . . . but they have this kind of thing where they kind of compete to see who can make the sickest comment about the females and they make all these comments and see who's the funniest and things like that, you know.

Bruce here identifies a particular mode of relating which is organized around quite specific norms or expectations. On one level, he seems to be suggesting that 'part and parcel' of being a heterosexual male involves an avoidance of emotions. This is reinforced through engaging in sexist practices as a principal mode of relating to other boys (see Willis 1977; Wood 1984; Kimmel and Messner 1989; Haywood 1993; Holland *et al.* 1993). He also highlights the role that competitive power plays among boys in performing heterosexual masculinity which is played out often in terms of who can make the 'funniest' or 'sickest' comment about females. However, Bruce does draw attention to the fact that this kind of behaviour does not happen all the time. It is, in fact, a very public display of performing hyper-heterosexual masculinity in peer group situations.

Bruce continues to elaborate on a generalized rule for behaving or relating, which he sees as being an important part of what constitutes heterosexual masculinity for many boys. However, the rule that boys should not show their emotions is also one that he identifies as constraining the way in which he would like to be able to relate to his male friends:

Bruce: Well I think it all comes back to rejection.

Wayne: What would they be rejected for then?

Bruce: Um, for showing their emotions because this attitude of mascu-
           linity and this stereotype has been built up for so long, passed
           on from their fathers, it just keeps getting passed on generation
           after generation.

Wayne: So it's not really just a stereotype, is that what you're saying,
           that it's kind of quite 'real'?

Bruce: It's 'real', definitely, with a lot of people. I'm not saying every-
           one's like that, but you will find a lot of it in most people. Even
           I must admit, um I feel uncomfortable say, giving my best friend
           a big hug in front of other guys . . . because that's not accepted
           by them, they reject that kind of idea of showing your emotions
           because you like this person even though it's platonic. There's
           nothing sexual about it, it's just that you really like this person,
           you can't show that because it's like that's reserved for the
           opposite sex, you don't do that kind of thing, that's showing
           your emotions too much and that's how we've been conditioned
           into being after so long, whereas females, they hug each other
           all the time, that's the way they are because they're friends and
           they like each other, they're not afraid to do that and other
           females condone that, they don't reject it . . . [But guys] they're
           still very, I don't know, closed. They're like that little town on
           Shame, the little closed community within themselves, they're not
           allowed to show the real them, they have to hide that. I guess
           that could be attributed to years ago when the male was the
           breadwinner, the woman stayed at home and that power that
           goes along with men and by showing your true emotions that
           kind of doesn't. It doesn't reflect your power, I guess, you could
           say. One of the attitudes and emotions that go along with power
           is that you are very, you're hard, you're cold, you strive to
           achieve, you, um, I don't know, it's hard to express. Powerful
           people aren't usually real kind, friendly, open people if you know
           what I mean? They have a mission or a purpose and they try to
           achieve that without letting emotions get in the way and I guess
           maybe that's been passed on through guys because guys have
           always been the powerful dominant figure, going back to say
           the 18/1900s and that's the way it's just come up and something's
           going to have to be done.

Bruce links boys' avoidance of expressing emotion to an 'attitude of masculinity' which has been 'passed on from their fathers'. In so doing, he emphasizes the pivotal role of fathers and adult men in establishing these norms for governing the behaviour of their sons. Moreover, what is significant is that Bruce has developed quite specific capacities for reading masculinity and is applying them to his own practices and to those of other boys. For example, his reference to the Australian film *Shame*, which dealt with the pack rape of a 16-year-old girl in a rural town, is pertinent in this respect. This film was studied in an English class which I conducted where issues around masculinity were discussed at length. Bruce is drawing on these understandings to make sense of his own lived experiences of masculinity. He reiterates the extent to which boys learn to self-regulate and police their masculinities (see Epstein, this volume; Frank 1993; Mac an Ghaill 1994; Connell 1995; Nayak and Kehily 1996; Flood 1997; Martino, 2000a). Within certain limits, expressing emotion and overt affection are circumscribed as sex-inappropriate for boys/men. Bruce accounts for such practices in terms of power, particularly when he makes the observation that powerful people 'aren't usually real kind, friendly open people'. In this sense, he highlights that behaving in accordance with certain rules, explainable in terms of being *hard*, constitutes for boys an exemplary instance of enacting a heterosexual masculinity.

What needs to be highlighted about this interview is Bruce's willingness to evaluate critically the social behaviour and practices of his peers. However, he is able to draw links between their behaviours and issues of masculinity. This is because certain links have already been explicitly made for him and, moreover, a certain knowledge about masculinity has been accessed at school (see Salisbury and Jackson 1996). In this sense, he actively takes up a position where he problematizes issues of masculinity in the lives of other boys at his school.

'They are teaching us pretty much crap'

Like Bruce, many of the boys interviewed talked at length about 'masculinity' and what it meant to them, but mentioned that they had not been asked explicitly to think about 'masculinity' at school. In a follow-up interview with Shaun, aged 16, what is highlighted is the extent to which he has reflected on the question posed in the previous interview three weeks earlier where he was asked to define 'masculinity'. He makes the point quite emphatically that:

> Right now they are teaching us pretty much crap that we will never need to know later on in life but this [masculinity] is something that is pretty important to a whole lot of people.

I want to focus more specifically on how he responds to some of the questions and to provide for teachers some access to the way he is thinking about and exploring issues of masculinity in his life. This is important because, through undertaking this kind of analysis, the limits and possibilities for encouraging boys to interrogate masculinities in schools can be discussed. In other words, what can be provided is some kind of 'contextualized guidance' (Gore 1992: 68) for teachers in terms of thinking about possible pedagogical strategies for addressing issues of masculinity in schools. Moreover, in this way, attention can be drawn to the already existing capacities for self-problematization that the boys we interviewed demonstrated, with some consideration being paid to how these capacities might be capitalized upon in teaching boys to reflect critically on the effects of dominant models of masculinity in their lives (Martino 1998, 2000b).

When I ask Shaun whether he felt many boys might feel threatened by talking about masculinity in class he comments that this might be a reason why it is not being addressed:

> Yes, I think that maybe that's why we don't have the opportunity, maybe that's the major reason. Guys do feel threatened about stuff like that. I know that if the teacher got up there and started talking about how to be male and the guys in the class thought that he wasn't being a guy, they might start giving him hassle and stuff. If the teacher had mannerisms, like if he was a gay guy or he did something or he did the most stupid things, guys would straight away go what are you on about, you're not masculine yourself; how can you teach us how to be that . . . So guys can be threatened by it but it also has to be presented in the right way.

Immediately, what is highlighted here is how students police male teachers through heterosexist and homophobic practices of surveillance. So those teachers who encourage their students to question dominant masculinity, risk having their own sexuality brought into question (see Epstein, this volume). Mills (1998: 77), for instance, states that for many boys 'homosexuality was associated with being supportive of feminist aims or of gay rights'. Hence, teachers' attempts to encourage boys to question their investment in dominant masculinities may well lead to the latter feeling threatened, as Shaun mentions above, thereby resorting to a homophobic tactic of questioning the male teacher's sexuality. Thus, the very homophobic and heterosexist practices which limit boys' learning and social relations may also impact on male teachers' commitment and willingness to encourage their students to engage in such critical thinking. For this reason, I ask Shaun about the story, *Manhood*, which I had discussed in class that term with my Year 11 English students (see Mellor *et al.* 1991). It is about a boy's dysfunctional relationship with his father, who expects him to behave in a stereotypically masculine way.

> *Wayne:* Do you think they [my students] were threatened by discussing *Manhood*?
>
> *Shaun:* No . . . I didn't think they felt threatened but maybe if they did they kept it to themselves because they wouldn't come out

saying it ... I suppose that if anyone did feel threatened they might have kept this to themselves.

Wayne: What I thought was that people were thinking about things that maybe they hadn't thought about for the first time and that it was important in some way that they thought about it. In their mind they were reflecting on it and that was basically all I wanted them to do.

Shaun: Yes, I know that, I myself I sat down because we had to analyse it and I sat down and I started drawing all this stuff out of it and it just helped me to figure out, I know that the stereotypes were there, but that also helped me to see them in different ways and might see them a little bit better and might see that *they are not just stereotypes and not just expectations but they're like this real big thing that does happen in real life* ... this is something that can happen in real life and that does occur and I suppose it started with everyone thinking about what they really are and what they should be and what they shouldn't be and how they are pressured to behave in certain ways.

So opening a space in the classroom for discussing how certain social expectations are related to 'being masculine' proved to be very important for Shaun. He went away and thought about the issues in relation to his own life, apparently drawing on already learnt practices of self-problematization. What is significant is his comment that the stereotypes about masculinity were not just fictions (Walkerdine 1990) but related very significantly to 'real life'.

I also ask Shaun to comment further on some of the points he raised about 'being a boy' in his previous interview:

Wayne: ... in the last interview OK, I asked you something about masculinity and what you thought about it ... about the problems that you think guys of your age experience and you said, one of the biggest problems of being a boy your age is that you don't exactly know what you are meant to be doing ... Can you elaborate on that? So there is some uncertainty then about being a guy?

Shaun: Yes, I know that the older you get and the more you learn about how things go and stuff, you learn and you think about this happened last time and I know it's going to happen next time, but you look at it from both sides, you feel like what's going to happen if you do something, either a whole bunch of things can happen from that, so it's almost as if we don't know ... *if we're guys we know that we play footy, I don't think they know why they do it, we don't know why we act that way and do what we do, we just do it because it's either natural or something*, but we don't know why we are doing it. It's pretty stupid when you think about it, but when guys play footy, because all guys play footy, they don't know why they are actually playing it or whether they like it that much or whether it's being drummed into them or they're just doing it to follow people. It's like almost as if no one is an individual, everyone sits down and waits for something to happen and then they watch the reaction of their friends and then they do what their friends do and so I don't think a lot of guys know how to act like how men are supposed to act or if there is such a thing that men are supposed to act in a certain way. A lot of guys will do something that they think is manly or they think is what they are meant to be doing, but it might not be what they are meant to be doing at all . . . like other people might see it as something that they are not doing properly or they are not being masculine and stuff like that. And it's also like you're damned if you do and you're damned if you don't, like there's a whole bunch of guys wrestling, if you don't then you are going to get laughed at by the other guys, but if you do you might get into trouble and stuff like that or the girls will think that you are an idiot and stuff like that and you will be called a meat head. So it's almost as if we get confused in what we have to do . . . It's almost as if we don't know how we are meant to act and there is no right way or a way of showing us how we are meant to act.

Here Shaun questions how boys' behaviour is somehow seen to be natural, but in posing certain questions about masculinity and in introducing him to a discourse about masculinity as circumscribed by particular social and cultural expectations, he is starting to problematize 'masculinity' in his own life and in relation to how he sees other guys 'acting'. For example, he is starting to problematize boys' engagement in football or their reasons for playing it and suggests that their investment in this sport is somehow related to social and cultural influences of which they are unaware (see Martino 1999). He elaborates further on these influences when I prompt him:

Wayne: Don't you think that boys learn the rules or what the right ways are? For instance, if guys play with certain kinds of toys and not others, if guys do certain things and not other things, don't you think that people bring them into line or their parents or society brings them into line really quickly.

Shaun: Yes, there is the thing about society how if a guy starts playing with dolls his dad is going to say what the hell are you doing, go and get your truck, stop playing with dolls and give them to your sister. That's how society and their parents think and the children are forced to do it that way. When they get old enough to start thinking about what they are doing I think they start to question what they are actually doing. Because I remember when I had the interview you asked me what it was to be masculine, I didn't have a clue because I never knew what masculinity was, I was thinking of when I was growing up I played with Lego, I did stuff like, I did the guy things, I go on and now I'm playing the drums which is pretty much a male instrument and I like to go out and play footy with my friends, I do male things and now when I look at it I see myself doing something that, it's as if like *there has been a ritual passed on by the parents and by society* and that each generation has to do what the last generation did when they were boys and they have to be guys and then they have to be men and men do it this way and then I started thinking about it and what's wrong with doing it the wrong way and what's wrong with doing it the other way. So I think that what happens to you at home is what happens to you in later life . . . *they teach you a way of being a man or a boy and they teach you the way that they think you should be*, though it might not necessarily be the right way or the way that you actually are meant to be, if you know what I mean . . . It's almost as if what the mother or parents teach you gets stuck in your head . . . You don't sit there and think about things or what would my dad think about it . . . I think that is just the way people are, they get set into the patterns from childhood by their parents . . . so we grow up with the expectations and then they are there. It's almost as if their expectations are there in the subconscious area but they are not out there and they are not evident until situations occur . . .

Here, Shaun highlights how boys are taught to act and behave in specific ways which are not somehow 'natural'. However, he highlights that boys may not always be conscious of what is driving them to behave in certain ways. This thinking is interesting in light of Shaun's previous comments about boys feeling uncertain and confused about what is expected of them. However, when prompted to explore the rules that boys learn for behaving in *appropriately* masculine ways, he is able to examine the issues of expectations and the role they play in boys' lives.

In the previous interview, Shaun mentioned how he had found the question requiring him to express his opinion about what he understood about masculinity a difficult one to answer. In fact, other boys we have interviewed throughout Australia, from diverse locations and backgrounds, have expressed similar views (see Martino and Pallotta-Chiarolli, in press). What is interesting about Shaun's response, which follows, is that in further reflecting on this question, he is led to consider what life must be like for a female.

Shaun: I can tell you now that I would much rather be male than female because I think that females have a lot more expectations put on them than guys have.

Wayne: In what way?

Shaun: In the way of being pretty and being good looking and being popular and stuff like that. When you asked me the question about being masculine I thought about the first thing that popped into my mind was being big and strong and stuff like that and then when I started to think about it I thought about, I sat down and I thought well, what's the other end of it, like what happens when females do it, like what would it almost be like if I had to be a female. I thought what happens to the females just in the school, I've seen in the school, there are a lot of expectations on them like if they are not pretty, people will hassle them because if you look there are a couple of groups around and the leader of that group is almost the best looking girl and a lot of her friends may not be as good looking as her and stuff like that and they might get hassled from the other guys, but that girl will never get that hassle. I know that a lot of the guys may hassle, they will turn around and talk about some girl and say oh look how fat that girl is, she is so fat. Then they look around and see that other girl is good looking and they go oh yes, she is really good looking, and be really nice to them and just because the girl who is ugly or she's fat or she's got something wrong with her . . . they will hassle her or other girls may hassle her . . . But with the guys it's almost as if it's pretty much who is cool, who can do stuff like that and that's how guys be friends with guys. I know that from my perspective, its like no other guy looks at another guy and says he's good looking or he's not good looking, he's not going to be my best friend, but it's almost as if the girls pick their friends and the leader of the group is the best looking girl in the group and you can see that almost nearly every time . . . That's how it is, a lot of expectations are put on the girls like looking good, being popular, doing stuff with other guys as well. If the girls talk to the guys then they will be more popular than the people that don't and so that there is a lot of pressure put on the girls and a lot more expectations put on the girls.

In fact, Shaun elaborates at length in this interview on how girls are harassed by boys if they are 'flat chested' or if they have 'huge tits'. This leads him to the following conclusion and realization about the gender politics governing social relations among boys and girls:

So that's how I see it that girls have a lot of expectations and a lot of pressure on them to be good looking and popular and stuff like that, whereas the guys don't really care, although they have their own little expectations amongst each other. *I think the guys don't really care what the girls think, I think they care more about what other guys think . . .* That is why

I thought that the guys have it pretty much easier than the girls, the only pressure that we really get is from other guys, whereas girls get pressure from guys and their friends to do stuff. That's why I wouldn't want it. I sure as hell wouldn't want to be female walking around these days.

So the question ultimately leads to Shaun thinking about the 'other side' and leads him to reflect on and to interrogate how hegemonic masculinities impact on girls in terms of the sexualized ways in which boys learn to relate to girls as objects (see Lees 1993). What is particularly interesting is Shaun's discussion about the power differentials in terms of how boys appear to dictate the way girls relate and regulate themselves whereas guys are more concerned about what other guys think. This highlights how powerful dominant masculinities are. It would seem that it might be very useful to ask students what life might be like if they were a member of the opposite sex (see Martino and Mellor 1995). This would lead to productive discussions about the kinds of expectations, and hence limits, that are placed on both boys and girls in terms of how they are required to behave, act and think. This commentary is interesting in light of the 'poor boy' rhetoric promoted by men's movement advocates and educators who buy into the competing victim syndrome as outlined by Foster, Kimmell and Skelton in the introductory chapter to this book (see also Foster 1994). What is often invisibilized in taking up such positions is the ways in which dominant masculinity impacts on the lives of girls, both in terms of how they are policed and learn to police themselves (see Hey 1997).

Implications: boys interrogating 'masculinity' in schools

Many boys have already developed certain capacities for self-problematization. The question for teachers is how to draw on these already existing 'techniques of the self' in relation to discussing and interrogating issues of masculinity in their classrooms and in their relationships with students. First, I believe that developing a particular kind of pastoral pedagogical relation with students based on mutual respect, care and trust is crucial for encouraging boys to reflect on these issues. While the safe space of the interview cannot be replicated to the same extent in teaching a class of 30 students, what can be achieved is the creation of a particular classroom environment where students feel comfortable and safe to discuss the effects of masculinity. Subjects like English and health education, for example, provide a productive site where these kinds of discussions can be conducted and where texts can be used to make explicit a certain knowledge about masculinity and its effects. Questions such as the following could be posed but need to be framed by particular theoretical understandings about gender (see Martino 1995; Martino and Mellor 1995; Gender Equity Taskforce 1997):

- What do you understand 'masculinity' to mean? What does it mean to be a man? In what ways do boys have to prove that they are men?
- What do you think is meant by the term 'versions of masculinity'?
- How are boys expected to behave? What stereotypes are you aware of? Where do these expectations come from? Who imposes these stereotypes?
- What happens to boys if they do not behave in stereotypical ways or according to the expectations of others?
- What is homophobia and what role do you think it plays in boys' lives?
- What do you think life might be like for a member of the opposite sex?

Such questions can provide a useful starting point or a 'threshold' for initiating students into interrogating how masculinities are constructed and influenced by already available understandings about what constitutes desirable or appropriate behaviour for boys within a culture at a particular point in time. However, as Gilbert and Gilbert (1998) highlight, any programme devoted to educating boys must avoid slipping into promoting problematic versions of masculinity which feed into biological determinist and essentialist arguments about the 'nature' of boys (see also Lingard and Douglas 1999). They must also encourage students to explore issues of diversity and difference among boys as a group rather than reinforcing differences between boys and girls. But, as Hey (1997: 130) points out, the 'formal pedagogy of schooling' has been about '. . . denying questions of differences to their subjects (Walkerdine 1985). There was little official encouragement to engage school students in discussions of the divisions and relations of power'.

The above questions, therefore, are presented merely as starting points for teachers in addressing these kinds of issues about power, difference and masculinities in schools. However, the context of a broader pedagogical relationship involving the ways in which teachers relate to students and the role that their own gendered understandings have to play in this need to be taken into consideration (see Martino and Berrill forthcoming).

Conclusion

In this chapter I have drawn attention to the willingness of adolescent boys to interrogate masculinities. I believe that one of the key issues for teachers is to find ways of drawing on boys' existing capacities for self-problematization. Given the opportunity, many boys will interrogate the limits of masculinity in their lives, and this can have positive effects in terms of encouraging them to re-evaluate their own social practices (Butler 1990; Simpson 1994; Nayak and Kehily 1996; Dixon 1997; Martino 2000b; Martino and Pallotta-Chiarolli in press). However, such critical work in the classroom cannot be undertaken unless students feel comfortable and respected in the classroom. In fact, establishing such a relationship is conducive to promoting effective classroom learning irrespective of the topic being addressed! But this cannot be executed effectively without taking into consideration teachers' own understandings and knowledge of gender. This needs further consideration.

Careful selection of particular texts can be used to encourage students to do this kind of critical work (see Martino 1995, 1999, 2000a, b). It would appear that posing certain questions and using specific texts could have quite positive effects in terms of assisting boys to deploy critical capacities for interrogating masculinities. This is supported by the claims made by boys themselves in this chapter and their willingness to engage in such discussions (see Lingard and Mills 1997). However, such pedagogies cannot somehow be divorced from the issue of the knowledge about masculinity that teachers need to provide for their students. As Skelton, Kimmell and Foster have highlighted in the introductory chapter to this book, biological deterministic arguments about boys as victims of the feminist movement appear to be driving public discussion and debate about boys, masculinities and schooling, not only in Australia but in the UK and the United States (Epstein *et al.* 1998; Hoff Summers 2000). This chapter is an attempt to move teachers beyond such limited and narrow understandings of the boys' educational agenda.

Note

1 This chapter is based on a presentation at the AERA Conference, San Diego, April 13–17, 1998. It is drawn from my doctoral research into the production of adolescent masculinities in school. I would like to thank Martin Mills and Libby Lee for their comments on earlier drafts of this chapter.

References

Arndt, B. (2000) The trouble with boys. *Sydney Morning Herald*, June 17.

Butler, J. (1990) *Gender Trouble: Feminism and the Subversion of Identity*. London: Routledge.

Capp, G. (2000) Boys fall behind girls in schooling. *The West Australian*, June 6: 11.

Connell, R.W. (1995) *Masculinities*. Sydney: Allen and Unwin.

Dixon, C. (1997) Pete's tool: identity and sex-play in the design and technology classroom, *Gender and Education*, 9(1): 89–104.

Epstein, D., Elwood, J., Hey, V. and Maw, J. (eds) (1998) *Failing Boys?* Buckingham: Open University Press.

Foster, V. (1994) What about the boys! The importance of theory/policy/curriculum nexus in the education of girls and boys. *Independent Teacher*, August, 24–7.

Frank, B. (1993) Straight/strait jackets for masculinity: educating for real men. *Atlantis*, 18(1 and 2): 47–59.

Gender Equity Taskforce (1997) *Gender Equity: A Framework for Australian Schools*. Canberra: Ministerial Council for Employment, Education, Training and Youth Affairs.

Gilbert, R. and Gilbert, P. (1998) *Masculinity Goes to School*. Sydney: Allen and Unwin.

Gore, J. (1992) What can we do for you! What can 'we' do for 'you'? Struggling over empowerment in critical and feminist pedagogy, in C. Lue and J. Gore (eds) *Feminisms and Critical Pedagogy*. New York, NY and London: Routledge.

Haywood, C. (1993) Using sexuality: an exploration into the fixing of sexuality to make male identities in a mixed sexed sixth form. Unpublished MA Sociology of Education dissertation, University of Warwick.

Hey, V. (1997)*The Company She Keeps*. Buckingham: Open University Press.

Hoff Sommers, C. (2000) The war against boys. *The Atlantic Monthly* 285 (5): 59–74.

Holland, J., Ramazanoglu, C. and Sharpe, S. (1993) *Wimp or Gladiator: Contradictions in Acquiring Masculine Sexuality*. London: Tufnell Press.

Kenway, J. (1995) Masculinities in schools: under seige, on the defensive and under reconstruction? *Discourse: Studies in the Cultural Politics of Education*, 16 (1): 59–79.

Kimmel, M. and Messner, M. (1989) *Men's Lives*. New York, NY: Macmillan.

Lees, S. (1993) *Sugar and Spice: Sexuality and Adolescent Girls*. London: Penguin.

Lingard, B. and Douglas, P. (1999) *Men Engaging Feminisms: Pro-Feminism, Backlashes and Schooling*. Buckingham: Open University Press.

Lingard, B. and Mills, M. (1997) Masculinity politics: an introduction. *Social Alternatives*, 16 (3): 4–6.

Mac an Ghaill, M. (1994) *The Making of Men*. Buckingham: Open University Press.

Martino, W. (1995) Deconstructing masculinity in the English classroom: a site for reconstituting gendered subjectivity. *Gender and Education*, 7 (2): 205–20.

Martino, W. (1998) 'Dickheads', 'poofs', 'try hards', and 'losers': critical literacy for boys in the English Classroom. *English in Aotearoa* (New Zealand Association for the Teaching of English), 25 (September): 31–57.

Martino, W. (1999) 'Cool boys', 'party animals', 'squids' and 'poofters': interrogating the dynamics and politics of adolescent masculinities in school. *British Journal of Sociology of Education*, 20 (2): 239–63.

Martino, W. (2000a) Policing masculinities: investigating the role of homophobia and heteronormativity in the lives of adolescent boys at school. *The Journal of Men's Studies*, 8 (2): 213–36.

Martino, W. (2000b) The boys at the back: challenging masculinities and homophobia in the English classroom. *English in Australia*, 127–8 (May): 35–50.

Martino, W. and Berrill, D. (forthcoming) Dangerous pedagogies: addressing issues of sexuality, masculinity and schooling with male pre-service teacher education candidates, in B. Frank and K. Davison (eds) *Masculinities and Schooling: International Practices and Perspectives*. Halifax: Fernwood.

Martino, W. and Mellor, B. (1995) *Gendered Fictions*. Cottesloe, WA: Chalkface Press.

Martino, W. and Pallotta-Chiarolli, M. (in press) *So What's a Boy?* Buckingham: Open University Press.

Mellor, B., O'Neill, M. and Patterson, A. (1991) *Reading Fictions*. Perth: Chalkface Press.

Mills, M. (1998) The human relationships education curriculum and gender and violence programs. *Change: Transformations in Education* 1 (2): 68–81.

Nayak, A. and Kehily, M. (1996) Playing it straight: masculinities, homophobias and schooling. *Journal of Gender Studies*, 5 (2): 211–30.

Salisbury, J. and Jackson, D. (1996) *Challenging Macho Values: Practical Ways of Working with Adolescent Boys*. London: Falmer.

Simpson, M. (1994) *Male Impersonators: Men Performing Masculinity*. New York, NY: Routledge.

Walkerdine, V. (1990) *Schoolgirl Fictions*. London and New York, NY: Verso.

Willis, P. (1977) *Learning to Labour: How Working Class Kids Get Working Class Jobs*. Westmead: Saxon House.

Wolpe, A.M. (1988) *Within School Walls: The Role of Discipline, Sexuality and the Curriculum*. London: Routledge.

Wood, J. (1984) Groping towards sexism: boys' sex talk, in A. McRobbie and M. Nava (eds) *Gender and Generation*. London: Macmillan.

Yates, L. (1997) Gender equity and the boys debate: what sort of challenge is it? *British Journal of Sociology of Education*, 18 (3): 337–47.

CHAPTER 7

Boyz' own stories: masculinities and sexualities in schools

DEBBIE EPSTEIN

Introduction

This chapter explores the role that sexuality plays in the formation and negotiation of masculinities for boys in schools. This focus is particularly important given the concerns that are being expressed about the boys in the public media (see Epstein *et al.* 1998). What is significant about the ways in which the boy problem has been framed is that issues of sexuality are invisibilized in a debate which Foster, Kimmel and Skelton in the introductory chapter point out has been carried on in vociferously anti-feminist terms with feminists being constituted as the villains of the piece and boys as the suffering victim/heroes. The effect of such a competing victim syndrome (Cox 1997) is to elide the very significant ways in which compulsory heterosexuality impacts on the lives of boys and girls at school, not only those who identify as gay. In this chapter I draw on research with gay boys and teachers in school to explore both the highly sexualized dimensions of schooling and the extent to which struggles around sexuality are intimately connected with those around gender (developed further in Epstein and Johnson 1998). This is particularly important given that macho and misogynist versions of masculinity draw on and feed the explicit and implicit homophobia and heterosexism to be found in playgrounds, classrooms and curricula. In fact, I have built on this argument elsewhere to suggest that boys have and produce problems in schools and in assessed achievement in part because of the demands made on them to be macho and, at all costs, not to appear feminized or gay (see Epstein 1998). The solutions are not to be found in anti-feminist masculinist (and masculinizing) politics, in the drums and 'nature' advocated by some, or in offering boys encouragement to do more of the same.

Understanding what happens to non-conforming 'sissy' and/or gay boys can help us think through how we can respond to the 'boy problem'. This chapter should be read as a contribution to that understanding.

Heterosexism and homophobia

While schools are constituted as public arenas – in contrast to the supposed private space of sexuality – they are nevertheless places where young people and their teachers do a great deal of cultural work on the construction of their identities in a whole range of ways, importantly around issues of sexuality. However, as I have pointed out, these struggles are intimately connected with struggles around gender (in this instance, primarily masculinity). Following Butler (1990), I also propose that it is impossible to develop a full understanding of gender relations without examining them in the context of compulsory heterosexuality, or, as she puts in, through the lens of the heterosexual matrix. In other words, sexism in schools needs to be understood through the lens of heterosexism. This is highlighted by the following boys' comments:

Steve: I mean, do heterosexual men and women actually debate with, y'know, why am I straight? . . . I don't believe so.

Clive: But everything that we see affirms their sexuality: books, TV, when you're out at work, people you meet on the bus, buying a newspaper, doing your shopping. Everything confirms, reinforces their sexuality . . .

Ranee: I mean, it's considered normal.

Steve: And yet, in my experience, I have a suspicion, y'know, basically heterosexual people are not very secure in what they are and that that is part of the hostility and the whole debate around homosexuality versus heterosexuality.

(Group discussion by KOLA, Birmingham Black Lesbian and Gay Group)[1]

When examining the level of hysteria generated in the mass media (especially the tabloid press) around issues of sexuality, particularly in relation to education, it is hard to avoid agreeing with Steve's conclusion. There is a level of uncertainty, of feeling threatened, which contributes to a form of moral panic, as illustrated in the Parliamentary debates (in the first half of 2000) about the possible repeal of Section 28 of the Local Government Act 1988[2] (see Johnson and Epstein 2000). I am particularly interested, therefore, in the importance that homophobia plays in the production of conventional, heterosexual masculinities. Nayak and Kehily (1996) argue that the performance of homophobia both polices and constructs heterosexual masculinities in schools and this has implications for the school lives of those boys/young men who resist conventional masculine identities as well as for girls/young

women. Moreover, homophobia and (hetero)sexism are themselves imbricated with racialized meanings. The normative heterosexual family is, by
implication if not definition, white and middle class; heterosexuality, masculinities and femininities are all played out in relation to the particular
'imagined community' (Anderson 1983) of this fantasy happy family.

Doing a thing on weddings

I have indicated above that sexism in schools needs to be understood through
the lens of heterosexism. Many examples of the use of sexuality as a form of
control and of resistance constitute both heterosexism and reinforcement to
particular versions of masculinity and femininity. For example, the instruction
not to be a 'Nancy-boy' is not simply about not being gay, but clearly also
about not being a 'real man' (of a particular type). Similarly, instructions to
girls/young women to behave in more 'ladylike' fashion are not only about
particular versions of femininity but also about behaving in ways that signify
heterosexuality. Equally, even successful resistance by girls/young women
to particular types of male teacher behaviour can become a way of reinscribing
heterosexuality. For example, one of our interviewees described how girls in
her class had adopted the wearing of high stiletto heels in order to stamp
'accidentally' on the foot of a male teacher who was sexually harassing them.
This had the desired effect of stopping him from touching them up, but at
the cost of wearing a particular signifier of heterosexual femininity (for a
fuller discussion see Epstein 1996).

Both heterosexuality and conventional gender relations are also often
(re)produced through the taught curriculum itself. For example, one of our
interviewees, Ayo,[3] told me a story about how, while in the infant school,
his teacher organized some 'mock weddings'. He did not remember the
particular context of this event, but knew that he had been about 6 years
old when it took place. It seems likely to me from his age that this was at
the time of the marriage of Charles and Diana. This was a time when infant
and junior teachers up and down the country were undertaking projects
about 'weddings' and 'marriage' (though I did not encounter any projects
about divorce to accompany their very public split and divorce negotiations
in the period after they split up and before Diana's death!):

Ayo: We were doing a thing on weddings.
DE: So, what, you were about 6 or 7?
Ayo: Yeah, and they decided that we should all play at getting married.
DE: They decided? The teachers?
Ayo: Yeah. As a fun thing to do, I suppose . . . And we, some, I think
two other 'couples' or, you know . . . they progressed up an imaginary aisle and had confetti and things thrown at them and this girl
who I was supposed to get married to didn't want to, and she
started screaming the place down, and I was really rattled.

DE: Yeah. Do you know why she didn't want to?

Ayo: No, it was just she didn't want to. And she started blubbering all over the place, and I remember this was just a lesson.

DE: Did she just not want to get married? Did she not want to do the getting married bit, or did she not want to do the getting married bit to you?

Ayo: I definitely think it was to me. And I was told it was to me. Some of the other kids were saying, 'Look, she didn't want to do that', and it made a really deep impression. I thought, oh, she doesn't like me. . . . but after the break period, the teacher got, I think had done things, or whatever, made things happen, and it was all done very quickly and rushed. You know, let's get this over with so everyone's satisfied, so we rushed through this pretend ceremony and stuff, and that was it.

DE: Did the kids sort of enjoy that? Did they think it was sort of . . .

Ayo: Yeah, they thought it was a giggle . . . And you know there were actual dresses and stuff, brides' dresses and little doll things that they got dressed up in and we were dressed in our ordinary clothes I think. We didn't do any Black history.

Here we see the mutual reinforcement of compulsory heterosexuality and of conventional gender relations inescapably intertwined. The playing out of the heterosexual marriage ceremony in its traditional (white, British) form with 'an imaginary aisle and . . . confetti and things thrown at them' assumes the desirability of marriage and institutionally heterosexist forms of relating and reinforces the fantasies of imaginary futures which children (and particularly girls) often express. Moreover, the dressing of the girls in 'brides' dresses' while the boys remained in their ordinary clothes represents a further reinforcement of particular ways of being boys and girls, of particular masculinities and femininities: girls wear pretty, frilly clothes and the teachers expect them to gain something from dressing up in 'brides' dresses and little dolls' things'; boys, on the other hand, are more careless about their appearance and would not enjoy or gain anything from dressing up in 'bridegrooms'' clothes. What we see here is the explicit production of macho versions of masculinity and what Bob Connell has called 'emphasized femininities' (Connell 1989).

Valerie Walkerdine has argued (1996, 1997), that popular culture in its various manifestations (in particular, advertising and pop songs and their videos, but also television programming) can frequently be read as eroticizing young girls (especially young working-class girls). In their turn, she suggests, the girls enter into these fantasies in ways which cannot be interpreted simply; these are neither examples of young girls-as-whores nor of child sexual abuse. Similarly, the pleasures of dressing up as brides is both about the fantasies of adults (in this instance teachers) and of the girls themselves. And the 'prettiness' of the 'wedding dress', the mythology of the 'blushing bride', enter into constructions of heterosexualized femininities, distinct from and Other than the masculine, 'rational' of the boys wearing their everyday clothes. In this way, the co-construction of masculinity and femininity as binary, heterosexual opposites is achieved.

Ayo's apparent leap from the weddings to the statement that 'we didn't do any Black history' is less random than it might at first appear. The particular form of wedding played out was, as I have already pointed out, traditionally white British, while the objection of the little girl to marrying him seems not to have been an objection to getting married as such, but a rejection of Ayo himself. Whether this hostility was, as seems likely, founded on racism is neither here nor there in terms of the way Ayo understood it. His immediate shift to black history is a clear indication that he experienced this episode as an example of racism. In this example, then, we see the intertwining of racism, sexism and heterosexism in a particularly powerful (and to Ayo painfully memorable) form.

They didn't bother me

The constant reinforcement of compulsory heterosexuality through particular sexist discourses about masculinity and femininity was a constant theme of all our interviews. Even in those few cases where respondents spoke about having no problem with being out at school (and as school students), this was in the context of being able to carry off particular gendered styles which are usually coded heterosexual. For boys, this was invariably to do with exhibiting those characteristics associated with 'real manhood'. For example, Simon[4] told me that:

> I ... came out at a very early age. I was rugby captain, very macho, very masculine, didn't have any problems with anybody picking on me. When you're six-foot-two, six-foot-one, six-foot at a very early age, you don't tend to have many problems ... So I eventually came out at school when I was 14, although I was aware of my sexuality, end of cubs, beginning of scouts, which would have been 10, 11 years of age. I'm an only child, so I had developed a very close friendship with a kid from school and negotiated puberty without too many problems at a relatively early age and so did my friend. And basically when we started secondary school at 11, sex between the two of us was more than a regular occurrence, whether it be in my house or in his house. It was only ever between the two of us, but as we went through school, there was no secret that the two of us were very attached to each other. Whether people thought we were best friends or whether they thought we were lovers was of no consequence to us. We were both in the rugby team and everybody left us alone.

Simon is very clear, here, that his ability to come out while still a school student without being, as he put it, 'picked on' rested on his size and perceived macho version of masculinity in what was, as he described it later, 'a very traditional school . . . very boys only, very Rugby orientated, very win, win, win, very academic'. This theme of his macho appearance and, at times, behaviour as a protection against being victimized for his gay sexuality reappeared frequently throughout the interview:

> People just left us alone. You just didn't mess with Simon and Peter, 'cos they would beat you up. But we never, ever had to beat anybody up whatsoever. When you were as tall and as powerful as we were, people just didn't mess, you know.

On occasions, he had recourse to homophobic abuse against boys who were not sufficiently macho:

Simon: But thinking back to when I was 13/14/15, if people weren't strong enough to play Rugby for the school, then my biggest upset is that 'oh, you're a pooftah, you Nancy boy', you know.

DE: And you would actually use those words?

Simon: And I know that I used those words, yeah. If people, if people, weren't strong enough to support the school, then I would certainly have a go at them. People who wanted to be in the school play, rather than play football, would get a lashing. And, you know, that's adolescence for you, you know, you, you would attack, perhaps rather than being attacked yourself . . .

DE: So, I'm interested in this business of the use of the abuse, and the use of the Rugby team macho image as a protection . . . but also using the abuse itself as a protection for yourself. Is that fair?

Simon: We, whether we were doing it knowingly or not, we felt that if we maintain this image, if we maintain this macho image, and we attacked others, we would be left alone, and nobody would attack us, you know. 'Look at Simon and Peter. They're not queer. Why don't we all strive to be like Simon and Peter?' you know.

From the perspective of a gay man now involved in all kinds of gay activism (for example the organization of Gay Pride), Simon remembered these moments with some embarrassment (hence, perhaps, the use of the word 'upset'). What is interesting, however, is that what was being required here both of him and by him was a version of masculinity which was not only apparently heterosexual because it was macho, but one which is particularly unfriendly to women (see also Connell 1995: Chapter 6). The misogyny and generally offensive sexist behaviour of groups of men in rugby clubs is legendary! Furthermore, other, less macho ways of inhabiting masculinity were derided: 'People who wanted to be in the school play, rather than play football, would get a [homophobic] lashing.'

Máirtín Mac an Ghaill (1994), quoting Lees (1987), also draws attention to the fact that:

For the students, the assimilation of non-macho behaviour to feminine behaviour was illustrated in relation to the ubiquity of the term 'poof' which, in 'denoting lack of guts, suggests femininity – weakness, softness and inferiority' (Lees 1987: 180).

(Mac an Ghaill 1994: 165)

This was confirmed time and again in our research. Frequently, the homophobia expressed towards non-macho boys was in terms of the assertion of their similarity to girls. That this takes place in primary as well as secondary schools is confirmed in my other research (Epstein 1995, 1997b) and that of Emma Renold (1999, 2000). Indeed, it is interesting to note that the behaviour of 'tomboys' within the primary context is much more acceptable than the behaviour of 'sissies'. This, I would suggest, is because for a girl to be more like a boy can be interpreted positively, while for a boy to be more like a girl is, almost invariably, seen as problematic because being a girl is, in some sense, disreputable. Insults like 'poof' and 'Nancy-boy' are used to control not only the sexuality of boys but also the forms of masculinity they are likely to adopt, at least within the school context. Interestingly, Mac an Ghaill (1994: 93) gives an example of a boy who was enabled to occupy a non-macho version of masculinity (including the achievement of academic success) by virtue of his previous association with a 'hard' gang and his consequent reputation as a 'hard man'.

Boys frequently seem to survive by dint of appearing 'hard' and macho, especially in boys-only schools. At the conference (held in April 1995) of the London Association for the Teaching of English, I attended a workshop on anti-sexist work with boys. Here the facilitator, Rav Bansal, pointed out that as soon as he started overtly antisexist work in his single-sex boys' school, he was labelled as gay and that, in order to retain any kind of credibility, he took care to drop remarks about having a girlfriend. Furthermore, in the tape of a lesson, which he played for the workshop, we heard him clearing the air for discussion of feelings and sexism with the remark that 'we know that none of us here are gay'. As he explained, he was distinctly uncomfortable about this but felt that it was the only way in which the boys in the class would even begin to entertain the ideas with which he was confronting them. In a context like this, it is hardly surprising that both teachers and students find it extraordinarily difficult to come out.[5]

Support for students

Of course, where lesbian and gay teachers feel unable to come out at school, they are often unable to provide support for those students identifying as lesbian, gay, bisexual or, indeed, unsure about their sexuality. Chris,[6] for example, spoke about her experiences in a coeducational setting:

I had a series of [threatening] letters put into my desk at school saying . . . 'if you don't meet me, I'm going to tell everyone in the school hall at lunch time' . . . There were about two letters that I received in the fifth year, and I actually showed them to my form tutor, and I told her how I was, you know, what was going on, and she said, 'Oh.' I thought she was a lesbian, but obviously she wasn't, because I wanted to talk to her about it and she just turned round and said, 'Well, I think you should just work harder. I think you're worrying about nothing. I think you should just concentrate on your exams.'

In this context, Chris assumed that the threatening letters had come from one of the boys. She had no proof of this, but had also met with overt adverse reaction from some of them. Furthermore, it seemed to her a reasonable assumption that the boys would want to attack her because her coming out as a lesbian seemed like a threat to their masculinities. It is also significant that the teacher (whether a lesbian or not) felt unable to support her. One might speculate that the overwhelming weight of masculine hostility was too much to confront.

In our interviews, those who had been 'sissies' felt the hostility of other boys and lack of support from teachers at least as strongly. Michael,[7] for example, in one of our group discussions, spoke about how:

There was absolutely nobody I could go to. There was, the teachers were just as bad as the pupils. There was no way that any of them were prepared to be supportive. Or if they were, it would be sort of, that smarmy liberal support you can get, about, well, oh great, that's really wonderful, you're making an alternative life choice. But I mean, it's not informative. You can't sit down and talk to somebody who, about, you know, specifically issues around coming out, around having boyfriends, trouble with that, about whether you're gay or not, if that person isn't themselves . . . I think it's really important at that point and stage in your life to have somebody around who is gay themselves, who knows what you're talking about . . .

I'm just very lucky in as much as, having been alienated all the way through my school, through having come from abroad, through . . . never having fitted in, it didn't, it wasn't a major trauma for me and I was able to get through it. But equally, I know friends of mine who, you know, reached that stage, that fatal age of 15 or 16, decided to come out, had no support at all and were completely scarred by it. Some of them still carry scars today. It took them years to get over what they went through. And it's simply not good enough to have somebody who says yes, that's fine, that's your alternative life choice and you're entitled to make it, because you don't have any social back-up.

The importance of Michael's statement, here, lies in the need he expresses for support from other gay men in the process of coming out. The appeal is not so much to a crude identity politics (though there may be something of that in it) but comes from an experience of lack of support from anyone who could understand the experience of being young and gay in school from a gay perspective. In this it has some similarities with the experiences of racism of those young black people who find themselves in predominantly white schools (Epstein 1993). Indeed, one of the things that Michael is saying here is that as a person of colour he had already learnt to deal with racism and this (in itself traumatic) experience enabled him to cope better when he came out as an adolescent. As one experienced gay teacher, active in the union and generally out, said, 'I wouldn't advise any kid to come out at school, even if their immediate circle is supportive.'

Michael's story is one of early identification of himself as 'different'. From nursery school on, he preferred playing in the 'Wendy House' [*sic*] and dressing up (as a girl) to playing more physical games with the boys. During primary school he made close friends with another non-macho boy, Alan:

> . . . we became really good friends and I remember one day actually just completely spontaneously, um, the bell went and we were off . . . And we just grabbed each others' hands and ran off, together, holding hands and all the other people in the class started shouting homo, homo, yurgh, homo, and I didn't understand what it meant, um, but I just realized that, you know, they were sort of shouting something abusive, and it was obviously something to do with Alan and something to do with us holding hands, so we stopped, and, um, felt quite guilty about it actually. I didn't really understand why and then a couple of days later there was this joke going around . . . Um, somebody would come up to you and say, so are you a, and you know this idea of homo somehow had stuck in my head as something bad and then somebody came up to me . . . and said are you a homo sapien [*sic*] and I didn't know what that meant, but I just heard the word homo and I thought, no no no, I'm not a homo sapien and everyone laughed at me.

In this case, Michael's friendship with Alan was made the subject of verbal harassment in such a way that both of them felt constrained to cool the friendship. Furthermore, the later teasing of Michael by others whose vocabulary allowed them to play on the word 'homo' was an additional punishment for his deviations from the norms of heterosexual masculinity. Michael was, then, made to feel guilty about being 'homo'(sexual) in the first instance and, through the later teasing, he was put in a situation whereby the denial of being 'homo' meant that he had also to deny being human. The joke, here, was not only about his naivety, but about the Catch 22 situation in which he was placed – a situation made more significant because the denial of full humanity to particular groups has, historically, been one of the ways in which a variety of oppressions have been held in place.

Teaching from the closet

As pointed out above, it is often very difficult for teachers to come out. Indeed, all the teachers (and whether they were out at school or not) we interviewed during the course of our project spoke of the risks both of coming out and of staying in the closet. Nigel, for example, spoke about how:

> I live very close to the school I work at, not actually in the catchment area – that was a deliberate choice. But two gay friends do live in the catchment area, and, horror of horrors, some new neighbours moved in ... and then it turned out that the children had been allocated a place at the school I teach in ...
>
> And then, just before Christmas ... the head summoned me. She said, 'I just wanted a word with you', and I went in and she said that this particular mother had been and complained. And I said, 'Why? I don't teach this child.' But she said, 'She thinks you are a danger to the children in your class', and I said, 'Well, why? Because I'm not adequate?' and she said, 'Well, let it just be said that she considers you to be, to have dangerous friends, friends who could be a danger to children.'

Here, the risk of being 'outed' at school (as against in the rest of his life) is vividly captured in the phrase 'horror of horrors'; the safety of the closet is dubious at best. This 'horror' is often avoided by dint of distancing oneself from anything to do with lesbian or gay sexuality and, for gay men, this can be most easily achieved through resort to macho styles of masculinity, as became particularly evident in another interview:

DE: You were saying that you felt like you had to definitely play a part?

Harry: Oh yes, yes!

DE: Can you tell me a bit about the part?

Harry: The part, I guess the part was to emulate the straight male teachers.

DE: What does that entail?

Harry: It entailed initially hitting pupils and being physically violent, or physically intimidating and [taking a deep breath] trying desperately not to appear soft.

DE: Yeah? Because that was the give-away?

Harry: That seemed to be the give-away, yeah ... I think that perhaps I was also steering clear of talking about anything that would suggest, give the children an opportunity to point the finger at me, or ask that awful question, which children in school are perfectly capable of asking.

Harry's evident distress during this part of the interview was compounded by his view that hitting children and being physically violent was both wrong in itself and constituted a truly terrible form of pedagogy. What is captured here is the strongly felt necessity to take any means available to avoid the inference that he was gay.

Later in the interview he talked about an incident in which he was 'outed':

> . . . I just panicked. All I could do really was play up the stereotype, as a defence. So I camped it up a bit, and died inside, and I managed to get through all the games and whatever we had to do on stage [during a teacher/student fundraising performance] and then walked off and I nearly just walked out of school.

This narrative captures a memory of terror. Harry's impulse to resign on the spot was not carried out. Here we see the opposite defence from the one he deployed in the classroom. Interestingly, Harry commented that this incident led to his 'relaxing' in the classroom, adopting a less macho teaching style and, in fact, improved his teaching. However, the choice he felt he had, between acting macho and acting camp is not a happy one.

Conclusion

Feminists interested in education have frequently written about the misogyny of schools (see especially Mahony 1985, 1989; Lees 1986, 1987, 1993). Sue Lees and Pat Mahony have also pointed to the homophobia of, in particular, boys. Their concerns have been primarily about what this means for girls in schools. Recent authors on masculinity have been primarily concerned about the effects of macho norms and behaviours on boys, particular those not conforming to these norms (Connell 1987, 1989; Mac an Ghaill 1994; Redman and Mac an Ghaill 1996). While I have focused here mainly on evidence from gay men, the argument of this paper is that misogyny and homophobia are not merely linked but are so closely intertwined as to be inseparable: misogyny is homophobic and homophobia is misogynist. The dual Others to normative heterosexual masculinities in schools are girls/ women and non-macho boys/men. It is against these that many, perhaps most, boys seek to define their identities. The psychic and social defences which they build up against contamination are damaging to their Others (who have to put up with more or less constant harassment), to themselves (for example, in relation to boys' attitudes to schoolwork and current debates around boys' 'underachievement', see Epstein 1998), and to the wider society (for example, in the social cost of macho behaviours).

If, as I have shown, homophobia is constitutive of normative heterosexual masculinities in schools and is also part of the daily misogyny of boys and male teachers alike, if boys have to appear to be super-heterosexual, macho studs to survive at school, then schools will be unhappy, painful places for girls, boys who do not conform and their teachers, who have to struggle against the macho behaviours of significant numbers of boys.

There are, however, (often fragmentary and fleeting) signs of change in available discourses of masculinity. While schools continue to lag behind somewhat timorously, television programming, films and bookshops are filled with representations of alternative masculinities and sexualities, many of them positive and some even downright subversive. For example, during April/May 2000, Boy George has graced the billboards in the UK, inviting people to 'be the first to come out' in an advertisement for a new type of bank account. This is only one of several such advertisements in English-speaking countries. A particularly striking example of the 'queer ad' was a television and film advertisement for Levis screened during the mid-1990s in the UK, Europe and the United States. It showed an extremely attractive young black woman, sexily dressed in jeans and top, hailing a New York cab. She sat in the back making up her face while the cab driver positively drooled over her sexiness. One's immediate reaction to this part of the advertisement was that this was astonishingly sexist and racist. Then came the denouement as the young woman felt her cheek and got out a battery operated razor with which she began to shave. 'She' was a 'he' and the expression on the cab driver's face said it all: disappointment; horror; disgust; desire. The final slogan was 'Levis, cut for men since . . .' Even this played/drew on gay double entendre. The subversion was of dominant discourses of both masculinity and sexuality.

This highlights that, irrespective of the role that schools play in regulating and policing sexuality and gender, students are exposed to a popular culture outside school which actively works to blur the boundaries between the homosexual/heterosexual, masculine/feminine. In this sense, teachers might want to consider the possibilities for strategically using popular culture texts to engage students in discussions about the formation, regulation and nego-tiation of cultural identities. The research drawn on in this paper indicates the possibilities for this kind of work.

Acknowledgements

This article was published in *Gender and Education* in 1997 (9 (1): 105–15) and has been updated for this book. I would like to thank Taylor and Francis for giving permission to reprint it. The first version of the paper was given as part of the British Educational Research Association Symposium at the American Educational Research Association Conference in San Francisco in 1995. I would like to thank the other contributors to and participants in that symposium. I would especially like to thank Fazal Rizvi for the thoughtful comments he made in his capacity as discussant at that session. Thanks to Birmingham University, the University of Central England and East Birmingham Health Authority for funding; to Richard Johnson and Peter Redman for their support and collaboration; to the interviewers on the project – Alistair Chisholm, Louise Curry (as part of her third-year undergraduate research placement), Mary Kehily, Gurjit Minhas, Anoop Nayak, Shruti Tanna; and to members of the Politics of Sexuality Group (David Abdi, Louise Curry, Richard Johnson, Adrian Kear,

Máirtín Mac an Ghaill, Peter Redman, Deborah Lyn Steinberg, Shruti Tanna) for the frequently exciting discussions we had around questions of sexuality which have informed my thinking on these issues (see Steinberg *et al.* 1997). Thanks also to Richard Johnson and Deborah Lynn Steinberg for reading earlier drafts and to the two anonymous referees and Chris Griffin for their helpful comments on the article as submitted to *Gender and Education*.

Notes

1 See also KOLA (1994). All names used are pseudonyms, unless participants have specifically requested that I use their real name.
2 Section 28 of the Local Government Act passed by the Thatcher government in 1988 (in)famously prohibited the 'promotion of homosexuality' by local authorities and said that maintained (i.e. state) schools must not teach that 'pretended family relationships' were equivalent to heterosexual ones. The Labour Government's attempts to have this law repealed in 2000 were defeated by the House of Lords.
3 While Ayo's parents were from Nigeria, he himself was born in London and identified as black, British and gay.
4 Simon was white, English and had attended a grammar school in south London.
5 This has been written up as part of his coursework for his MA (Bansal 1995).
6 Chris was white, English. She had been to a selective and very middle-class secondary school followed by a girls' sixth form college.
7 Michael's father was white, English and his mother was Indian. He had attended several different schools, some in the UK and some in other countries, especially during his early and primary years.

References

Anderson, B. (1983) *Imagined Communities: Reflections on the Origin and Spread of Nationalism*. London: Verso.

Bansal, R. (1995) Looking over your shoulder: a study of anti-sexist discussions in an all-boys classroom. Unpublished MA course work, University of London Institute of Education.

Butler, J. (1990) *Gender Trouble: Feminism and the Subversion of Identity*. New York, NY and London: Routledge.

Connell, R.W. (1987) *Gender and Power: Society, the Person and Sexual Politics*. Cambridge: Polity Press.

Connell, R.W. (1989) Cool guys, swots and wimps: the interplay of masculinity and education. *Oxford Review of Education*, 15 (3): 291–303.

Connell, R.W. (1995) *Masculinities*. Cambridge: Polity Press.

Cox, E. (1997) Boys and girls and the costs of gendered behaviour, in *Gender Equity: A Framework for Australian Schools*. Canberra: Department of Employment, Education, Training and Youth Affairs.

Epstein, D. (1993) *Changing Classroom Cultures: Anti-Racism, Politics and Schools*. Stoke-on-Trent: Trentham Books.

Epstein, D. (1995) Girls don't do bricks. Gender and sexuality in the primary class-room, in J. Siraj-Blatchford and I. Siraj-Blatchford (eds) *Educating the Whole Child: Cross-Curricular Skills, Themes and Dimensions.* Buckingham: Open University Press.

Epstein, D. (1996) Keeping them in their place: hetero/sexist harassment, gender and the enforcement of heterosexuality, in L. Adkins and J. Holland (eds) *Sexualising the Social.* Basingstoke: Macmillan.

Epstein, D. (1997b) Cultures of schooling/cultures of sexuality. *International Journal of Inclusive Education,* 1 (1): 37–53.

Epstein, D. (1998) Real boys don't work: boys' 'underachievement', masculinities and the harassment of sissies, in D. Epstein, J. Elwood, V. Hey and J. Maw (eds) *Failing Boys? Issues in Gender and Achievement.* Buckingham: Open University Press.

Epstein, D. and Johnson, R. (1998) *Schooling Sexualities.* Buckingham: Open University Press.

Epstein, D., Elwood, J., Hey, V. and Maw, J. (eds) (1998) *Failing Boys? Issues in Gender and Achievement.* Buckingham: Open University Press.

Johnson, R. and Epstein, D. (2000) Sectional interests: sexuality, social justice and moral traditionalism. *Education and Social Justice,* 2 (2): 27–37.

KOLA (1994) A burden of aloneness, in D. Epstein (ed.) *Challenging Lesbian and Gay Inequalities in Education.* Buckingham: Open University Press.

Lees, S. (1986) *Losing Out: Sexuality and Adolescent Girls.* London: Hutchinson.

Lees, S. (1987) The structure of sexual relations in school, in M. Arnot and G. Weiner (eds) *Gender and the Politics of Schooling.* London: Hutchinson/Open University.

Lees, S. (1993) *Sugar and Spice: Sexuality and Adolescent Girls.* London: Penguin.

Mac an Ghaill, M. (1994) *The Making of Men: Masculinities, Sexualities and Schooling.* Buckingham: Open University Press.

Mahony, P. (1985) *Schools for the Boys? Co-education Reassessed.* London: Hutchinson.

Mahony, P. (1989) Sexual violence and mixed schools, in C. Jones and P. Mahony (eds) *Learning Our Lines: Sexuality and Social Control in Education.* London: The Women's Press.

Nayak, A. and Kehily, M. (1996) Masculinities and schooling: why are young men so homophobic?, in D.L. Steinberg, D. Epstein and R. Johnson (eds) *Border Patrols: Policing the Boundaries of Heterosexuality.* London: Cassell.

Redman, P. and Mac an Ghaill, M. (1997) Educating Peter: the making of a history man, in D.L. Steinberg, D. Epstein and R. Johnson (eds) *Border Patrols: Policing the Boundaries of Heterosexuality.* London: Cassell.

Renold, E. (1999) Presumed innocence: an ethnographic exploration into the construction of sexual and gender identities in the primary school. Unpublished PhD thesis, University of Wales, Cardiff.

Renold, E. (2000) 'Coming out': gender, (hetero)sexuality and the primary school. *Gender and Education,* 12 (3): 309–26.

Steinberg, D.L., Epstein, D. and Johnson, R. (eds) (1997) *Border Patrols: Policing the Boundaries of Heterosexuality.* London: Cassell.

Walkerdine, V. (1996) Popular culture and the eroticization of little girls, in J. Curran, D. Morley and V. Walkerdine (eds) *Cultural Studies and Communications.* London: Edward Arnold.

Walkerdine, V. (1997) *Daddy's Girls.* Basingstoke: Macmillan.

CHAPTER **8**

'Learning to laugh': A study of schoolboy humour in the English secondary school

ANOOP NAYAK AND MARY JANE KEHILY

Introduction

In this chapter we explore how adolescent boys use humour to exhibit a particular form of masculine identity and establish a peer group social hierarchy. Our ethnographic study[1] of the English state school system suggests that 'learning to laugh' is a practice through which male students negotiate the transition into adulthood. By exploring the social interactions of young men, our work suggests that forms of masculine identity are organized and regulated through humour. Here, humour can be an unofficial resource through which boys learn about the culture of manhood and test out these values among one another. Thus, we argue that humour is a technique that can be seen to produce differential positions of domination and subordination within the peer group. In other words, it is a means by which boys are able to assert power over their peers. But, as we demonstrate in this chapter, such power relations are dynamically negotiated and reworked within the competing cultural codes of schoolboy humour.

To date, pupil humour has been understood as an 'antidote to schooling' (Woods 1976: 179) on the one hand, that offers an escape from boredom, routine and tedium. On the other, it has been interpreted as a class cultural form of resistance that challenges the middle-class ethos of the school establishment (Willis 1976, 1977; Dubberley 1993). By way of extension, for the working-class 'lads' in Paul Willis's (1976, 1977) classic study, having a 'laff' was regarded as preparation for the workplace, the styles and rituals whereby young men 'learn to labour'. Here, a parallel between the roughhouse rules of the 'lads' and the industrial culture of the work-place was established in a mutually enforcing bond of white, working-class masculinity. In particular we are indebted to the insights of Woods and Willis, where pupil humour can be understood, respectively, as both a coping strategy and a product of class cultural tensions. However, our study further suggests that humour is less an 'outcome' or 'effect' of working-class masculinity than a means by which boys are able to fashion these very identities. In this sense humour can be a style utilized by young men to substantiate their heterosexual masculinities. Although some styles of joking may enhance feelings of equality, we focus on how boys use humour to regulate and police their masculine identities.

In fact, it was the pervasive nature of 'wind-ups', joke telling, 'funny stories', spontaneous gags and mimicry that led us to consider seriously how boys use techniques of humour to construct their masculinities. It was through this 'unseen' form of communication and relating that values, meanings and appropriate forms of masculine behaviour were rejected or validated in young people's peer-group cultures. One of the aims of this chapter, therefore, is to enable teachers to gain further insights into how culture can impact on boys' social relationships in school. In short, we seek to address why many Anglo male students 'learn to laugh' in a way that is detrimental to teachers, girls and one another. However, we argue that only by investigating the 'informal', hidden culture of boys' peer group relations can we develop a better understanding of how dominant versions of heterosexual masculinity impact on boys' lives at school.

Local and global context of the study

Our research with boys was undertaken in schools located in the West Midlands region of the UK. The area has a history of factory employment as well as a former industrial heritage related to skilled craftwork such as the art of jewellery making. More recently the region has witnessed widescale deindustrialization with the dismantling of the former car and 'metal-bashing' industries and the emergence of a competitive global economy. Furthermore, in the postwar period the region has become synonymous with the influx of diasporic communities from the New Commonwealth countries as well as large numbers of settlers who have arrived from Pakistan and Ireland. In these 'new times' of global change and development it is the convergence of time and space within the meeting place of the local that has now radically transformed the everyday English working-class culture, of which the national trait of humour is but one expression. Thus, while this collection makes a comparative reference to three continents – Australia, Europe and North America – our study also highlights the importance of scale. It does so by alluding to the cultural specificity of local spaces (the neighbourhood, playground or street) and the complex interaction with wider global processes related to migration, the economy and culture.

At a local level the very fabric of the West Midlands region seems to speak of an industrial heritage that can no longer be realized, functioning as symbol of post-industrial alienation. In the post-Fordist era, it appeared the young men in our study were hardly 'learning to labour'. Yet as we will find they remained every bit as dedicated to the counter-culture of humour as the 'lads' in Willis's (1977) research. In this post-industrial environment, 'masculinity may be less about having power than about feeling entitled to it' (see Chapter I). We contend that heavy, industrial humour may become a means for recuperating masculinity in a post-industrial economy. The values embedded in schoolboy pranks, jokes and funny stories, then, act as symbolic codes through which young men may learn to be 'masculine' in the absence of secure manual work.

Humour and schoolboy masculinities

One of the ways in which the boys in our study 'tried out' masculine identities was through the ritual of humour and game playing. Such games included forms of verbal and physical sparring such as 'play-fighting', 'cussing' or 'blowing' matches and the use of ritualized insults. We suggest that it is through these displays of verbal and physical performance that young men are able to display an English heterosexual masculinity.

'Cussing matches'

The practice of 'cussing matches' or 'blowing competitions' was reported as a recurrent mode of schoolboy humour. The term 'blowing competition' was used as a metaphor to illustrate how the game involved the production of an inflated, 'pumped-up' hyper-masculine ego. The object of the game involved puncturing the ego of an opponent through ritualized forms of abusive name calling. One teacher, Mr Carlton, reflected on the hidden violence embedded within these exchanges.

> We get things like, we used to have, 'Your mom's a dog.' What does that mean, y'know? [laughs] 'Your mom's a sweaty armpit.' It is purely an insult and kids had competitions here called blowing competitions to see who could give the worst insult, right. Now we've managed to stamp it out, but my God, you should have heard some of the things that were said. And it was always about their mother, right, because that is the one thing that everybody has in common. They all know their mother and that's very personal. They know where they come from, very personal and it hurts. And you get all these brash kids who've been reduced to tears by some of the comments that have been thrown at them.

'Blowing competitions' were hotly contested verbal duals that tended to occur between two invariably male opponents, usually in lunch periods away from the intervention of teachers. As such, these activities occurred at the edges of school life, in the 'informal' zones carved out by pupils. According to Mr Carlton, the object of 'blowing competitions' was 'to see who could give the worst insult'.[2] The competition involved the giving and taking of ritualized insults where wit and language became the stage for the performance of masculinity. Here, the ability to absorb 'very personal' comments with seeming indifference, and to respond sharply, are the weaponry required for successful verbal jousting. That 'brash kids' could be 'reduced to tears' indicates that a publicly recognized version of masculinity can be momentarily punctured and secured through these contests.

These rituals show the techniques young men may utilize to make each other vulnerable, while emphasizing the power of dominant versions of masculinity to produce anxieties within the structure of a competitive 'game'. 'Blowing competitions' have the effect of creating clear-cut masculine identities, crystallizing who is 'hard' or 'soft' through the public exposition of power and vulnerability. Mr Carlton noted how 'blowing competitions' were 'always about their mother' because it's 'the one thing that everybody has in common, they all know their mother and that's very personal'. In a discursive manoeuvre, young men are able to mobilize a sexist discourse of power against other males through a verbal attack on their mothers. In doing so they can achieve a superior masculine subject position within the peer group.

The informal cultures of schooling, however, are not set apart from the institutional production of masculinities. In this respect student/student relations may at times chime with the attitudes, values and culture endorsed in teacher/student relations. For example, a milder form of 'cussing' could exist between boys and male teachers, a practice that rests on shared and established gender codes:

Smithy: Some teachers treat you like a mate, dayn't ay?
Shane: Like Carlton. Me and Carlton 'ave cussing matches . . .
Jason: He [Mr Carlton] calls me mum a slag he does! Me and Carlton, we 'ave a laugh man.

In this sense the 'unofficial' culture of the 'cussing match' may be replayed in the 'official' space of the classroom. The implication for teachers lies in the recognition that gender identities are constituted as much through the everyday fabric of schooling as by way of the official pedagogy and its concern with the personal and social development of pupils.

Formulaic insults

Although mother insults were regularly employed during the highly charged showdown of a 'cussing match', at other moments young men drew upon these familiar codes to generate humour among friends out of school. However, the meanings of these insults were *transformed* in the contexts of friendship groups, and away from the intensity of classroom cultures. Wzithin the male friendship group the telling of jokes and relating of insults is structured through the context of peers and situation (Walker and Goodson 1977). Schooling cultures are then central to interpreting the shouting rituals of 'cussing matches'. However, outside school young men were able to decode mother insults differently according to the variable circumstances in which they deployed them.

The importance of context suggests that mother insults, as invoked for the public appraisal of masculinities, may take on different meanings. This goes some way to explaining how an insult during a 'cussing match' may be treated as offensive and capable of reducing males to tears, yet is bandied around between mates (or male teachers and students) at another point under the guise of 'play'. Such examples of mother insults, nevertheless, remained highly misogynistic and often explicitly sexual in whatever contexts they occurred. A school student called Macca related two typically formulaic ritual insults to us that were passed around within the male peer group and used as a resource for humour among friends:

> Your mom's been raped so many times she puts a padlock on her fanny.

> Your mom's got so many holes in her knickers you can play Connect Four.

These 'jokes' have a 'well articulated structure' (Labov 1972: 334) and demonstrate the power of sexual taboo in the masculine peer group.[3]

Punch 'n' run

The object of punch 'n' run is to hit an opponent and run off before he or she has time to retaliate. The punch 'n' run game is usually initiated by young men, though some young women could be drawn into participation. The following is an example of mock fighting which we have termed punch 'n' run. Here, a young woman responds to the masculine physical gaming in school.

> *Tina:* I don't really like Darren that much now. He's always competitive ain't he? Have you seen him with Clive? Clive punched me in my arm and he punched me three times, and so Darren did. So I went [demonstrating] one-two-three!

The extract shows how punch 'n' run may be a competitive intra-male contest to see who can deliver the most blows. Such continual, competitive jockeying for status within male peer groups leads Jordan (1995: 79) to suggest that 'many of the disadvantages as suffered by girls and women are the result of being caught in the crossfire in a long-standing battle between groups of men over the definition of masculinity'. Masculinity is performed through the supposedly humorous repetition of sequences such as punch 'n' run. Punch 'n' run is also structured around certain implicit conventions, where Tina tolerated Clive engaging in these interactions but disliked Darren's attempt to join in.[4]

The examples provide insights into the way male power is negotiated and contested through the bravado of ritualized humour and social exchanges in schools. Such humour may be regarded as 'funny violence' (Beynon 1989: 198) by some students yet experienced as 'deeply marginalising and oppressive' by others (Edley and Wetherell 1996: 10). Moreover, some British researchers have documented the relationships between such types of competitive game-playing more generally, linking them to forms of masculinity and working-class occupational culture (Willis 1977; Back 1990; Hollands 1990). The practice of gaming can also be a coercive technique exerted by certain male peer cultures to establish and maintain power over other subordinated masculine schooling cultures. The routines of 'cussing', banter and punching may also be seen to substantiate male heterosexual identities by expelling 'femininity' from 'self' onto 'others' (Freud 1905). Physical and verbal gaming rituals are thus an important route for trying out 'masculine' forms of behaviour in schools.

Mythic events and the making of men: the use of 'classic stories' in schoolboy culture

Alongside the rituals of gaming, we found collective story telling played a central role in framing classroom humour and consolidating versions of heterosexual masculinity. Certain events achieved a lasting appeal in school and could be reinvoked for the shared pleasure of mutual retelling. The various identifications made when relating certain events elevated these stories to mythic status; they were described as 'classics' and understood as key reference points for making sense of young men's time and place within the education system. Indeed, Sara Delamont (1989: 191) has also encouraged teachers and researchers to explore 'cautionary tales, jokes, urban legends, atrocity stories' and so forth within school contexts to achieve a richer understanding of pupil lives. It is to these informal anecdotes and mythic events that we shall now turn.

Paddy's story – the nun, the clay cock and the Irishman

The classic story or mythic event serves as the cultural apparatus around which students can collectively assemble and reassemble their social lives. The repetition of particular stories enables students to define a meaningful pathway through the labyrinthine corridors of schooling existence. During our time in school we heard several stories involving teachers having nervous breakdowns, falling through trapdoors, having their flasks of coffee spat in, being chased by pupils and chasing pupils (Kehily and Nayak 1996). The comic narratives celebrate oppositional forms of behaviour in the classroom and emphasize pupil power in oppressive circumstances. Like flags being unfurled, these narratives were unfolded with pride and thrust down as markers of resistance, a symbolic victory against the odds.

The attraction of these stories to adolescent male culture can be seen in the rapid ease with which the tales are 'sparked'. In this example Paddy is spotted walking past the room, where an immediate link is made between Paddy as a person and an event in his past which is prioritized by pupils. Incredibly, the event occurred in another school and was not witnessed by the pupils in our research yet its *resonance* for the male peer group informs us of the cult status of this story. The interview took place with a mixed group of girls and boys and displays a dramatic style of masculine resistance that appears to be enjoyed by most of the pupils. The mythic tale was repeatedly referred to, becoming a touchstone for pupil experience, while providing evidence of how male resistance to schooling can be fashioned and celebrated through humour. It is difficult within the written format to capture the flavour of the regional accents, the speed of delivery, intonation and excitement embedded in the dialogue, so these must be left to the reader's imagination.

Smithy: There's Paddy!
Jason: He's the one you want to question – Paddy.
All: [laughter] Watch him go red.
    Why what's he done?
Clive: He's a nutcase!
Samantha: He's a nutter! [all laugh]
Jason: You'll have to go and fetch him and watch him go red.
Clive: Ask him about his old school days.
[Savage enters]
Samantha: Savage, go and fetch Paddy.
Savage: Paddy's just beat me up! [all laugh]
Jason: Paddy's beat him up!
Samantha: Is he coming?
Jason: Watch his face. He's going red already! [all laugh]
Samantha: Oh, leave him. He's probably doing something for his own
    house group.
[Swelling laughter]
Smithy: What's he say?
[Paddy enters]
Clive: Ask him why he got expelled from his old school.
Jason: Say why d'yow git expelled, aye.
    We don't wanna embarrass him.
[Increased laughter]
Jason: [loudly to Paddy] Why d'yow git expelled from your last
    school? [all laugh]
Samantha: Go on, tell 'em!
Jason: Jus' tell 'em Paddy!

All: Tell 'em! You've said it before.
Smithy: They're curious.
Jason: Nothing gets said.
Samantha: Go on!
              No, don't embarrass him.
Clive: Jus' say it Pad, go on.
Paddy: I made a cock outta clay an' give it to a nun!
[Mass laughter]

Paddy's story, in keeping with previous aspects of male humour, can be understood as a 'verbal performance' structured through the social interplay of 'audience' and 'situation' (Volosinov 1973). Here, the social act of story telling is reliant upon recognition with others, as the group of pupils collaborate and interact as both actors and audience. Within the research dynamic we felt that the research group were providing an audience for Paddy, staging a show for us (and one another) while watching our reactions. Watching Paddy – and watching us watching Paddy – generates great excitement in the school context.

The research group began by mediating relations between ourselves and Paddy, presenting us as an interested party ('they're curious') and a confidential one ('nothing gets said'). At the same time we are informed about Paddy that 'he's the one you want to question' and asked about 'fetching' him in. Our role as audience is central to the building excitement, where our comments about not wanting to embarrass Paddy serve only to fuel the exhilaration. The references to being beaten up by Paddy, and the laughter this produces, refers to the punch 'n' run gaming discussed earlier.

The celebratory fervour of this story stems from the violation of norms produced in the mythic event. Making a 'cock outta clay' and presenting it to a nun can be seen as an ultimate transgressive expression, with all its symbolic masculine overtones. Here, the cock as a symbol of phallic power has the ability to threaten and shock, a means through which Paddy can use a masculine discourse of power against female teachers in a Catholic school. The act of defiance is further exaggerated where a nun is said to be the recipient of the clay cock. The narrative humour is produced through seeing the nun as a symbol of passivity and purity, with Paddy's gesture of defiance crossing religious and sexual boundaries. The gendered juxtaposition of cock and nun is a symbolic moment of masculine resistance forged in asymmetric relations by which the pupil momentarily 'gets one over' the teacher. As Valerie Walkerdine (1990) has illustrated, such transformations in the dynamics of power are possible through the multiple positions subjects can occupy in discourse. The multiple and contradictory subjectivities of teacher/nun/ adult/female or pupil/adolescent/male are thus neither unitary, simplistic, or in any way straightforward. Consequently, Walkerdine indicates that not all acts of resistance against school authority have revolutionary effects; they may be 'reactionary' too, especially when we consider the dynamic of gender.

The pleasure in the mythic story derives from the various transgressive practices and the infringement of multiple boundaries: religious/sexual, teacher/pupil, male/female, public/private. The event brings each of these borders into sharp relief and reveals the complexities of power within school arenas. Paddy is ushered in by the pupil group for comic reasons, to tell his story and 'watch him go red'; he was immediately dispensed with after the performance. The group operate as supporting actors and provide the context for Paddy's delivery of the infamous one liner. Paddy's masculinity is continually appraised through the retellings of the narrative sequence and the collective 'remembrance' of his expulsion. In recounting the mythic sequence, pupils keep alive the notion of Paddy as 'mad' or 'a scream' and a 'nutter' – a mythology that in itself is rooted in English stereotypical representations of the Irish. While there is not scope in this paper to address the serious issue of racism in schools there was certainly evidence to suggest that racist epithets could be deployed in the making of a white, English working-class masculinity. Moreover, if the mythic event is to be believed, the celebratory humour conceals the tragic underside of Paddy's expulsion. Here, we have been less interested in the 'facticity' of events and more concerned with the investments made by young men in particular incidents, and their desire continually to retell and relive the experience in the mythic imaginary. The narrative functions to consolidate Paddy's display of resistance and the masculine values of the group more generally.

The arthritic tongue

Although a main feature of the narratives is their anti-authoritarian structure, sexual stories concerning other pupils could also become mythic events (Canaan 1986). Here, sharp retorts and humorous barbed remarks could be used to question the heterosexual masculinity of other young men. Willis (1977) found intra-male conflict to be a means of bolstering working-class masculinities which were not simply fashioned against girls and women but also against conformist boys, the 'ear 'oles'. We found that although clear hierarchies existed between those who saw themselves as 'lads', and those they labelled 'snobs', peer group status was continually being reshuffled when young men engaged in quick-fire exchanges. The following example illustrates the ways in which humour can be used to put down another male and at the same time consolidate the heterosexual masculinity of the teller and the rest of the group. Here, Macca was asked to remind us of why Tom had become a recent target for abuse.

> OK, he was going out with this girl for, like, three months and he never did anything with her, like get off with her or anything. And she went to get off with him and he pulled away. So after this, this kid goes to him, 'You've got an arthritic tongue, that's why you've not got off with Sally.' A classic.

The metaphor of an 'arthritic tongue' was deployed to indicate that Tom embodied the medical condition of arthritis when it came to making sexual moves on members of the opposite sex. The assertion was that he would freeze, cramp up and so reveal a retarded male heterosexual identity. His reluctance to be sexually assertive and 'French kiss' Sally was regarded as a reflection of his passive masculine status within the peer group and acted to confirm that his tongue was, indeed arthritic. In this reading Tom becomes the living embodiment of an emasculated, sexually impotent young man. The meanings inscribed in these stories serve to make them memorable signposts or points of direction in young men's sexual coming-of-age.

The narrative concerning Tom and his legendary 'arthritic tongue' becomes 'a classic' in similar ways to the story of Paddy and the clay cock. The arthritic tongue narrative questions Tom's heterosexual masculine performance and his hesitance with Sally, 'He never did anything with her.' The use of a 'put-down' has the effect of asserting the status of the teller, which in turn consolidates the male peer group who impose their values upon the target male (Stebbins 1980). This may further explain the admiration for Paddy as someone who was said to be expelled for sexual exhibition. The arthritic tongue narrative also reveals the various performative levels of masculinity: the need to perform sexually with Sally, the need to boast about the 'sexual performance' with other young men and the 'put-down' itself as a performative regulator of masculine behaviour. Sex/gender identities are, then, stringently policed by male peer groups within school when Tom is humiliated and laughed at for gender inappropriate behaviour and Paddy is celebrated as school rebel for his phallic performance. Recollecting mythic events serves to commemorate the hyper-masculine versions of self that display sexual daring and an audacious resistance to authority. At the same time the values encoded in these tales operate as regulatory reminders or performative rehearsals for the constitution of heterosexual male identities.

The 'gay student'

In keeping with the folklore of student humour a series of myths ran concerning students and teachers alleged to be gay (see Nayak and Kehily 1996 for further discussion). Homophobic displays not only consolidate the identities of the individual but speak to the wider masculine culture of the peer group. Thus, young men who did not cultivate a hyper-masculinity were subject to brutal forms of homophobic abuse. This implied that masculinities were continually being asserted and appraised in school arenas, as this victim narrative reveals:

> *Miles:* It's a sort of stigma ain't it? A quiet person in a class would be called 'gay' or summat. I was for a time 'cos I was fairly quiet in the classroom and for a while everyone was callin' me gay . . . I think my grades have suffered 'cos of disruptive members of the

> class. They're not really interested in getting a qualification so
> it's, 'Well what can we do for a laugh today? Disrupt the history
> lesson or something like that.'

As Miles indicates, calling other young men gay is seen as a 'laugh'. It is
used as a cultural axis for charting dominant and subordinate heterosexualities
within male peer group culture. The oppressive effects of homophobic humour
are seen in Miles's articulation of the social stigma of being called 'gay' and
his belief that his 'grades have suffered'. The empirically grounded comments
may be placed in the context of wider international debates concerning
male underachievement as signalled by authors in Australia and the UK
(Chapter 1). This style of humour is a technique for disciplining the enactment of heterosexual masculinities where '[h]umour is a powerful device
for celebrating one's own identity and for enhancing one's status, and for
whipping others into shape' (Woods 1990: 195). Hence, we see young men
laughing at the lack of physical attention a friend shows to an attentive
female, a pumped-up display of masculinity in 'blowing competitions' and
homophobic epithets invoked against academically minded males 'for a laugh'.
Thus, as the masculine peer group becomes more important in the lives of
working-class boys the rewards to perform socially and sexually may increasingly outweigh the need to perform academically where the material
realities of an unstable local political economy form a hollow promise for
the future. These incidents indicate humour may offer a temporary reassur-
ance. More importantly, for teaching practitioners such discourse serves to
create and consolidate heterosexual hierarchies in male peer groups through:
regulation of self and others, enhancing reputations, disparaging reputations,
demarcating those who belong from those who do not.

Implications for teachers

Our research indicates that it is important for teachers to develop an understanding of the powerful role that humour and sexuality play in how boys
learn to fashion and negotiate their masculinities within the informal peer
group situation at school. The ways in which boys perform their masculinities
and how these impact on their social relationships and learning need to be
targeted for specific discussion in schools, both with students in the classroom
and teachers in professional development forums.

Moreover, we believe that it may be helpful to situate local performances
of heterosexual masculinities in boys' lives at school within the broader
socio-cultural context of changing patterns in the post-school labour market.
It may well be that the changing pattern of labour has most significantly
impinged upon the lives of working-class young men with its emphasis on
the dismantling of centralized mass production and a new accentuation upon
changing times and 'flexible accumulation' (Harvey 1990). As long-term

manual work declines, in a so-called 'feminized' world of flexible workers and new technologies, these male pupils are practising other ways of being 'proper' men that aim to accentuate heterosexuality beyond the 'emasculating' existence of unemployment. What is now needed for the 'new times' of global change and uneven development is less rigid masculine templates. Ironically this would be more in keeping with the uncertainty of the post-industrial economy and the increasing flexibility of gender roles now required in the global market place and the recently changing domestic arena.

In this sense – in terms of helping boys to be more flexible – teachers can play a major role in assisting them to interrogate their adherence to rigid and constraining gender stereotypical behaviours and roles. Boys need to be encouraged to reflect on their practices of masculinity with the view to opening up possibilities for embracing alternative ways of being male which are not discordant with those forms of masculinity required in the changing labour market. The role of teachers in undertaking such a critical practice with their students should not be underestimated (see Salisbury and Jackson 1996).

Conclusion: the last laugh?

Our study suggests that humour is an *organizing principle* in the lives of young men within English school arenas. Humour was seen as a regulatory technique in the way that the boys performed their masculinities. Young men who did not subscribe to an exaggerated practice of masculinity were ridiculed through humorous rituals. Consequently, those who worked hard at school, or exposed sexual vulnerabilities in relationships with young women, were targets for banter and abuse. The development of 'cussing matches' and other rituals of abuse offered a practical means of testing male prowess that avoided the dangerous, and somewhat more determining, consequences of fights. In this sense, humour was a means by which the boys were able to construct their masculine identities in school: macho behaviour was mythologized in stories of defiance, some pupils were ridiculed as 'gay' for conforming to teacher authority, while others were regarded as sexually impotent with 'arthritic tongues' if they failed to perform sexually with girlfriends. Here, humour was a style for the perpetual display of 'hard' masculinity and also a means of displacing fears and uncertainties.

In light of this analyisis, we have also argued that it may still be of value for teachers to place young men's contemporary interactions within an understanding of the changing local political economy. A little over twenty years ago, Paul Willis (1977) persuasively argued that having a 'laff' provided young men with the preparatory tools for cultural life on the shop floor. The similarity between being part of a school counter-culture against teachers and grafting for an existence under the ever watchful eye of a factory steward was exemplified in the trickery, subversion and humour common to pupils and workers in each social sphere (Willis 1976). However, a decline in the region's industrial base and the erosion of trade union activity has exacerbated long-term unemployment in the West Midlands area of Britain. Whereas the 'lads' of '77 may have found recognition in the familiar, albeit constrained, enclave of factory life, the young men in our study seemed less optimistic about full-time employment and job security. It may be the case that in today's economic climate young men are no longer able to attain a socially recognizable masculinity through manual labour, so are seeking to authenticate this identity in postures of male heterosexuality. More research is required to determine the exigency of these claims, though we may speculate on the continuing presence and practice of 'lads' in school, despite changes to the manufacturing base. If boys are no longer 'learning to labour', then why do they continue to 'learn to laugh' in a manner appropriate to the shop floor?

We believe that teachers can play an important role in helping boys to reflect on and understand these practices of masculinity. Spaces in schools need to be provided so that boys can be given the opportunity to critically evaluate the motivations driving the manner in which they learn to relate. They need to be encouraged to consider the consequences of how they fashion their masculinities, not only in terms of how they impact on their social relationships and attitudes to schooling, but on how they affect their relation to new forms of labour. What can be achieved at the local level of schooling, therefore, is an attempt to help boys to problematize their social practices of masculinity. In this way, spaces can be provided for discussion about the effects of masculinity on boys' lives with the view to helping them to move beyond the limits of the rigid templates of an exaggerated masculinity to which many of them subscribe in their everyday lives at school.

Notes

1 The term ethnography refers to 'the writing of culture' through the method of long-term observation, interviews and the use of field diaries and documentary evidence.
2 See Labov (1972) and Lyman (1987) for further discussion of verbal sparring.
3 Although our study has been based in secondary schools, other researchers have indicated that the use of sexism and racism in name calling is also a feature of preschool and primary years classrooms in the English system (Walkerdine 1990; Troyna and Hatcher 1992; Connolly 1995).
4 Punch 'n' run performed similar interpersonal functions as the 'duelling play' and 'back slap and chase' games that feature in Les Back's (1990) youth club research.

References

Back, L. (1990) *Racist Name Calling and Developing Anti-Racist Initiatives in Youth Work*, Research Paper in Ethnic Relations No. 14. Coventry: University of Warwick.

Beynon, J. (1989) A school for men: an ethnographic case study of routine violence in schooling, in S. Walker and L. Barton (eds) *Politics and the Processes of Schooling*. Milton Keynes: Open University Press.

Canaan, J.E. (1986) Why a 'slut' is a 'slut': cautionary tales of middle class teenage morality, in H. Varanne (ed.) *Symbolising America*. Lincoln, NE: University of Nebraska Press.

Connolly, P. (1995) Boys will be boys? Racism, sexuality, and the construction of masculine identities amongst infant boys, in J. Holland and M. Blair with S. Sheldon (eds) *Debates and Issues in Feminist Research and Pedagogy*. Clevedon: Multilingual Matters.

Delamont, S. (1989) The nun in the toilet: urban legends and educational research. *Qualitative Studies in Education*, 2 (3): 191–202.

Dubberley, W.S. (1993) Humour as resistance, in P. Woods and M. Hammersley (eds) *Gender and Ethnicity in Schools: Ethnographic Accounts*. London: Routledge.

Edley, N. and Wetherell, M. (1995) Negotiating masculinity: young men's discourse on sexuality. Paper presented at Discourse Analysis Workshop, Nene College, Northampton, May.

Edley, N. and Wetherell, M. (1996) Masculinity, power and identity, in M. Mac an Ghaill (ed.) *Understanding Masculinities*. Buckingham: Open University Press.

Freud, S. (1905) *Jokes and their Relation to the Unconscious*, Pelican Freud Library, 6. Harmondsworth: Penguin.

Harvey, D. (1990) *The Condition of Postmodernity*. Oxford: Blackwell.

Hollands, R. (1990) *The Long Transition: Class, Culture and Youth Training*. London: Macmillan.

Jordan, E. (1995) Fighting boys and fantasy play: the construction of masculinity in the early years of school. *Gender and Education*, 7 (1): 69–86.

Kehily, M.J. and Nayak, A. (1996) The Christmas kiss: sexuality, story telling and schooling. *Curriculum Studies*, 4 (2): 211–27.

Labov, W. (1972) *Language in the Inner City: Studies in the Black English Vernacular*. Pennsylvania, PA: University of Pennsylvania Press.

Lyman, P. (1987) The fraternal bond as a joking relationship: a case study of the role of sexist jokes in male group bonding, in M. Kimmell (ed.) *Changing Men*. Buckingham: Open University Press.

Nayak, A. and Kehily, M.J. (1996) Playing it straight: masculinities, homophobias and schooling. *Journal of Gender Studies*, 5 (2): 211–30.

Salisbury, J. and Jackson, D. (1996) *Challenging Macho Values*. London: Falmer.

Troyna, B. and Hatcher, R. (1992) *Racism in Children's Lives*. London: Routledge.

Volosinov, V.N. (1973) *Marxism and the Philosophy of Language*. London: Seminar Press.

Walker, R. and Goodson, I. (1977) Humour in the classroom, in P. Woods and M. Hammersley (eds) *School Experience*. London: Croom Helm.

Walkerdine, V. (1990) *Schoolgirl Fictions*. London: Verso.

Willis, P. (1976) The class significance of school counter culture, in M. Hammersley and P. Woods (eds) *The Process of Schooling*. London: Routledge.

Willis, P. (1977) *Learning to Labour*. Farnborough: Saxon House.

Woods, P. (1976) Having a laugh: an antidote to schooling, in M. Hammersley and P. Woods (eds) *The Process of Schooling*. London: Routledge.

Woods, P. (1990) *The Happiest Days? How Pupils Cope with School*. Lewes: Falmer.

CHAPTER 9

'Sad, bad or sexy boys': girls' talk in and out of the classroom

VALERIE HEY, ANGELA CREESE, HARRY DANIELS, SHAUN FIELDING AND DIANA LEONARD

> *Girl 1:* [Boys usually have] very boring conversations about science.
> *Girl 2:* What else do they talk about? . . . they talk about really weird things.
> *AC:* Well, what do girls talk about that's so interesting then?
> *Girls:* We talk about interesting stuff. We talk about boys.
> (Transcript, girls' group interview, Mill Bank)

Introduction

The girls in Mill Bank Primary School in London are not the only ones 'talking about boys'. So is the government, the newspapers and the popular media. There is also a great deal of popular and academic educational research about the *problem* of boys (Byers 1998). However, as numerous feminist critics note (Francis 1999; Epstein *et al.* 1998; Lingard and Douglas 1999), the rush to rewrite gender equity as the discourse of *male* disadvantage is misguided and premature. As we intend to illustrate in this chapter through our research (Daniels *et al.* 1999), a rather more complex and contradictory story about boys' and girls' learning cultures in schools emerges. We write about the combined and persistent effects of other social differences on gender such as social class, all of which, along with the effects of learning context, are elided by the mainstream discourses on boys' underachievement (see introductory chapter, this volume).

About the study

Our study focused upon primary classroom learning cultures in 12 schools for detailed investigation (six in Birmingham and six in London), but in this chapter we draw on the London sample. Our selection included schools we ranked as high, average or low achieving as well as reflecting comparable and contrasting socio-economic and ethnic profiles. At the top of our 'performance' tables were Cityscape and Mill Bank, less ethnically diverse and serving affluent communities of highly educated 'consumers', in the middle were the contrasting 'aspirational' school of Marsh Hill (with its predominantly working-class and black communities) and the more middle-class and Anglo Trafnell Park, while the least successful schools of Georgian and Parkside constituted the low-achieving cases.

We used headteacher interviews, ethnographic classroom observations, teacher interviews and children's same-sex group interviews, as well as videoing children in a researcher-determined set task to frame detailed case studies of how teachers set up the conditions of learning. We were especially interested in their use, management and hence rationale for constructing large or small group, individual or pair work as teaching and learning opportunities (Daniels *et al.* 1999). Within the context of this study we were able to investigate how girls understood the sexual politics of learning in specific classroom contexts. By this we mean how they understand themselves as specifically *gendered* learners in relation to boys in unequal conditions of power. In this chapter, therefore, we are concerned to explore the classed dimensions of particular versions of femininity in terms of how they inform girls' talk about boys in classroom learning cultures. In this sense, the focus is on how girls understand boys through the broad categories of cooperation or competition, and how girls' talk emerges as a distinctly gendered critique of the boys' social practices.

One of the major issues we consider is the 'underground' (see and cf. Gilligan, Lyons and Hanmer 1990) nature of girls' resistance that enables them to elaborate a version of femininity that is much more contradictory than allowed for in some accounts. For example, Becky Francis claims pessimistically (cf. Walkerdine 1985) that the 'femininity valued by primary school girls (is that) which emphasises being sensible and selfless, (and) leads them to abandon power to the boys who position themselves, in opposition to them, as silly and selfish' (Francis 1997: 20; cf. Pattman nd). Yet, our research shows that this tendency of 'abandonment' is far less likely in some classrooms and among some groups than others. In short, on the basis of this study we argue that there is a need to think in more nuanced ways about gender and power as variable by learning contexts. We will show girls having interests beyond the controlling gaze of boys, and while some of them can, through dint of class power or pedagogic contexts of support, 'escape', all of them come to understand themselves within the (contested) terms of learning as a gender struggle. The significance of their teachers, their girl friendships, their social class and their experience of contrasting learning and teaching styles all play a part in the resistant capabilities and capacities of 'girls' talk'.

Derision and desire: how some middle-class girls talk about boys

In this section we include a focus on a discussion of helping behaviour with a group of high-achieving girls from Mill Bank Primary School as a means of exploring their account of the classroom learning culture. We see the school as offering a particularly individualistic pedagogy (see Hey *et al.* 1999). By this we mean a setting that *does not* use the characteristically 'progressive' form of group work. The house pedagogy is one in which the teacher tends to use a highly stylized narrative transmission form. This is followed through in the dominant use of individual work. This is pedagogy for bright individuals and it particularly favours middle-class boys. We have argued in other papers (Hey *et al.* 1999; Creese *et al.* 2000) that the ethos of Mill Bank School reflected the aspirations of a particular classed fraction that predominated among its parents (see for example Bernstein 1996).

In this context, individualistic high-flying or *'standing out'* was almost required by the competitive pedagogy. Nevertheless, some learning/friendship alliances were formed 'around the edges' of the classroom. This fragment of girls' talk captures how they view Oscar and Henry's idiosyncratic way of making informal talk:

Pupils: No, they help each other.
Pupil: Well yes, that's each other.
Eliza: Sometimes Oscar and Henry help each other but they speak in such a loud voice we hear them. Sergeant Major, they call each other . . . amazing. Sergeant Guy.

Here we are invited to see the world of middle-class masculine friendship as strange and as 'other'. It has a militaristic register – a surprising but dominant theme of other elite boys' discourse (see and cf. below).

Girls' views on boys are little researched but they offer a fascinating insight into girls' sense of emergent identity (cf. Padfield 1997; Pattman nd). To our surprise, questioning the girls about the formal domain of classrooms flipped over very quickly into how they understood boys beyond their public personas. Girls' interest in the nature of personal and interpersonal group interactions generated more complex and thus more (potentially) subversive notions of boys.

Most middle-class girls were fluent in talking to us about the boys in their classrooms. They were also funny and our tapes were punctuated with giggles, in this case prompting a reprimand from one of them: 'Eliza, calm down; we're on tape.' Being sensible is, as we have noted, a major expectation of girls (Walkerdine 1985; Pattman n.d.), yet, in providing an 'all girls together' research situation, we had emulated some conditions of 'girls' banter' (Hey 1997) and the girls included us (VH and AC) in this sort of non-sensible 'disrespectful' talk. A major topic of the banter was boys' respective (heterosexual) status as 'sad' or 'sexy'. Often our formal agenda was recast, as the following extract shows:

VH: Do you ever work with any of the boys?
Girl: Yes.
VH: Which subjects do you work with the boys?
Eliza: We're doing a play for assembly, me and Andrew and Emmalie
        are working with Bennie as well. That's the one with the cheeky
        grin. He's got dimples . . .
VH: What about Bennie?
Girl 1: He's cool and he's got two dimples.

Bennie appears here as 'cool' – a 'sexy' male in contrast to the risible 'boys' with their childish obsessive interest in 'science' and other equally cultish 'masculine' games. These 'sad' boys were often compared with, and seen to be similar to, brothers:

Girl: All my brother talks about is computer games, football, football on
        computer games. Whereas like girls . . .
VH: Well, what do you talk about then?
Girl: Well we just talk about the latest gossip. We talk about boys don't
        we?
Girl: My brother he just talks about his favourite hero.

These girls (at least three of them close friends) rehearse a shared set of discreditations and distinctions. At the same time they propose (gender) positions for themselves. The business of appreciating desirable boys is very efficient for staking their *own* place as desiring, mature girls – self-evidently superior to sad boys who are discounted as 'nerds'.

The private confession of non-sensible desire can of course subsist *alongside* public positions as 'sensible'. As such, this informal talk accomplishes the neat subversion of the dominance of male talk by converting it into the pejorative indicator of 'nerdyness'. This is achieved through a reversal of the customary relations of male = active/female = passive relations.

Moreover, the production of the 'sexy' position for Bennie is worth considering further. It is not simply that his looks are appreciated (though this is an important correlate of sexiness); it is his likeable personality.

Girls and boys both find adult control irksome at times. Girls, ability to 'have a laugh' (cf. Woods 1977) with a 'charming' boy is, as we might imagine, a very scarce commodity(!) and thus a prized cultural pleasure. Boys who have the skill to 'make you laugh' without disrupting your learning are distinguished from the rest and given immense prestige. Bennie's ambiguous role was that of a 'maverick' (see and cf. introduction in Cohen 1997; Hey *et al.* 1999). We think this points to the need to pay far more attention to the role of the (hetero)sexualization of learning cultures (Epstein and Johnson 1999). We have data to show that the middle-class 'nerdy' boys are well aware of their asexual positioning and resent it.

The tastes of certain middle-class girls were fine-grained (Bourdieu 1984) and the powerful 'big, bold and beautiful' girls reported above held a 'taken-for-granted' feminine superior common sense, against which lesser mortals like boys had to become attractive (being charming, being funny) to make any claims to their attention. In one sense what such discourses reveal is a class power – that is gendered. We are talking to self-confident daughters of professional (post-feminist?) women who feel entitled to express preferences and are used to expressing as well as achieving distinctions.

At another of our study schools (Cityscape) we found the same sort of discourses. This is what some high-status white girls in Cityscape say about one key boy: 'There are people who are good, like, working with because they'll muck about a little bit and then they'll still get on with their work. I mean people like . . . Ned, he's not bad'. These girls return to the theme later: 'He's so funny', (but, crucially) 'he's not going to distract you from your work and you know he'll make you laugh.'

These girls were extremely clear about the way they valued boys as good learning companions. Even in this inclusion-orientated school with a collaborative pedagogy, the girls (and, significantly, also the boys) were conscious of one boy (Remo) who did not 'fit in'. The 'star girls' construed him as 'naughty' or 'dumb' because he hadn't understood that 'showing off', i.e. acting and standing out, was seen as witless. Such bids for attention could only be redeemed through being entertaining, as they said '. . . they don't make you laugh either!' As testament to the ethos of the school and the range of masculinities made possible there, the admired Ned resisted 'writing off' Remo. Instead, Ned sought to reposition him as a novice (a newcomer to the school and its values) as well as insisting that he was 'very clever' (Creese *et al.* 1999).

Disturbance, disruption and danger: How some working-class and middle-class girls talk about boys

Not all of the girls in our study were as powerful, nor as 'sophisticated', nor as articulate as 'the big, the bold and the beautiful' of Mill Bank and Cityscape (Gordon *et al.* 1998). It was painful to see (these interviews were videoed) the inadvertent silencing of some working-class girls by our asking the same set of questions and adopting similar manners and approaches. There was not the same space for banter or their views.

Thus not all the girls we spoke with produced or performed that classed confidence we have come to describe as 'star girl' self-assertion. On the contrary, the contrasting levels of social confidence and power among girls was startling. Moreover, there were clear differences between and beneath what superficially appeared as similar classes cultures of learning that effected the talk of middle-class and working-class girls. The relative solidarity of girls' social relations also played a part in providing shared classed understandings about the 'causes' of boys' difference.

White working-class girls in another school, Trafnell Park, were initially scathing about the misogyny they experienced in the informal/formal classroom. Again, aspects of masculine 'otherness' were understood but less benevolently than at Mill Bank, despite the 'therapeutic' (overwhelmingly middle-class liberal) ethos of their school (Hey *et al.* 1999; cf. Bernstein 1996). Their experiences could well be a function of their own subordinate class positioning in relation to the elite 'top boys'. Here a member of a (friendship) group known as JAZZ (after their initials!) are talking about Travis's learning style:

> Travis is like . . . you put that over here and then it would be like this, and everyone's going like, 'We're trying to work *this one* out' and he gets – and in the middle of Miss's specific statement he'll just ask a question and then he'll – and she'll go, 'Yes, Travis' and he'll go something like, 'Miss, what happens when you square the number of light years wrong?'

Their voices take on the intonation of weary 'maternal' irritation with boys 'being difficult'. Again, the posture of Travis can be read (and *is* read by the girls) as deliberately subversive – a maverick again (see earlier) who spends his ingenuity trying to wrest (intellectual?) control away from his teacher (cf. Redman and Mac an Ghaill 1997). Points of identification with the care and control work of their female teacher are clear in many girls' discourses. How these find expression is to be the source of another article. As they added succinctly, 'Travis is always going off in the wrong direction.' Metaphors of direction are worthy of deeper analytic attention than we can offer here but they signal issues of control and resistance.

Our field notes are dotted with instances of Travis's 'pitch' for the floor. He seemed to see himself as taking up his 'masterful' inheritance by bids to reoccupy the pedagogic public space.

Travis was also the leader of the elite middle-class boys' group and a singular uniting feature of this group was their rejection of football and alternative cultish adherence to Warhammer. This fraction of boys could be said to have taken up a bourgeois variant form of 'extreme' masculinity (cf. Barker 1997). Certainly their teacher ceaselessly resisted their efforts to initiate Warhammer topics in whole-group literacy work. The girls we interviewed in Trafnell Park also noted the elite boys' use of specialized and stylized language – 'they speak in code', and it is the exclusion and 'otherness' of boys' different vocabularies that places these girls (and we would argue their teacher) as non-cognoscenti outsiders looking in on a masculine world. Here are elite 'lads' doing and learning to keep out femininity.

The girls also comment about the boys 'trying to make each other laugh'. Yet, the girls remain dismissive not so much because of the humour but because the laughter is *not,* as in the case of Ned or Bennie, social or inclusive *of them*. They also note the slide from 'having a laugh' (Woods 1977) to 'Travis is quite distracting to his friends.' Like so much of girls' talk, the working class girls at Trafnell Park constantly understand boys through the categories of moral and instructional regulation (Bernstein 1997), mainly because their experience is of boys pulling against its force:

Girl 1: Yeh, me and Susie, Barbara and Andrea were in a group. So um, and so – but we were singing and nobody was joining in so Miss said, 'We'll do the song that we're going to do for Leavers' Assembly' and we all stood up and we started singing it. And John and Patrick . . . Miss went over . . . and John and Patrick . . . and John said . . .

Girl 2: He said . . . 'This is crap, it's just like the Scouts.'

But in this school, and significantly, the girls privilege an explanation that often recontextualizes boys' 'bad' behaviours as signs of deeper levels of personal trauma and disturbance. Their account is a discourse of sympathetic therapy and 'understanding' that echoes their teacher's voice. This means they do *all the work* of rescuing boys from themselves – the level of shared feminine understanding and compassion, i.e. emotional labour in the class (and certainly in their interview data) is phenomenal. Individual boys are placed in contexts of relationships, histories and circumstances and girls adopt a stance towards them that was part 'annoyed teacher', part sympathetic 'counsellor', part exasperated mother. The girls knew about Paul's psychotic mother, Tony and George's dead mother, individual boys' 'strong personalities' or 'loner' status. These social psychological facts then cross-cut the emergent 'feminist' reading of why boys appear as 'spoilers' or non-cooperators.

Could it be that the 'discourse of understanding' was pressed in to service to rehabilitate some boys at Trafnell Park, because it also rehabilitated girls' and their teacher's anger? Valerie Walkerdine suggests that feminine emotions including rage are generally converted into interpersonal feelings and thus depoliticized forms of understanding (Walkerdine 1985; cf. Bernstein 1996 on invisible and visible pedagogies).

Boys do not seem trained in or encouraged to take on the social responsibilities of *understanding* (see and cf. Gilligan 1993; Ohrm 1998). This is not a source of knowledge that is valued. This is *not* incidental to their progress and performance in classrooms; on the contrary, it partly explains it. One instance may be indicative of this.

When we asked how Travis helped, the girls made the distinction between girls who *'explained'* and boys who 'just told'. Indeed, with Travis 'you'd have to go up to him'. They drew a distinction between him and Zara, who, if she happened to see your work in the queue (for example) would 'point it out to you'. Here, encapsulated in a vignette, are paradigmatic instances of our qualitative data – an overall tendency for girls to support others' learning (extroverted orientation: she points it out to you – she explains it – learning-centred?) compared to boys' preference for individual or pair work (introverted orientation: you'd have to go up to him – he would just tell you – teacher-centred?).

Elite boys' excluding work (not only through cultural exclusions but also through 'rationing' helping) could be said to constitute pedagogic 'border work' (Thorne 1993), and it enables elite able boys to retain power. The working-class girls we spoke with in Trafnell Park did not consider 'rationing' their understanding of boys. Indeed, these girls did an enormous amount of emotional labour in getting behind the barricade. Clearly in some schools and in some circumstances boys' quest for and success in dominance persists, despite the best intentions of their feminist teachers. Elite boys' strategic retreat to cliquey macho masculinity may be designed to thwart such discourses and practices.

It is not that girls (nor teachers) meekly acquiesce; we have seen how powerful girls in Mill Bank reconstrue this 'retreat' as 'sadness'. Yet, in the particular learning ethos of Trafnell Park, girls take their cue from their teacher and are compelled to reconsider aspects of boys' 'disruption' as psychological 'disturbance'. After all, the dominant discourse (especially for working-class girls) assumes and rewards a caring femininity – and obversely punishes the withdrawal of caring. Girls rescue boys from themselves and (like their teacher) to that extent are disarmed from further critical insights.

We are not asserting claims of intrinsic or essential modes of feminine (or masculine) discourse and positioning. On the contrary, we next consider the different readings of badly behaved boys proposed by the 'top' girls at Marsh Hill. In this predominantly working-class multi-racial school, it was not required to redeem boys' bad behaviour through 'understanding'. Here 'star girls' like their female mentor teacher adapted a much more individualistic 'masculine' controlling position. Whatever else they were into it was not 'rescue'.

Powerful post-feminism: 'mad, bad boys'

When we talked with 'top girls' in Marsh Hill, we were intrigued to find how they asserted their strong academic position through different narratives about individual badly behaved boys. Their talk also heavily identified with their teacher but this time was dominated by stories of anti-helping behaviours such as comments about boys' 'moods'. 'Said sulks, when he doesn't get his own way, he just moans', Suria 'could be awkward', Johan can be 'very annoying'. This reflects the exasperated tone taken by their female teacher when she too is talking to us about her struggling to get certain boys to 'cooperate'. One of the girls summed up their feelings in the following: 'Most of the boys in our class, if they don't get their own way they just moan and groan and sulk.' They later develop the reasons for what they take as a disparity in attitudes to learning that bear upon boys' lack of persistence:

And I think, like, the boys – if they – not all of them but some of them, maybe most of them – they like, if there's a lesson that they don't like and they're doing something that they don't like they'll start to mess around. And talk to their friends. And some of the girls – they – even if they don't like it a lot they'll still try to do it.

Sometimes they, too, 'muck around a lot' but stop (sensibly!) when 'Miss tells them to'. But when boys are told 'they just carry on . . . they get really angry . . . they get into tantrums, 'slam the door', but girls are 'more serious with their work' while boys 'encourage' door slamming, 'they slam the door and think it's funny'. Again the topics of disruption, 'anger' or 'challenge' and 'humour' pose themselves and these girls quite literally 'take their teacher's side'. But what also emerges is their wider awareness about the circular dynamics of boys' complaints of 'unfair treatment'. The complaint discourse of male disadvantage' (i.e. the 'poor boys' discourse; see Epstein *et al.* 1998; Foster, Kimmel and Skelton, Chapter 1, this volume) is very strong in this class (see and cf. Hey *et al.* 1999). Moreover we think such resentment is akin to what Foster, Kimmel and Skelton (Chapter 1) calls 'deadly petulance'. But as they point out:

> And, like, if we put our hand up for a question, sometimes they complain that Miss chooses girls quite a lot, but it's usually that girls are at the front and she can't see the boys as well. 'Cos they're at the back, and they're mucking about!

When these girls take on the boys in the competition for answering questions first (which they did), when they take up responsibilities (which they did), when they secure 'top place' in the literacy groups (which they did), the boys attempt to derail this by 'moaning, sulking, moodiness or anger'. This is a more explicit but equally classed form of dissidence than the position taken up by middle-class boys at Trafnell Park. In this context, the fearsomely effective friendship/learning group of the 'top girls' was one of the most sustaining networks we had met. Both they and their teacher knew the value of the combination. What they also knew was the difficulties posed by their success for some 'wannabe boys'. Marsh Hill was one of the most aggressive settings that we visited. It is tempting to be glib and call what some boys were suffering from as 'aspiration rage'! And what the girls are picking up on and refusing to therapize away is the sense of boys' resentment at their displacement (cf. Hey *et al.* 1999). Top girls' powerful talk was fuelled by an uncompromising successful application of girls' collaborative orientations to a competitive situation. In this light 'top girls' were in a 'win win' situation. What are the implications for teachers of what all these differently placed girls are saying about boys they share their learning with?

Discussion: achieving girlhood

As teachers know, attention has been focused on pupils' academic public performances (Reay and Wiliam 1998) and within that on 'boys' underachievement' (see Epstein *et al.* 1998 for a critique of the debate in UK and see Gilbert and Gilbert 1998 for a clear overview of how this discourse is played out elsewhere). But pupils are equally, if not more, preoccupied with the crucial social tasks of 'achieving' a 'normal' sexed sense of self (Hey 1997; Kehily 1998). Gender 'normality' has to be constantly performed (according to Butler 1997); being properly feminine and masculine requires repetitive conformity to a code of behaviour, attitudes and orientations that is literally 'written on the body'. Here is what Bronwyn Davies says:

> Far from sex giving rise to gendered practices, it would seem that the possession of a particular set of genitals obliges the possessor to achieve ways of being that appear to be implicated in the particular set of genitals they happen to have.
>
> (Davies 1989: 237)

Moreover, the enormous work that goes into femininity and masculinity as 'opposites' clearly goes on within the formal settings of classrooms when girls and boys make sense of themselves as 'opposite' sort of learners. Such polar tendencies are tied into the 'heterosexual presumption' (Rich 1980; Connell 1987, 1995; Kehily and Nayak 1997). Carrie Paechter's recent review of the literature on the social and cultural making of gender (1998: Chapter 4) draws attention to a principal feature of western gender discourses, *dimorphism*, 'gender as embodied and oppositional'. This ideological feature of gender serves to write the conditions for the enforcement of what has been referred to (see Chapter I, this volume) as ' "the sexual contract" whereby the functions of caring, nurturance and emotional support are seen as belonging to women'. Our study clearly reveals evidence of this emergent sexual (pedagogic) contract.

Boys resent girls looking out for themselves rather than for them. This can intensify the oppositions between 'sensible' girls and 'non-sensible' boys and is likely to reproduce highly gender-differentiated behaviours with consequences for schooling outcomes. Clearly also some classrooms produce boys who do not demand girls take all the social responsibility for learning/ supporting. Moreover, girls value boys who 'make them laugh' and are good at communicating.

We have discussed how different girls develop different degrees of reflexivity about boys' behaviour and disposition. The most powerful of them assert a feminist common sense. We also think these 'feminist' and 'would-be' feminist narratives are extraordinarily 'local' and context-sensitive – girls echo their teachers' (mothers') voices. It is noticeable that girls taught by teachers who take up a 'masculine' stance of 'control' (the teachers at Mill Bank and Marsh Hill) as opposed to a feminine stance of 'care' (the teacher at Trafnell Park), are far less likely to 'take up' what we have called the apologetic 'mini-teacher' position (adopted from Mauthner 1998). By this we mean a surrogate teacher role which is modelled on the style and orientation to others demonstrated by their own teacher. We provisionally suggest that teachers need to take more reflexive account of how they structure the learning of their groups and classes. Girls' investment in discourses and practices of 'social' responsibility and boys' unspoken assumption that they should be the recipients of attention may make boys resentful if the learning context privileges 'top' girls. If circumstances of classroom organization mean that girls withdraw their emotional and pedagogic support from boys then boys feel a loss of a 'right'. Some of our evidence has indicated the problematic conditions that can arise when 'girls do become boys' equals as learners and stop being their caretakers' (Foster, Kimmel and Skelton, Chapter 1, this volume).

In other classrooms it is important to draw attention to how class privilege releases invaluable critical resources, which works for some girls rather than others.

We want to raise some implications of this analysis for the further professional development of teachers' work. We think it a difficult but essential task to ask teachers to recognize, reflect upon and reconsider the gendered (often unconscious) relations of pedagogy and power.

Sense and sensibility: lessons from girls on boys

Edward Sampson speaks about

> the power that some groups have to manage the very discursive practices by which their own group's identity is constituted on the basis of their ability to manage the identity of others.
>
> (Sampson 1993: 1223)

One such group is teachers. Therefore, putting it at its most banal, how teachers construe the behaviour of pupils matters. We think a focus on the way that gender and learning relations are currently played out in terms of the binaries – girls = sensible and boys = risky behaviour – cast light upon the intricate ways that learning implicates children's identities.

All of this suggests that the 'successful' subject of primary schooling (especially in the context of literacy) is much more likely in reality to be female, not because girls are *essentially* 'sensible' but rather that it is their orientation as cooperators that makes them better able to support their own and others' learning. We think girls' competency as learners is misread as sensibleness and trivialized. We urge professionals (along with policy makers) to re-read the pejorative 'sensible' through another lens. Our own work draws on several social theories, namely post-Vygotskian accounts of learning as social activity and a post-structuralist feminism that considers the sort of 'identity work' involved in teaching and learning. We think this allows us to conceptualize important systemic features of our data such that we can tease out how girls and boys make themselves up and recognize themselves as 'properly' gendered.

If girls are rewarded for being 'sensible', boys gain prestige (from their peers) and wider culture for being competitive 'risk-taking' individuals – which currently means they are rewarded for being and asserting their *self* – in a society that privileges individualism.

The lack of explicit recognition – indeed the impossibility of the recognition – of girls' social and hence educational *competence* lies in this binary logic (Walkerdine 1987). Paechter notes that when girls do better, boys are said to lack 'motivation' due to social circumstances. Boys could by implication do better *if they wanted to*. Conversely, when boys do well then this is confirmation of a natural superiority (see Epstein *et al.* 1998: Introduction).

The school that seems to provide girls and boys with the least polarized account of learning and gender (and difference as 'other') is Cityscape. This school encourages *all* its pupils to collaborate by modelling for them how to communicate in styles that support learning through listening and sharing. Girls identify one such excellent communicator whose charm and the ability to communicate with them (perhaps signalling a more equitable relationship) is clearly highly valued. In other settings, boys' border work and exclusion and cliquey domination is intensely disliked. Bennie's maverick *individual* charm is recognized as almost unique.

Where are we now with the debate about gender and learning? We must move beyond obsessing about boys. Along with others, we do think there have been some shifts 'behind the back' of these dominant positions. The emergence of powerful 'big, bold and beautiful' girls is one such indicator. In some (as yet) unspecified and indeed contradictory ways, both the moral panic about boys and the earlier feminist critiques (Epstein *et al.* 1998; Myers 2000) have shifted the ground from underneath boys' feet. Boys as a result are now *as ever* foregrounded in schooling discourses (Epstein *et al.* 1998) but we think in a much more ambivalent way than previously. Suddenly it is not so 'cool' to be a boy.

Moreover, it is the working-class schools and working-class and black boys who come under far greater scrutiny. This in turn provokes increased greater performance anxieties (at the levels of institution and pupils). How teachers are to intervene here around boys' learning is not straightforward. Bright/middle-class boys can continue with their preference for individual work. But what about those boys (including some middle-class boys) who need help? Girls at least have the potential chance of engaging each other informally about work even in the most individualistic classrooms.

We would argue that all boys need radical forms of educational work about how they relate to each other, let alone how they relate to girls and their female teachers. Yet, it is this essential process work that seems relegated in the rush for 'outcomes'. Paradoxically, boys seem completely unaware how much learning can be gained from sharing, talking and *listening to each other*. Thus the performance drive seems to compound boys' general orientation to ends rather than means and may add to their experience of underachievement. Certainly girls are aware of their own room for greater manoeuvre. They are far more likely to have learned collaborative orienta-tions. They can in some circumstances shift between collaborative and competitive styles and some have learned to adopt individual and group orientations to their advantage.

We have suggested in this chapter that the sorts of (gendered) learner identifications made possible relate to the local contexts of learning in the classroom, the corridor and the playground. Do some institutional discourses and practices encourage respect for the 'other' – sex, gender or 'race' – and thus refuse to see difference as deficit? Do some schools put children into settings where communicative practices encourage the recognition and cel-ebration of difference as diversity rather than as polar opposites? Do some settings and competitive practices ensure that a consolidation of cultural, educational and social power prevails?

There are some general pointers that arise from our work that could assist professionals in other classrooms.

It is quite noticeable that more antagonistic accounts about boys came from classrooms that were structured within a competitive as opposed to a more collaborative ethos. Gender wars were rife in four out of our six London primary schools. In only two schools was it possible for a more egalitarian notion of difference to emerge. We have pointed to one here – Cityscape.

We would tentatively suggest that the 'in-between' space of classrooms, i.e. the talk that gets done to relay 'outside' (culture, community, social difference) to 'inside' (curriculum, pedagogy, assessment), is a marker of how the learning context does or does not divide on stereotyped gender lines.

We tentatively suggest that teachers see girls' friendship/group work skills as an important aid to learning – they make up what we think is misunder-stood as girls 'sensibleness'. Getting group work right might assist in sup-porting learning if that in turn reflects a school ethos that makes inclusion central. Girls who make and retain (!) effective friendship/learning group combinations clearly create a potentially powerful (and under-researched) set of learning resources – cf. Gordon *et al.* 1998. If all is going well in the friendship/learning groups these pedagogic settings can centre them in in-credibly useful support systems that are capable, we suggest, of scaffolding learning beyond the power of their teachers.

We should, therefore, perhaps not be surprised that when girls are centre-staged (as they were in our female-only friendship group interviews) ideas and insights that are traditionally viewed as 'background' and may not have been voiced explicitly among them collectively before reveal themselves as important insights (hopefully to girls and, we hope, helpfully to teachers). Here we have focused upon the capacity of their talk as critique and insight into the gendered nature of classrooms.

Such views show not only the power of their understanding but also its limits. They tell us just how insightful and confident some girls are in reflecting upon the gendered nature of classroom life. How girls read boys as peers/friends or as enemies/aliens clearly indicates their awareness about the very different ways boys see them in turn. Are the genders behind or in front of the gender barricade? And what are the impacts on all the pupils' learning? The challenge remains of making available to all our pupils effective learning styles that do not depend on traditional binary lines. We would not want to suggest to girls that they should stop being 'sensible'. On the contrary, we would want to make the 'feminine' position of collaboration and support more widely distributed among the boys. Tony Blair's (in)famous mantra in the UK election of 1997, 'education, education, education', captured the New Labour core message of using schools to build the way towards social inclusion. But as heretic critics suggest, it takes a redistributive rather than a rhetorical move to deliver such important goods (Mortimore and Whitty 1997; Daniels et al. 1999; Young 1999; Bullen et al. 2000). One of the goods that clearly is in need of redistribution in girls' favour is gender power.

Conclusion

The 'Learning and Gender Study' has shown girls contesting boys. This chapter has centred on a little-known aspect of girls' language of evaluation. Here is an alternative language of boys as variously 'charming', 'nerds', 'moaners', 'moody' or 'troubled'. Girls' accounts of boys' talk and classroom behaviour question the way that the boys' underachievement debate has worked to fracture wider concerns with social equity and education (cf. Epstein et al. 1998; Gilbert and Gilbert 1998). On the contrary, our analysis of classrooms sees the relations of teaching and learning (pedagogies) as forms of sexual politics that work through the social differences of class, ethnicity and age. We agree with comments made in Chapter I that what we need to focus upon is less the uncontested reality of universal male domination than the consequences for girls (and boys) of the ideological assumption of 'masculinity' as domination. This may be 'less about having power than feeling entitled to it' (our emphasis). We have come to a very similar conclusion in our idea of 'wannabe' dominant boys (see Hey et al. 1999). As we have seen in this chapter, girls talk within and against that assumption.

References

Barker, M. (1997) Taking the extreme case: understanding a fascist fan of Judge Dredd, in D. Cartmell, I.Q. Hunter and I. Whelehan (eds) Trash Aesthetics. London: Pluto Press.

Bernstein, B. (1996) Pedagogy, Symbolic Control and Identity. London: Taylor and Francis.

Bernstein, B. (1997) Official knowledge and pedagogic identity: the politics of re-contextualisation, in I. Nilsson et al. (eds) Teachers, Curriculum and Policy: Critical Perspectives in Educational Research. Umea: Department of Education, University of Umea, Sweden.

Bullen, E., Kenway, J. and Hey, V. (2000) New Labour, social exclusion and educational risk management: the case of gymslip mums. *British Educational Research Journal (forthcoming)*.

Butler, J. (1997) *Excitable Speech: The Politics of the Performative*. London: Routledge.

Bourdieu, P. (1984) *Distinction*. London, Routledge.

Byers, S. (1998) Co-ordinated action to tackle boys' underachievement. Speech presented to the 11th International Congress for School Effectiveness and Improvement, University of Manchester Institute of Science and Technology, 5 January.

Cohen, P. (1997) *Rethinking the Youth Question*. Basingstoke: Macmillan.

Connell, R.W. (1987) *Gender and Power: Society, the Person and Sexual Politics*. Cambridge: Polity Press.

Connell, R.W. (1995) *Masculinities*. Cambridge: Polity Press.

Creese, A., Hey, V., Daniels, H. *et al.* (1999) Within firing range? Targeting the performance of gender. Revised version of a paper given at the British Association of Applied Linguistics, The Open University, Milton Keynes, 18–19 October.

Daniels, H., Hey, V., Leonard, D. *et al.* (1999) Learning and Gender: A Study of Underachievement in Junior Schools. Final report to the ESRC Learning and Gender. R000237346.

Davies, B. (1989) The discursive production of male/female dualism in school settings. *Oxford Review of Education*, 15 (3): 229–41.

Epstein, D. and Johnson, R. (1999) *Schooling Sexualities*. Buckingham: Open University Press.

Epstein, D., Elwood, J., Hey, V. and Maw, J. (eds) (1998) *Failing Boys? Issues in Gender and Achievement*. Buckingham: Open University Press.

Francis, B. (1999) Lads, lasses and (New) Labour: 14 to 16-year-old students' responses to the 'laddish behaviour and the boys' underachievement' debate. Paper presented at 'Voices in Gender and Education' Conference, University of Warwick, 29–31 March.

Gilbert, R. and Gilbert, P. (1998) *Masculinity Goes to School*. London: Routledge.

Gilligan, C. (1993) *In a Different Voice: Psychological Theory and Women's Development*. Cambridge, MA: Harvard University Press.

Gilligan, C., Lyons, N.P. and Hanmer, T.J. (1990) *Making Connections: The Relational World of Adolescent Girls at School*. Cambridge, MA and London: Harvard University Press.

Gordon, T., Holland, J. and Lahelma, E. (1998) Friends or foes? Interpreting relations between girls in school. Paper presented at the 'Ethnography and Education' Conference, Department of Educational Studies, Oxford University, 7–8 September.

Hey, V. (1997) *The Company She Keeps: An Ethnography of Girls' Friendship*. Buckingham: Open University Press.

Hey, V. and Creese, A. with Daniels, H., Fielding, S., Leonard, D., and Smith, M. (1999) Hegemonic, traditional and reflexive discourses of emergent masculinities in primary schools: contextualising gender and class identifications in different pedagogic practices. Paper presented to the 'Education Policies and Practices' Seminar, Kings College, University of London, 7 December.

Kehily, M.J. (1998) Learning about sex and doing gender: teenage magazines, gender enactments and sexualities, in G. Walford and A. Massey (eds) *Studies in Educational Ethnography*. London: JAI Press.

Kehily, M. and Nayak, A. (1997) 'Lads and laughter': humour and the production of heterosexual hierarchies. *Gender and Education*, 9 (1): 69–87.

Lingard, B. and Douglas, P. (1999) *Men Engaging Feminisms: Pro-feminism, Backlashes and Schooling*. Buckingham: Open University Press.

McCann, R. (2000) *On their Own: Boys Growing Up Underfathered?* NSW: Finch.

Mauthner, M. (1998) Bringing silent voices into a public discourse: researching accounts of sister relationships in J. Ribbens and R. Edwards (eds) *Feminist Dilemmas in Qualitative Research: Public Knowledge and Private Lives*. London: Sage Publications.

Mortimore, P. and Whitty, G. (1997) *Can School Improvement Overcome the Effects of Disadvantage?* London: Institute of Education.

Myers, K. (2000) *Whatever Happened to Equal Opportunities? Gender Equality Initiatives in Education*. Buckingham: Open University Press.

Ohrm, E. (1998) Gender and power in school: on girls' open resistance. *Social Psychology of Education* 1: 341–57.

Padfield, P. (1997) 'Skivers', 'sadies and "swots": pupils' perceptions of the process of labelling those 'in trouble' at school. Paper presented at the Scottish Educational Research Association Annual Conference, University of Dundee, September 18–20.

Paechter, C. (1998) *Educating the Other: Gender, Power and Schooling*. Brighton: Falmer.

Pattman, R. (n.d.) Throwing jelly beans at people in suits – maturity, immaturity and how boys and girls position themselves and each other in interviews, personal communication.

Reay, D. and Wiliam, D. (1998) I'll be a Nothing: structure, agency and the construction of identity through assessment. Paper presented at the British Educational Research Association Conference, Queens University of Belfast, Northern Ireland, August 27–30.

Redman, P. and Mac an Ghaill, M. (1997) Educating Peter: the making of a history man, in D.L. Steinberg, D. Epstein and R. Johnson (eds) *Border Patrols: Policing the Boundaries of Heterosexuality*. London: Cassell.

Rich, A. (1980) Compulsory heterosexuality and lesbian existence. *Signs: Journal of Women in Culture and Society*, 5 (4): 631–60.

Thorne, B. (1993) *Gender Play: Girls and Boys in School*. Buckingham: Open University Press.

Walkerdine, V. (1985) On the regulation of speaking and silence, in C. Steedman, C. Urwin and V. Walkerdine (eds) *Language, Gender and Childhood*. London: Routledge and Kegan Paul.

Walkerdine, V. (1987) Femininity as performance. *Oxford Review of Education*, 15 (3): 267–79.

Woods, P. (1977) Having a laugh: an antidote to schooling, in P. Woods (ed.) *The Process of Schooling*, Open University Block 2. Milton Keynes: Open University.

Young, M. (1999) Some reflections on the concepts of social exclusion and inclusion: beyond the third way, in A. Hayton (ed.) *Tackling Disaffection and Social Exclusion: Education Perspectives and Policies*. London: Kogan Page.

CHAPTER 10

Transgressing the masculine: African American boys and the failure of schools

JAMES EARL DAVIS

Not all boys are the same. This simple point is not an obvious one given all the talk about the 'boy problem' in the United States. But where are African American boys? It's apparent from the national conversation on troubled boyhood that the inclusion of black boys' experiences muddles the discussion. The image that comes to mind of boys victimized by a feminist agenda and the conspiracy of not letting 'boys be boys' is clear and consistent: white and middle class. We have created a separate discussion and agenda, particularly about schooling, that removes black boys from an important national debate. The 'other' boy crisis (Chapter I, this volume) that many black males face is defined by racism, poverty, and violence. African American boys are not only a major problem for schools, they also trouble our cultural analysis of boyhood. The difficulty for schools, at least, rests in their inability to deal with 'where these boys are coming from'. While schools acknowledge that these students often bring diverse backgrounds and perspectives, little is known about the complex lives African American boys, in part, create at school.

Indeed, the current plight of young black males in American schools is the focus of much concern for teachers, parents and communities. The dismal statistics of the achievement gap and behavioural programmes have captured the attention of a nation (Jencks and Phillips 1998; Polite and Davis 1999; Majors 2000). However, the predominant perspective on understanding the 'black boy problem' calls for solutions without much attention to the active role African American boys themselves play in creating their own school experience. This is not to say that how schools structure students' opportunities to learn isn't important. For sure, inequalities in schooling have potentially lifelong consequences for black male educational attainment, employment and family relations. Access to quality academic programmes, curricula and teacher quality are extremely important for these students who bring to school many skills, dispositions and behaviours that are considered marginalized at best and criminal at worst. But always to cast these young males as victims strips them of any agency in how they make meaning of who they are at school.

Based on a previous study of black boys in middle school, this chapter highlights for teachers how African American boys make sense and construct meanings of masculinity and sexuality. What emerges from conversations and observations of boys is an insight into their roles in male identity development and behaviour in school. Implications for teacher practice, both at a curricular and personal level, are numerous. This chapter focuses on critical issues identified by black boys that inform teachers about valuing diversity in masculinity. The active voices and behaviours of these boys serve as new texts about their role in the crisis that affects them. Their perspectives not only frame conditions confronting African American boys as learners but also inform teachers and administrators of potential interventions.

Researching black boys at school

In the mist of trying to get a handle on the education crisis of black boys, we have learned too little about how boys construct personal meaning for their social and academic lives. We do know that black boys are both loved and loathed at school. They set the standards for hip-hop culture and athleticism, while at the same time experiencing disproportionate levels of punishment and academic failure. This juxtaposition leads to a range of behaviours and strategies within school that set the tone for the overall problematic educational experience of black boys (Sewell 1997). How do these boys respond to a context that defines them as both 'sexy and as sexually threatening' and create a space that they can call their own?

Although black boys as well as black girls are having hard times at school, some research suggests that the problems facing black boys are more chronic and extreme, thus deserving special programme and curricular attention (Watson and Smitherman 1991; Garibaldi 1992). Negative cultural messages about black males in the media and in everyday life abound (Belton 1995; Blount and Cunningham 1996; Harper 1996), portraying them as violent, disrespectful, unintelligent, and hyper-sexualized. These cultural messages carry over into schools and affect the ways black male students are treated. For instance, black boys' demeanours are misunderstood by white middle-class teachers and seen as defiant, aggressive and intimidating (Majors *et al.* 1994). Further, in almost every category of academic failure, black boys are disproportionately represented (Entwisle *et al.* 1997). In addition to lags in test score performance and grades, African American males are referred for special education placement at a much higher rate than all other students and they are much more likely to be suspended or expelled from school (Harry and Anderson 1999). There is growing evidence that black male disengagement with school develops in the early grades and continues to intensify as they progress through school (Carter 1999). By all indicators black males consistently fall behind other students in school performance and lead their peers in school infractions and other negative outcomes.

Although the body of research on black boys in school is limited, it provides some useful insights. Much of this work, comparative in nature, examines the academic experiences and outcomes of black boys relative to other students. Slaughter-Defoe and Richards (1994) suggest that, as early as kindergarten, black males are treated differently from other male and female students. Throughout elementary and middle school, black boys consistently receive lower ratings by teachers for social behaviour and academic expectations (Irvine 1990; Rong 1996). In their study of factors related to school outcomes for black males, Davis and Jordan (1994) suggest that boys' school engagement reflected in study habits and attendance were positively related to achievement and grades. Black boys who spend more time on homework and attend school regularly also perform better academically and are more engaged in their schooling. They also found that remediation, grade retention and suspensions induce academic failure among black boys. The research that exists on black males in school is relatively recent, and typically focuses on factors that characterize or place these students 'at risk' as learners. Little attention is given to how black males construct personal meaning for their lives in and out of school. Particularly, discussion about how black boys make sense of their own masculinity has been noticeably absent.

Schooling black masculinity

During the past two decades, a variety of journal articles, reports, scholarly and popular books have detailed the precarious nature of black males in school and society (Gibbs 1988; Holland 1989; Majors and Gordon 1994; Mincy 1994; Polite and Davis 1999; Brown and Davis 2000). Related to this work, an array of programme initiatives has captured the attention of school administrators, local communities and parents as possible solutions to school-related problems associated with black males. These programmes seek to support current school activities by providing a positive presence of adult black men. Mentoring programmes that assign professional black men as role models for young boys, typically in elementary and middle schools, have been established in many school districts. Professional black men serve as teachers' aids, tutors, and reading partners for black boys needing academic support and guidance. The justification for these initiatives points to the need for consistent and positive black men in educational settings who provide models for young black males to emulate (Holland 1992). Others contend that the increased presence of committed and successful black male adults in educational environments is essential for enhancing black boys' academic and social development. This positive male presence diffuses traditional masculine behaviours and counters negative gender role socialization of black boys (Cunningham 1993). The development of conceptions and expressions of masculinity that match positive behaviours and deportment in school settings is the primary objective of these interventions.

Approaches such as all-male schools and classrooms take a more radical approach to current schooling conditions. Given the severity of problems associated with black boys in schools, advocates for race- and gender-exclusive schooling defend these strategies that reorganize the gendered nature of schools and classrooms as the best approach (Watson and Smitherman, 1991). Many advocates for black boys see teachers as responsible for imposing feminine standards of behavioural expectations on black boys that induce oppositional behaviours in academic attitude and engagement (Holland 1992). These all-male academies serve as compensatory devices aimed at restoring a normative masculinity to the centre of black boys' schooling experiences.

Afrocentric models of masculinity are being proposed as alternatives to European conceptions of masculinity. These 'new' conceptions of masculinity seek a shift from western ideas of male socialization to a cultural awareness grounded in the experiences and history of African people (Akbar 1991; Jeff 1994). The intent of these models are transformative, however images of a normative masculinity being either unfulfilled or misdirected still dominate. Recent studies on the effectiveness of culturally themed and Afrocentric school experiences for black boys have been mixed. Fifth-grade black boys enrolled in a cultural immersion school were found to take more personal responsibility for their intellectual and academic achievement than their peers in a traditional school. The immersion school, however, appears to account for no other achievement or esteem differences (Sanders and Reed 1995). Additionally, Hudley (1995, 1997) identified potential effects on academic self-concept for black males enrolled in separate Afrocentric classrooms, but found limited effects. Specifically, the achievement motivation and academic self-concept of black boys participating in immersion programmes at the school or classroom level improve marginally, if at all. Reasons for these limited outcomes, however, may be more related to methodological limitations rather than programme effectiveness (Davis and Polite 2000).

Black boys in middle school project

Based on a study of middle school black males, using observations, interviews, and small group discussions, in this section I present and link black boys' ideas about masculinity to their dynamic experience of being black and male. As part of a research team on a larger research project, I collected data at a middle school (grades 6–8) during three academic years (Davis 1999). This medium-sized (798 students) middle school was located in a large suburban county in a north-eastern state. The middle school enrols students from a range of socio-economic and racial backgrounds, including a significant number of black students from a nearby urban centre. African American students are bussed daily from their inner-city neighbourhoods to an upper middle class suburban community where the school is located. Black boys (ages 10–13) are from diverse social and economic backgrounds. While most reside in the city and are from working-class families, a few also live in suburban neighbourhoods near the school.

The research project was organized to document how students talk about race and gender in a middle school environment. Team members attended various school activities during and after school and observed and talked to students during class, between class and at lunch. These frequent and prolonged observations of students in a natural school setting provided rich information about the everyday lives of students at school. These observations are supplemented by small-group and in-depth individual interviews.

All the small group interviews were both video and audiotape recorded. We were particularly interested to facilitate conversations with and between students about their experiences, interactions and ideas around race and gender. So in the small groups we encouraged students to talk as members of their racial and gender groups. For instance, we asked questions such as 'What is it like to be black and male in this school?' In my thematic analysis of the student data, I have searched for patterns and topics that characterize typical thinking of black boys at the school. My intent here is not to offer findings that generalize to all black boys in all school settings. Rather, my purpose is to understand the voices of black masculinity in one school and how meanings of masculinity play themselves out socially for these boys. The following section represents some overarching themes that were generated from the project database. I provide examples of how black boys think and talk about what it means to be male, particularly their feelings about the expectations for boys at school.

A masculinity of their own

Data from small group and individual interviews inform most of my understanding of the vulnerable and complex school lives organized by black males. Black boys create a very distinctive culture for themselves – one that's shaped by a unique racial and gender position in this middle school. Black boys clearly understand and embrace traditional conceptions of masculinity. Drawing on my reading of this alienating schooling environment for black boys, I found that a social responsive subculture around masculine expectations and acceptability has emerged. This subculture is different from traditional school cultural behaviours and norms for white boys in middle school because joining the distinct racial school experience of black boys with maladaptive notions of what constitutes appropriate boyhood creates a reactive social environment.

To get an initial sense of how black boys think of their peers, I asked them whom they considered the most popular black boys at the school. There were two young males who were consistently mentioned. Most boys said they were popular because of their physical appearance, the clothes they wore, and their rapport with girls. Surprisingly, one of the boys mentioned is lauded because of his strong academic record. He is also an athlete and very popular with girls. A 7th grade student's guarded admiration for a popular black boy revolves around traditional masculine attributes such as physical characteristics and prowess:

> He's really cool and he dresses nice. And he helps you when you are in need. One time, he really helped me out. One time I was about to get banked[1] near the corner store where I live by a bunch of other guys 'cause I had fought one of the guy's brothers and he came up there and help me out. He's a good guy.

In a collective manner, black boys are engaged in producing and reproducing what they consider an authentic black masculine identity. Since they are well aware of their marginalized academic and social status at the middle school, they create their own rules for resisting schooling that excludes and labels them as at-risk city boys. This subcultural space they create in turn functions as a vehicle where their version of masculinity becomes protest and defiance in the face of negative expectations of teachers and peers.

These boys carry a heavy load of expectations from fellow students and teachers. For instance, they bear the burden of racial stereotypes surrounding issues of sexuality coupled with the mark of troublemakers inside and outside class. Unfortunately and unknowingly they reinforce these racial and sexual stereotypes. But the potential benefits of their hyper-sexualized status make it difficult for most boys to counter these notions. According to Michael, a very thoughtful and articulate 8th grade black male who is well liked by teachers and consistently appears on the honour roll, sexual stereotypes of black boys are common at this school:

> Right now black guys are very popular. It seems like white guys have lost their status, they are more invisible. I think a lot of white girls buy into the myth of black guys.

It should be noted that interracial dating is generally an unacceptable practice at this middle school. Most students are uncomfortable, at least publicly, in endorsing romantic relationships between black and white students. When these relationships do occur, however, they are almost exclusively between black boys and white girls who are very discreet due to fear of peer criticism. Recently a few black boys in the 8th grade have become romantically linked to white girls at the school. A black 8th grader, Juan, comments and reflects on this taboo topic while acknowledging that he likes white girls and enjoys socializing with them at school:

> Before coming to school here, I went to school with all black people. I lived in an all black neighbourhood and only associated with other blacks. Now I live in the suburbs, mostly white neighbourhood. Since being in a school that's mixed, I've gotten to know all different kinds of people. Before, I really didn't have contact with white girls. But being at this school you get to know them and I like that.

Juan also feels that some black boys have become very popular at school primarily because of the 'sex thing'. He reflects on his personal trials and the unstable nature of this social status at school. He complains, 'Last year I was in the most popular in-group at the school, but I was kicked out this year, I don't know why.' Unlike Juan, Michael, who has been criticized by other black students at the school for acting like a 'geek' and not 'knowing how to dress', feels the social pressure to date or at least talk about his desire for white girls. By doing so, he knows he would present himself in a more conforming masculine way at school.

Among black students, the dominant masculine script for boy–girl interactions provides some insights to the state of gender relationships. Generally, black boys are not allowed to have meaningful friendships with black girls. While the social climate among black boys and girls is generally friendly and mutually supportive, these relationships are based on their shared racial status. Black boys tend only to deal with black girls from their mutual position of racial solidarity. For the most part, however, strong platonic friendships between black boys and girls are non-existent, unless the friendship can be recognized as possibly leading to sex. It should be noted that there is very little evidence to suggest that there is a great deal of sexual activity among boys and girls at this middle school. Relationships that are considered 'sexual' are in fact merely constructed around the talk and intent of sex, not actual sexual relations. For instance, black boys know what's the appropriate social interaction style that should occur between males and females. Friendship is usually not an option. Due to the limited nature of boy–girl interactions, potential academic benefits are also limited. One exception, however, are honour classes where very few black students, boys or girls, are enrolled. Given the small number of black students in these classes, cooperative work relationships are more pragmatic. For example, Rob is the only black boy in his 7th grade maths honours class. He comments on how he interacts with black girls in his class:

> I can talk to these girls about school and stuff. Since we are the only blacks in the class, we have to stick together. Usually, guys and girls don't hang, unless they are trying to hook-up. They do their own thing, we do ours.

Boy victims of labels at school

Black boys tend to organize around ideas that reflect who they are and how they want to be seen as black males. These conceptions of masculinity are a means of challenging a school climate that excludes and labels them as at-risk boys from the inner city with very few academic skills. The counter-culture that these boys create functions as a vehicle where a hyper-masculine style serves as a form of protest and defiance. Sadly, the resulting behaviours only confirm negative opinions that teachers and peers already hold. It seems that black boys at this middle school are both victimized and liberated by their self-constructed identity. They enjoy the power and social benefits of social agency and self-expression, but they are stymied by racial stereotypes they seek to undermine.

The restrictive masculine culture of black boys also serves as a policing agent for normative masculine enforcement. Black boys enforce their meaning of masculinity by sanctioning other boys who do not adhere to their definition. What can be said of the few boys who do not always adhere to the prescribed masculine orthodoxy? I refer to them as transgressor because they go against the accepted notions of proper masculinity at the school. Often severe social punishment is directed towards these black boys who act counter to the behavioural code. Shunning and ridiculing black boys who transgress the masculine standard accomplishes this objective. One area of notable transgression is presentation style. Black boys make very clear what's accepted masculine presentational behaviour including hallway walk, how boys talk, school attire, trainers, lunchroom interaction style, and how boys carry their books and book bags. The shared experience of being African American at this school is not enough to forge tolerant social alliances.

Severe masculine transgressions are more than likely about issues of sexuality. For instance, positing alternative views on sexuality as well as questioning any aspect of the traditional masculinity could result in social harassment. Several common labels are selected to describe these boys. These pejorative slurs are employed by boys to belittle, distance, insult and injure. Labels like 'gay', 'sissy' and 'fag' are freely used to produce the highest level of emotional fear and hatred. With these markers boys are given the ultimate sanctioning – removal from the friendship circle of black boys to the exclusive company of black girls. But they also may be relegated to the social networks of a variety of white student social groups. Publicly, how boys position themselves relative to girls and 'soft' boys is important in maintaining a normative masculine image at school. A 7th grade student, Anthony, is consistently recognized as someone who falls outside the domain of the black masculine authority at the school. This position, in part, derives from his social manner and behaviour characteristics. Anthony is physically larger than most of the boys in his grade. Although he is effeminate, he is not tolerant of students' taunts and sneers. One of Anthony's 7th grade peers describes him this way:

He's like gay, a real fag! He swishes when he walks and he talks like a girl. Once he came up behind me at the water fountain and he was just there acting like a girl. It made me nervous so I got away from him as far as I could. Ah, you know that he's gay. He likes guys. He'll say that he is not gay. He says he likes girls. That's not true. It doesn't matter what he says. He's still gay. He doesn't care what people think about him. That's why he gets into a lot of trouble. He has to fight a lot. People at school can't stand him.

Another black 7th grade student offers his views about why Anthony is socially rejected and held in low regard by other black boys at school:

People make fun of this guy because of the way he walks and the way he talks. He's soft so people make fun of him and this voice . . . I wouldn't want to be like him. He tries to be hard and tough 'cause of the way he acts, but people still don't like him. He goes around thinking that he is really hard, but he isn't.

Unfortunately, little attention has been paid to the plight of boys who go against the masculine value system. Black boys who are considered out of the masculine mainstream by their peers are severely stigmatized because of the dual weight of racial stereotype and gender norms (Carter 1999). Black boys who do not meet the standards of an acceptable masculinity are treated as masculine mistakes; including boys who dare to verbalize alternative views on masculinity. Those who do transgress occupy a very complicated and vulnerable social position at the school. Since they defy both racial and gender regulations, these boys are constantly juggling and negotiating their identity of being black and male. Usually their efforts for legitimacy and recognition fall short.

Teaching boys to transgress

Teacher accountability is a dominant theme in school reform efforts across the US. Much of this concern for accountability centres on student learning and achievement outcomes (Boykin 1994). But should teachers be held responsible for the social outcomes and experiences of black boys? It goes without saying that teachers play a very significant role in the school lives of students. Since most of the school day is spent in classrooms under the supervision and guidance of teachers, their influence on black boys should never be taken for granted. Although teachers are blamed for many problems boys face, ironically most of the proposed solutions aimed at remedying the educational plight of African American boys have excluded teachers. The rationale for this position is that teachers are blamed for students' poor levels of academic performance and engagement (Holland 1992). Teachers' influence on black boys is too important, however, to silence them and reduce their contribution to background noise. Responses from boys at this middle school, in fact, tend to recognize both teachers' potential and problems in their education:

> Black males at this school have a bad reputation. Some of the teachers have had trouble with them. But if she doesn't know you and what you are like, there usually is a problem. But once she gets to know you, then you have a better reputation with her.

> I think they should take the time to talk to us and let us know what's going on and how we are doing in our life and everything, I think they would feel better about black males if they knew something about us and what's behind our background. The problem is they don't know what's going on in our life.

Black males in general share this desire for a more personal connection with teachers. They feel they are often misunderstood and wrongly judged because of how they look and act. Teachers bear a disproportionate role in monitoring social relationships, not only in their classrooms, but also in other social settings at the school. Traditionally teachers have felt that their student social networks and relationships were off-limits to them. As teachers are being held accountable for structuring students' learning opportunities, so must teachers take a more active role in understanding black boys and intervening when necessary with social lessons that cultivate an appreciation for a variety of ways that boys can behave at school.

Teaching strategies need to be refocused and centred on the lives created and lived by black boys in schools. Understanding how black boys make sense of who they are in school and their relation to a school culture of masculinity offers new points of entry for teachers. While it is true that school is an important site of critical social and cultural intervention (Browne and Fletcher 1995), teachers need to be informed by where black boys are positioned in school. These multifaceted and complicated school lives of black males regrettably are too often ignored, misunderstood and rendered invisible. Teachers need to make meaningful interventions that promote positive portrayals highlighting the possible selves of school-aged black boys – new images that link masculinity to the importance of schooling, academic achievement and a diversity of relational styles.

In order to effectively teach boys to transgress, teachers must become full partners in promoting positive interventions that broaden the range of masculine behaviours, talents and other social resources available to black boys. This work must include non-traditional gender projects in curricular and non-curricular activities. The middle school years are appropriate to include studies that focus on anti-homophobic, anti-sexist and anti-racist topics. Also a rethinking of current course material in middle school that relates to new masculine objectives, particularly in social studies, is essential. In music, art, physical education and other subject areas, teachers are responsible for creating a safe academic and physical space where boys are encouraged to explore non-traditional gender activities without the ridicule and threats of other students. The work will be difficult at times, but the responsibility for cultivating healthy zones for masculine nurturing and self-discovery, where black boys are not deprived of imagining their whole selves, falls where it should – with teachers.

The thought of black boys as victims of female (mostly white) teachers continues to create a groundswell of activity directed towards improving educational outcome. In Chapter 1 it is argued, and I concur, that it's not the school experience that feminizes boys but rather a traditional notion of masculinity that inadequately informs boys about what success in school means. In almost every school where there are significant numbers of black males, programmes are in place to rescue black boys. Rite of passage, mentoring, male tutoring, and manhood training programmes continue to grow in popularity in schools around the country. Interestingly, these pro-grammes emerge out of concern for black boys' relative lack of educational success, but too many of them do not question the negative consequences of normative masculinity. Regardless of the flaw in the approach, the message to teachers in elementary and middle schools is clear: race and gender matter in educating black boys.

Conclusions: lessons in masculine diversity

As I have tried to illustrate in this chapter, middle school is a place where black boys make sense about what it means to be a black male. In the process, a counter-culture is created that feeds upon a traditional masculine hegemony of behaviour and attitude. I am well aware that the development of black boys' social identity is complicated by the heavy dosages they get from immediate and distance sources, such as family, community, church and the media. Indeed, these social messages provide young males with information about their place and purpose. Schools, for sure, are contested sites where black boys learn to endorse and participate in a masculinity project that restricts their possibilities. The current schooling experience of many black boys is yet another disappointing aspect of their young lives. For many of them, schools ignore their aspirations, disrespect their ability to learn, fail to access and cultivate their many talents, and impose a restrictive range of masculine options. Within this overwhelming oppressive schooling context, too many black boys simply give up – beaten by school systems that place little value on who they are and what they offer.

Certainly a broader and more diverse definition of acceptable masculinity is needed at this middle school (Connell 1995). But from this reading of student culture, only a narrow conception of masculinity is readily available to black boys. Any thought, action or response counter to the masculinity norms at the school is considered inappropriate and subject to peer punishment.

This regulation of masculinity requires a level of gender 'know-how' that must be understood by boys in order to survive socially at school. To be sure, the dynamic nature of negotiating identity categories is difficult for all black boys, but some boys, due to their non-traditional masculine style or appearance, bear a disproportionate level of criticism and social estrangement. Ultimately all boys are disadvantaged by these strict gender norms. Conformity to these valued masculine behaviours not only increases the level of anxiety about being socially ostracized, but also dictates boys' range of social, emotional and academic experiences in school. The inability to explore and embrace other possibilities of boyhood reduces the kinds of options and opportunities African American boys can have and desperately need at school. In turn, the development of a school culture that acknowledges diversity in how boys can be boys will continue to be arrested unless proactive teaching is realized.

Note

1 Banked refers to being violently jumped, physically assaulted, or beat down.

References

Akbar, N. (1991) *Visions of Black Men*. Nashville, TN: Winston-Derek Publications.

Belton, D. (1995) *Speak My Name: Black Men on Masculinity and the American Dream*. Boston, MA: Beacon Press.

Blount, M. and Cunningham, G.P. (eds) (1996) *Representing Black Men*. New York, NY: Routledge.

Boykin, A.W. (1994) Reformulating educational reform. Toward the proactive schooling of African American children, in R.J. Rossi (ed.) *Educational Reforms and Students at Risk*. New York, NY: Teachers' College Press.

Brown, M.C. and Davis, J.E. (eds) (2000) *Black Sons to Mothers: Compliments, Critiques, and Challenges for Cultural Workers in Education*. New York, NY: Peter Lang.

Browne, R. and Fletcher, R. (1995) *Boys in Schools: Addressing the Real Issues – Behavior, Values and Relationships*. Sydney: Finch Publishing.

Carter, P. (1999) *Balancing Acts: Issues of Identity and Cultural Resistance in the Social and Educational Behaviors of Minority Youth*. PhD dissertation, Department of Sociology, Columbia University, New York, NY.

Connell, R.W. (1995) *Masculinities*. Berkeley, CA: University of California Press.

Cunningham, M. (1993) Sex role influence on African American males. *Journal of African American Males Studies*, 1: 30–7.

Davis, J.E. (1999) Forbidden fruit: black males' constructions of transgressive sexualities in middle school, in W.J. Letts and J.T. Sears (eds) *Queering Elementary Education: Advancing the Dialogue About Sexualities and Schooling*. Lanham, MD: Rowman and Littlefield.

Davis, J.E. and Jordan, W.J. (1994) The effects of school context, structure, and experience on African American males in middle and high school. *Journal of Negro Education*, 63: 570–87.

Davis, J.E. and Polite, V.C. (2000) Early schooling and academic achievement of African American males. Commissioned paper presented at the African American Male Achievement Symposium, US Department of Education, Office of Educational Research and Improvement, December 4.

Entwisle, D.R., Alexander, K.L. and Olson, L.S. (1997) *Children, Schools, and Inequality.* Boulder, CO: Westview Press.

Garibaldi, A.M. (1992) Educating and motivating African American males to succeed. *Journal of Negro Education,* 61: 12–18.

Gibbs, J. (1988) *Young, Black, and Males in America: An Endangered Species.* Dover, MA: Auburn House.

Harper, P.M. (1996) *Are We Not Men? Masculine Anxiety and the Problem of African-American Identity.* New York, NY: Oxford University Press.

Harry, B. and Anderson, M.G. (1999) The social construction of high-incidence disabilities: the effects on African American males, in V.C. Polite and J.E. Davis (eds) *African American Males in School and Society: Policy and Practice for Effective Education.* New York, NY: Teachers' College Press.

Holland, S. (1989) Fighting the epidemic of failure: a radical strategy for education inner-city boys. *Teacher Magazine,* 1: 88–9.

Holland, S. (1992) Same-gender classes in Baltimore: how to avoid the problems faced in Detroit/Milwaukee. *Equity and Excellence,* 25: 2–4.

Hudley, C.A. (1995) Assessing the impact of separate schooling for African American male adolescents. *Journal of Early Adolescence,* 15: 38–57.

Hudley, C.A. (1997) Teacher practices and student motivation in middle school programs for African American males. *Urban Education,* 32: 304–19.

Irvine, J.J. (1990) *Black Students and School Failure: Policies, Practices, and Prescriptions.* Westport, CT: Greenwood.

Jeff, M.F.X. (1994) Afrocentrism and African-American male youth, in R. Mincy (ed.) *Nurturing Young Black Males: Challenges to Agencies, Programs and Social Policy.* Washington, DC: Urban Institute Press.

Jencks, C. and Phillips, M. (eds) (1998) *The Black–White Test Score Gap.* Washington, DC: Brookings Institution Press.

Majors, R.G. (2000) (ed.) *The Education Revolution.* London: Taylor and Routledge.

Majors, R.G. and Gordon, J.U. (1994) *The American Black Male: His Present Status and His Future.* Chicago, IL: Nelson-Hall.

Majors, R.G. and Mancini Billson, J. (1992) *Cool Pose: The Dilemmas of Black Manhood in America.* New York, NY: Lexington.

Majors, R.G., Tyler, R., Peden, B. and Hall, R.E. (1994) Cool pose: a symbolic mechanism for masculine role enactment and copying by Black males, in R.G. Majors and J.U. Gordan (eds) *The American Black Male: His Present Status and His Future,* pp 245–59. Chicago, IL: Nelson-Hall.

Mincy, R.B. (ed.) (1994) *Nurturing Young Black Males: Challenges to Agencies, Programs, and Social Policy.* Washington, DC: The Urban Institute.

Polite, V. and Davis, J.E. (eds) (2000) *African American Males in School and Society: Policy and Practice for Effective Education.* New York, NY: Teachers' College Press.

Rong, X.L. (1996) Effects of race and gender on teachers' perception of the social behavior of elementary students. *Urban Education,* 31: 261–90.

Sanders, E.T. and Reed, P.L. (1995) An investigation of the possible effects of an immersion as compared to a traditional program for African-American males. *Urban Education,* 30: 93–112.

Sewell, T. (1997) *Black Masculinities and Schooling: How Black Boys Survive Modern Schooling*. Stoke-on-Trent: Trentham.

Slaughter-Defoe, D.T. and Richards, H. (1994) Literacy as empowerment: the case for African American males, in V.L. Gadsden and D.A. Wagner (eds) *Literacy Among African American Youth: Issues in Learning, Teaching, and Schooling*, pp 125–47. Cresskill, NJ: Hampton Press.

Watson, C. and Smitherman, G. (1991) Educational equity and Detroit's male academies. *Equity and Excellence*, 25: 90–105.

CHAPTER 11

'Someone has to go through': indigenous boys, staying on at school and negotiating masculinities

LEE SIMPSON, MARK MCFADDEN AND GEOFF MUNNS

Introduction

This chapter is concerned with the stories that some indigenous Australian boys tell of their continued engagement with schooling. These stories reveal that within the interplaying dynamics of community, family, peers and school, the boys are involved in constant negotiations over multiple and intersecting identities: as members of an involuntary minority group (Ogbu and Simmons 1998), as males, and as students at school. The outcome of these negotiations is critical for their cultural acceptance and identity construction as both indigenous and male.

The study[1] from which this chapter is drawn explored the lives of indigenous Australian boys who were remaining at school in the post-compulsory secondary years. What compels them to remain in schools and classrooms which historically have denied them access and equality is a vital issue to address for those who want to encourage engagement with school and education, and thereby enhance educational outcomes for indigenous students. It is also important to understand the terms on which they participate in the structures and relationships of school and adjust to the patterns of schooling they find there (Connell 2000). Their negotiation of subject choice, relationships with teachers and attitudes to and involvement in sport all influence a particular kind of indigenous masculinity that impacts on their engagement with school. Both Mac an Ghaill (1994) and Sewell (1997) have illustrated how particular forms of racial masculinities can lead to both resistance and over-conformity in the school setting and to differential academic outcomes.

Indigenous students: school participation and retention

The relationship of indigenous students to schooling is a significant issue in many post-colonial countries. There is convincing evidence to suggest that school is a battle for the majority of indigenous students in countries that include Australia, New Zealand, Canada and the US. Indeed, it is a battle that is frequently lost.

Statistics show in post-colonial countries that many indigenous students do not reach or complete post-compulsory education. In Australia, government reports show that the retention rate for indigenous Australian students is 25 per cent, which compares to 78 per cent for non-indigenous Australian students (Commonwealth of Australia 1995). In New Zealand official figures tell a similar story. In 1997, 64 per cent of 16-year-old Maori students were enrolled at school compared to 89 per cent of non-Maori students. Figures for 17-year-old students showed that 39 per cent of Maoris were going to school compared to 65 per cent of non-Maori students (New Zealand Ministry of Education 1998). Statistics and research from Canada reveal that half of First Nations students complete high school in comparison to other groups, and that only 23 per cent of those that graduate proceed to college. These completion and attendance rates are significantly lower than those of the general population (Wright 1998). Likewise in the US, only 52 per cent of American Indian students finish high school, and of the 17 per cent that attend college, only 4 per cent graduate (Meyers 1997). These figures reflect a drop-out rate for American Indians that is double the country's average. In some communities the reported drop-out rates approach 100 per cent (Hatch 1992, cited in Sanchez and Stuckey 1999).

The statistics further show that it is indigenous boys who lose school battles in greater numbers. In Australia, the federal government has gathered data demonstrating that 'starting from the early years of secondary school, Aboriginal and Torres Strait Islander boys and men are less likely to participate in education than Aboriginal and Torres Strait Islander girls and women' (Commonwealth of Australia 1995: 100). Similarly, the New Zealand government reports that there are rapidly widening gaps in post-compulsory education participation rates between Maori and non-Maori students, particularly among Maori males (New Zealand Ministry of Education 1998). Clearly, there is a consistent and disturbing statistical picture of large numbers of indigenous students, and particularly male indigenous students, who do not remain at school. Such a picture underscores the importance of the development of educational policies, pedagogies and resources to improve rates of retention among this school group.

Even though government statistics indicate that the retention rate for indigenous Australian students is 25 per cent, that figure still represents a significant number of indigenous students remaining at school in the post-compulsory years. There are dangers when these boys who remain are ignored by researchers in favour of those who drop out. First, this affords a research privilege to a particular expression of indigenous masculinity. Second, this narrows the focus about school retention, attempting to consider engagement at school from the point of view of the disengaged. Finally, it renders invisible the significant decisions made by those who remain at school. As Riseborough (1993: 33–4) argues, too much research focuses on intractable, 'non-ideal', 'deviant' students at the expense of less visible, or invisible, tractable, 'good', 'conformist' students. This, he argues, has created a 'conformist-blindness' in the sociological literature which has deflected critical attention away from and restricted theoretical understanding of ' "the conformist's" educational identity and career'.

The indigenous boys who stay on at school in post-compulsory years are in an obvious minority from an already marginalized group.[2] They make their decisions to remain at school against seemingly overwhelming odds and statistics. The telling of the stories of such indigenous boys is a recognition that, despite all the obstacles, some students in disadvantaged groups succeed and find in education a gateway to opportunity rather than a pathway to further oppression (McFadden 1996). This need for a different approach to researching the relationship between education and disadvantage has been recognized in both the US (Nieto 1994; Lavin and Hyllegard 1996; Levine and Nidiffer 1996 and O'Connor 1997) and the UK (see National Commission on Education 1996).

Theoretical underpinnings

Identity, resistance and masculinity

The brutal dilemma for many indigenous students remaining at school is that they often have to make choices between striving for success in the dominant white culture or looking for acceptance in their own culture. This is because success at school is regularly interpreted as 'acting white', an obvious risk to cultural identity for indigenous students (Fordham and Ogbu 1986). On the other hand, leaving school may help students to be culturally accepted within a collective identity that is often defined by difference from the dominant white group. It is this difference for indigenous male students that often finds expression in stances of school resistance and particular forms of protest masculinity.

For indigenous Australian boys, most of whom are fighting both lack of school success and acceptance, it is quite understandable that many would have a strong belief that the education system is not working for them. When this is the case, relationships with education are affected by how individuals and groups work on collective solutions to their shared school and education problems (Ogbu and Simmons 1998). Research has frequently focused on how these solutions, critical to the formation of cultural identities, repeatedly find articulations in resistant and protest stances. This is a means by which many indigenous boys express a particular form of subordinated masculinity (Connell 1993). That this masculinity is developed in opposition to the school is hardly surprising, given the school experiences of many indigenous boys. Among other difficulties, these experiences invariably bring them into direct conflict with forces of discipline and control. Connell (1994: 9) notes that 'masculinity may be constructed *against* the discipline system through defiance of authority' (emphasis in original) and that 'the dialectic of masculinity and authority is one of the dynamics producing drop-out'.

Research into boys and their resistances to school has also shown that the school experiences of marginalized groups are played out within class-determined contexts and positions. The mechanisms of male resistance and protest masculinity have often been described in working-class communities (Willis 1977; Corrigan 1979; Mac an Ghaill 1994) where the school represents the oppressive and exploitative power of the state as it systematically undermines, restricts and denies future life chances. However, research has also identified male resistance to racial oppression (intersecting with issues of class) as expressed in and around school structures (Mac an Ghaill 1988; Bowser 1991; Poynting *et al.* 1999. See also Chapter I, this volume). In this study of indigenous male students' responses to schooling, there are specific questions that arise around issues of masculinity, particularly in light of their social marginalization.

Another form of subordinated masculinity?

The indigenous boys who participated in this study, in choosing to stay on at school, appear to be looking to win an educational battle in which many of their cultural peers have decided not to engage. Why they have made this decision is a central question to pursue. After all, history shows that the battle they are fighting is one that most of their community have been unable to win. There are also salient questions around whether, as Ogbu suggests, there are cultural prices to pay for continued engagement and perhaps success in the *whitefellas'*[3] world of education and what success in education has to offer. Critical in these cultural risks is the negotiation of a different form of masculinity than is apparent for many of their resistant peers. The very real peril is that their engagement with schooling will bring about cultural subordination and alienation from within already subordinated cultural forms of masculinity. This is a danger because continued engagement with schooling, for these students, runs against cultural support for school resistance. The concept that cultural support is a key element that encourages and bolsters resistance to school is fundamental to the research reported in this chapter. Also fundamental is an understanding of the way in which resistance and cultural support is conceptualized.

Resistance and cultural support

While this study utilizes elements of resistance theory[4] it also brings different theoretical perspectives and research foci to the understanding of the educational experience of Australian indigenous school students. A critical theoretical difference to be applied to the analysis of issues surrounding students who chose to stay on at school, including those from indigenous Australian backgrounds, has been developed by Munns and McFadden (2000). Although they explored the complex group and individual processes around school rejection, they also focused on what can encourage enagagement with education. Significant among their findings were ideas about *cultural support.* Ironically, they found cultural support could either operate to entrench educational rejection or, conversely, was critical in helping students remain in education.[5]

Importantly, there are two connected elements to cultural support. The first concerns students' feelings about school. The evidence suggests (see Munns 1996) that the majority of indigenous Australian students leave school because they believe that school is not a place that works for them.[6] The second element of cultural support is concerned with the way indigenous Australian communities respond to their students leaving school. There is evidence to suggest that indigenous Australian communities accept both their students being pushed out of school and school rejection. This is, however, no happy acceptance, more a perception that their children have been let down by the system. Indigenous Australian communities do not want it to happen, hope desperately that it does not, but when it does, the student is not rejected by the family, peers or their community for being a 'failure' at school. Clearly, indigenous Australian communities believe that the institutional offer to be educated does not include equitable access and outcomes (Munns 1996).

For indigenous Australian students, being pushed out of school and/or school rejection is often followed by cultural support from within their own community, and for the majority, leaving school early is seen as inevitable. For most indigenous Australian students, it is argued that leaving school offers a sense of cultural solidarity; just another individual in the group struggling against oppression. Leaving school and the shoring up of cultural solidarity for many indigenous Australian male students is an expression and identification of their masculinity that exists in tension with the hegemonic masculinities of the dominant class and race.[7] However, and paradoxically, it is also clear that indigenous Australian communities value education and it must be understood that they also support those students who remain at school. What makes the difference for these students in helping them to remain at school is at the heart of this study.

The discussion of interview data that follows brings forward important insights into why these indigenous boys have chosen to remain at school and how they see themselves positioned in relation to their peers, their families, their community and the school. It also highlights a particular form of masculinity which is, interestingly, subordinate both to white hegemonic masculinity and the dominant anti-school values shared by a majority of their indigenous male peers. These insights highlight issues that have implications for educators looking to respond to the challenge of finding pathways for educational opportunity and success for indigenous Australian students when educational rejection often has cultural support (Munns and McFadden 2000).

We begin the discussion of the data in the next section with a poignant comment about the pressures that indigenous males must cope with if they are to remain at school.

Talking about life at school

'Different but connected'

> I've gotta lot of mates out of school and they try to talk me out of it . . . It's pretty hard, because you are sittin' up there, it's 10 o'clock at night and they say, 'Just stay here the night, don't go to school.' And I say, 'I have to go home and go to school.'
>
> (Ben)

The students who participated in this study have strong rationales for their choice to stay at school and describe both the pressures and rewards, at this stage, of their decision to remain. In addition, they detail some of the factors that led them to make an 'against the odds' decision to stay on. Importantly, they define themselves as different from those peers who have left but still feel connected to them. There is a powerful sense of independence as they renegotiate their relationships with their friends who have left school in a way that maintains their cultural solidarity. Here peer pressure to leave school is challenged and rejected while still keeping a place as 'one of the boys'. This is explained by Tim:

> I think that they don't make fun of me or nothin'. Like they're pretty supportive . . . they know that I'm doing my HSC[8] . . . but when I see 'em after school and they say, 'Hello', it doesn't matter where I'm going.

The boys describe the out-of-school activities of the peers who have left as 'wandering' or 'walking around', highlighting a sense of aimlessness and lack of direction. They do this in a way that does not place blame, but rather understands that their mates have made a different choice from them. Ironically, however, the data raise significant questions for further exploration about, in particular, curriculum tracking and choices and the way in which school may be just another site for 'wandering around' for those who choose to remain. Here too aimlessness and lack of direction is a possibility. We will return to these curriculum issues in the final section of the chapter, after discussing in more detail the rationale behind the students' decisions to stay at school and their relations with family, peers and teachers.

Being at school – doing something and wanting to do something

As stated above, each of the students interviewed had a well-developed justification for staying on at school. The most comprehensively developed rationale related to jobs. No one wanted to end up in 'dead end', 'part-time' or labouring jobs, although trades were considered by the few who mentioned them as being outside any definition of 'labouring'. Each was clear about the tightness of the labour market and believed that success in education was the way in which they would make the most out of a difficult and competitive job market. Perhaps the most engaging concept to emerge here was the notion of 'doing something' and 'wanting to do something' constructive rather than wasteful or aimless with your time. As Ernie says, 'After I finish school, I just want to get a good job!' And John articulates the relationship between education and employment:

> I know how hard it is to get a job . . . There aren't many places that give a 15- or 16-year-old kid who's only just scraped in to get his Year 10 certificate a full-time job.

Rather than turning their perceptions of restricted future chances into stances that reject what school is offering, they are keen to work hard and get through school to maximize their chances. This invariably means accepting the kind of academic work and learning that has often been the focus of masculine anti-school stances. The boys' determination makes it all the more crucial for schools to provide access to curriculum and pedagogy that will help these boys get what they want educationally and not turn their choice to remain into a period of limbo before they inevitably rejoin their wandering friends on the streets.

Family support and cultural identity

Although we have previously identified cultural support as a factor in strengthening resistance to school, it is important to understand that support is delicately balanced around both staying and leaving. Each of the boys has a 'community safety net' (Munns and McFadden 2000) recognizing, understanding and supporting their position should they start to withdraw their allegiance to the school and education. However, in these stories, family support was bolstering their being at school. Each student stressed the importance of the family in their decision to remain at school. There are interesting tensions, however, around family support that need further exploration. Pressure, and support, may come from families that are breaking the educational barrier for the first time. Consider, for example, the comments of Michael: 'I am the first one to do Year 12 in my whole generation . . .

you've got pressure on you, you don't want to pull out.' Tim also shares the pressure of being the only one in the family to go the distance:

> My dad rings up and he goes, 'Make sure you study and make sure you go to school' but out of my whole family I'm the only one that went through to Year 12. Like there's five of us and three of them have already left and the other one he's leaving in a couple of years. Someone has to go through – can't have everyone dropping out.

Others, like Ernie, come from families who have a recent history of school completion and he feels a strong sense that he must do the same: 'They say [his brothers and sisters] I should stick in there because they had to do it; I've got no choice.'

Perhaps most telling are the comments that show that, far from seeing that their identity as indigenous boys is to be defined by the development of a protest masculinity that will result in school rejection, these boys believe that their indigenous identity is encouraging them to stay on. Here is a different form of masculinity that is mobilized in support of educational achievement. It is not, as Ogbu and Simmons (1998) predict, defining identity by difference from the dominant group, but instead, as Ogbu (1999) advises, using the 'beat them at their own game' framework of thinking. As Michael puts it:

> I said to Mum, 'What about pulling out?' And she says no, to stay in there. I keep on thinking to myself 'I want to do it, I want to do it!' . . . Because I'm Koori,[9] she wants me to get the HSC, because you don't see many Koori kids achieve at that level.

Adam takes this further: 'They [Koories] want to make a point that they can do it. All the other schools – most of the Koori people have already dropped out.'

Being at school – relations with peers and teachers

As already shown, the students saw themselves as different from those indigenous peers who had left school early but they still referred to them as 'their mates'. Those who remained exhibited a quiet independence about the job ahead of both themselves and their school colleagues and saw school as a site for constructing new friendships and positive patterns of influence with both indigenous and non-indigenous students. Tim expresses it this way:

> I feel like I sort of miss them because they were my friends and then I just started hanging around different people, people that wanted to stay on at school and do well, and so, yeah, it helped me . . . it's actually better for me.

In addition they exhibited a sense of support for their cultural peers who were 'sticking in' and 'doing good', as much as for those who were finding school work not so easy. At this critical point they seemed individually to be challenging the solidarity so often expressed through not becoming an achiever, and a 'big noter'.[10] Tom makes this point clearly:

> In the seniors [the post-compulsory years] I haven't heard anyone put anyone down or like to bring anyone down, back down to their level. If someone is going good, then that's good.

This is noteworthy and perhaps indicative that cultural solidarity was a critical factor in relationships with the dominant white group at school. Previous studies of white working-class boys (see for example Willis 1977) had found that the quest for and achievement of academic success created cultural barriers separating groups at school.

Although the indigenous boys in this study did not go out of their way to talk about school issues and progress, they were sensitive to how their friends were going academically. Note Gary's observations: 'I reckon they are going all right the ones that are stayin' on. They want to learn, I think they think the same way about me . . . I'm not sure.' Intriguingly, the students saw themselves as positive role models for younger students and were clear that the younger indigenous students had to be careful not to 'muck around' too much or things would 'get harder' for them. In these comments by Michael and John we clearly can see challenges to culturally supported school rejection:

> . . . the juniors kind of have a laugh [during meetings] and you just tell them to have a good listen. You kind of tell them not to muck around when they are mucking around.
>
> (Michael)

> You've got the little cheeky ones that are coming up through Year 7 and that and they are just going to have a harder time, it gets harder for them.
>
> (John)

Their attitudes to teachers were illuminating. School, they said, was a place where teachers ruled. The game was theirs and they always came 'out on top'. As John says, '. . . you've got to play their game and play it by their rules. That's what I learnt.' Note, however, our earlier point that by staying on at school the boys were attempting to be winners in the dominant group's educational game. They now recognized the concessions and accommodations to be made. Curiously, in the post-compulsory years, these students experienced teachers very differently from in their junior years. The rules of the game had shifted for the students too. The students experienced a respect that was new and noted the shift in teacher expectations and responsibility. Here was a small group of boys from a marginalized group who after a cruel war of educational attrition were now seemingly accepted into the centre. It was a different and surprising space:

Teachers actually start talking to you with a bit of respect. A lot of the teachers that are pricks all of the time. Yes. That sort of swung me out: come to school with a big white shirt on and actually different from the rest of them. You would walk past and teachers would actually say hello without staring at you.

(John)

Regardless of this shift, almost all spoke about their reluctance to approach all but a few teachers for help with academic work or to ask questions about what they did not know. Here the concept of 'shame' was crucial to a number of students.[11]

A final point to be made regarding teachers is that all boys spoke of one or two supportive teachers whose approach they appreciated both inside and outside the classroom. Indeed some teachers spent considerable extra time helping students with their studies, as Tom testifies:

The teachers help me – like push me if I want tutoring. Nearly every class I got tutored for after school so I'd come to school quarter to nine in the morning and wouldn't get home until five.

'Wandering around' out of school, wandering around in school?

In this section we return to the curriculum issues about direction and relevance. According to the students interviewed, those students who are not at school 'walk around all night . . . just wander around'. It is the aimlessness of the wandering metaphor that is both captivating and ironic here: captivating because it characterizes so well the directionless life these students wish to avoid through education. Ironic because school can, in itself, be a site for curriculum aimlessness and lack of direction. There is a fascinating curriculum tension developing in the data around sport and academic work. This connects with an associated tension between academic curriculum choices and so called 'easy option' subjects.

Sport looms large in the lives of these young indigenous men (see also Connell 2000). For a few, the chance to play football for the school was a 'major reason' for staying on and assumed the status of 'top priority'. Certainly this is a significant school site in which they can assert power and enact their masculinity. It is also an important cultural connection that they can maintain with their community and their out-of-school peers. For the majority, it was a significant life interest and one around which critical choices were constructed. In Australian society, particularly for indigenous people, success in sport has been held up as a pathway to opportunity and status. At school sport also played a central part in their reasons for being at school and the way they were being positioned by the teachers. It was clear that playing football afforded the students some school status that helped in their making it through to the post-compulsory years. In a significant way it provided an opportunity to enact a form of masculinity that was a counterpoint to their acceptance of academic work that may have otherwise threatened them as both boys and indigenous Australians. However, again, it is a mark of their independence of thought and action that most of these boys realized that there were 'no guarantees' with sport, and placed the 'Australian dream' (and indigenous Australian 'only way out') of sporting success in relative perspective. 'Until about Year 9 I thought sport, sport and don't worry about school and that . . . I woke up to myself because sports aren't going to take you very far' (John). The dream, regardless, remains potent and to a suggestion that a major sporting club would show some interest in him comes Michael's response, 'Stink it [school]! I'd be up there training straight away.'

Sport is also important because it is central to the kinds of curriculum choices that face these students, choices that often come down to that between relevance and rigour. It is important here to understand that when students choose subjects they invariably do so under a considerable teacher influence. There is clear evidence to suggest that teachers were encouraging the students in their continued movement towards sport and sport-related subjects. Perhaps this was to bolster their feelings towards school and self-esteem; perhaps it was to improve classroom discipline; perhaps it was about furthering the school's reputation as a top football school. Whatever the motivation for this 'tracking' by the teachers, there is a real danger that the indigenous students were being 'side-tracked' at school into curricular options which might restrict their future academic outcomes.[12]

So not only is sport seen by both students and teachers as an important reason for many indigenous students to remain at school, but it is used as a curriculum pathway in subjects like 'sports, leisure and lifestyle'. Where that kind of pathway might lead is open to further exploration. Some students saw the kinds of curriculum choices that sport and leisure studies represented as 'easy choices'. Others saw such 'easy options' as time wasting and equated learning with intellectual challenge. Compare the comments of Ernie and John:

> They [some other students] pick out subjects, real good ones that they know how to do and that . . . the easy courses, trying to pick all the easy ones.
>
> (Ernie)

> With all the new electives we got to choose from I chose business studies and legal studies . . . I find that very challenging . . . hard but I am learning as well.
>
> (John)

It is the latter expression of independence that characterizes many of the difficult choices that these students continue to make as they negotiate their current and future identities.

Conclusion

Listening to these indigenous Australian boys talk about their school experiences raises the question of whether their life choices are similar to those made by indigenous students in other post-colonial countries. No doubt there are others like them in these countries who are remaining at school against all odds and who also face the brutal dilemma of potentially trading cultural identity and acceptance for educational success. This is an important research focus to pursue because it is important to track whether such trade-offs translate into opening up life and further educational opportunities or are, once again, a false promise. Such research would provide important opportunities to bring to light and make explicit the complex social and cultural support processes behind why some indigenous males choose to remain at school when the majority of their peers leave before they gain the credentials that lead to pathways of educational success. Importantly, it will also highlight the way in which particular forms of indigenous masculinity find expression and support.

In addition, how indigenous males and females in urban and rural settings are differentially positioned in relation to school, and the consequences of that differential positioning, are central social and cultural complexities to be further explored. Also, given the historical centrality of reproductive arguments in sociological explanations of disadvantage, continued research would clarify how much needed strategies of support might be shared and reproduced for others so that pathways to educational opportunity and success may be broadened.

Notes

1 The boys were interviewed for the *Widdin Pindari* Research Project. (*Widdin Pindari* is *Wiradjuri* language for 'remain on higher ground'. The *Wiradjuri* people are indigenous Australians who have lived and live in areas of southern and western New South Wales.) The study uses ethnographic methodologies to look at the interplay of community and school experiences among groups of indigenous Australian students who are remaining at school in the post-compulsory years in both urban and rural contexts. Data is collected by teams of indigenous Australian and non-indigenous Australian researchers in urban and rural schools. In its design and implementation, *Widdin Pindari* recognizes the epistemic responsibility of the researchers to the studied community: the challenge to reconceptualize objectivity, subjectivity and representation (Lawrence-Lightfoot and Davis 1997).
2 See Malin (1994) for a history of the shameful treatment of indigenous students in Australian schools.
3 Whitefellas is a term commonly used by indigenous Australian people to refer to non-indigenous Australians. Quite often it carries a connotation of grudging acceptance of the differential power relations between the groups in all aspects of Australian society.

4 A key theorist is Willis whose theory of resistance and cultural production (1977, 1981, 1983) has as its central idea that there is a relationship between structure, culture and agency in social change. We acknowledge, of course, that there is ongoing debate about and critique of resistance theory (see for example McFadden 1995 for an overview).

5 It was further argued by Munns and McFadden (2000) that support was critical in helping students reaccess education and was associated with mending a sense of *cultural fracture* when education had been previously experienced as a 'first chance' failure.

6 We recognize, of course, that students may not so much reject school as experience a sense of being pushed out (Rumberger 1995). The history of Aboriginal education in Australia confirms that students both reject and are rejected by school.

7 As Munns (1998a) proposes, there are notable empirical arguments for considering that leaving school for many indigenous Australian males may well be a culturally supported response produced through the interplay of community, school and educational factors.

8 The Higher School Certificate (HSC) is the final school examination for students in NSW secondary schools. These students were in the final year of the HSC, Year 12.

9 'Koori' and 'Koories' are the names used by many Aboriginal people when referring to Aboriginal people from most parts of NSW.

10 A 'big noter' is a derogatory term used by some indigenous Australian people to put those who seem to be achieving in their place. This may be applied even though the person is not making a point of their achievement. Similarly, in Australia, whites talk about cutting down 'tall poppies' when undercutting achievement.

11 Shame is a cultural response by many indigenous Australian students which is heightened and intensified in the process of schooling to the point where it often becomes a determinant of behaviour. Shame is particularly apparent when indigenous Australian people stand to lose face in their relationship with institutions in mainstream Anglo-Australian society (see Munns 1998b; Munns *et al.* 1999).

12 See Carrington (1983) for a discussion of this phenomenon with African Carribean students.

References

Bowser, B. [ed.] (1991) *Black Male Adolescents: Parenting and Education in Community Context*. Lanham: University Press of America.

Carrington, B. (1983) Sport as a side-track. An analysis of West Indian involvement in extra curricular sport, in L. Barton and S. Walker (eds) *Race, Class and Education*. London: Croom Helm.

Commonwealth of Australia: Reference Group Overseeing the National Review of Education for Aboriginal and Torres Strait Islander Peoples (1995) *National Review of Education for Aboriginal and Torres Strait Islander Peoples*. Canberra: Commonwealth of Australia.

Connell, R. (1993) The big picture: masculinities. *Theory and Society*, 22 (1): 597–623.

Connell, R. (1994) Knowing about masculinity, teaching boys and men. Paper presented at Pacific Sociological Association Conference, San Diego, April.

Connell, R. (2000) *The Men and the Boys*. Sydney: Allen and Unwin.

Corrigan, P. (1979) *Schooling the Smash Street Kids*. Basingstoke: Palgrane.

Fordham, S. and Ogbu, J. (1986) Black students' school success: coping with the burden of acting white. *The Urban Review*, 18 (3): 1–31.

Lavin, D.E. and Hyllegard, D. (1996) *Changing the Odds: Open Admissions and the Life Chances of the Disadvantaged*. New Haven, CT: Yale University Press.

Lawrence-Lightfoot, S. and Davis, J. (1997) *The Art and Science of Portraiture*. San Francisco, CA: Jossey-Bass.

Levine, A. and Nidiffer, J. (1996) *Beating the Odds: How the Poor Get to College*. San Francisco, CA: Jossey-Bass.

Mac an Ghaill, M. (1988) *Young, Gifted and Black: Teacher Relations in the Schooling of Black Youth*. Milton Keynes: Open University Press.

Mac an Ghaill, M. (1994) *The Making of Men: Masculinities, Sexualities and Schooling*. Buckingham: Open University Press.

McFadden, M.G. (1995) Resistance to schooling and educational outcomes: questions of structure and agency. *British Journal of Sociology of Education*, 16 (3): 293–308.

McFadden, M.G. (1996) 'Second chance' education: accessing opportunity or recycling disadvantage? *International Studies in Sociology of Education*, 6 (1): 87–111.

Malin, M. (1994) Aboriginal education, policy and teaching, in E. Hatton (ed.) *Understanding Teaching. Curriculum and the Social Context of Schooling*. Sydney: Harcourt Brace.

Meyers, B. (1997) Keeping students in colleges: what's working? *Winds of Change*, Winter: 58–9.

Munns, G. (1996) Teaching resistant Koori students: towards non-reproductive education. Unpublished PhD thesis, University of New England, Armidale.

Munns, G. (1998a) Let 'em be king pin out there all on their own in the streets. How Koori boys respond to their school and classroom. Refereed paper presented at the American Education Research Association Annual Conference, San Diego, April.

Munns, G. (1998b) 'A lot of 'em get so shamed': Koori students, risks, shame and the classroom curriculum, *SET Research Information for Teachers*, 2.

Munns, G. and McFadden, M.G. (2000) First chance, second chance or last chance? Resistance and response to education. *British Journal of Sociology of Education*, 21 (1): 59–75.

Munns, G., Simpson, L., Connelly, J. and Townsend, T. (1999) Baiyai '. . . meeting place of two parties . . .' (Wiradjuri) The pedagogical literacy relationship. *Australian Journal of Language and Literacy*, 22 (2): 147–64.

National Commission on Education (1996) *Success against the Odds: Effective Schools in Disadvantaged Areas*. London: Routledge.

New Zealand Ministry of Education (1998) *Annual Report on Maori Education 1997/98*. Wellington: New Zealand Government.

Nieto, S. (1994) Lessons from students on creating a chance to dream. *Harvard Educational Review*, 64 (4): 392–426.

O'Connor, C. (1997) Dispositions toward (collective) struggle and educational resilience in the inner city: a case analysis of six African-American high school students. *American Educational Research Journal*, 34 (4): 593–629.

Ogbu, J. (1999) Minority groups and education: Invited Address at American Education Research Association Annual Meeting, Montreal, April.

Ogbu, J. and Simmons, H. (1998) Voluntary and involuntary minorities: a cultural–ecological theory of school performance with some implications for education. *Anthropology and Education Quarterly*, 2 (2): 155–8.

Poynting, S., Noble, G. and Tabar, P. (1999) Intersections of masculinity and ethnicity: a study of male Lebanese immigrant youth in Western Sydney. *Race Ethnicity and Education*, 2 (1): 59–77.

Riseborough, G.F. (1993) Learning a living or living a learning, in I. Bates and G. Riseborough (eds) *Youth and Inequality*. Buckingham: Open University Press.

Rumberger, R.W. (1995) Dropping out of middle school: a multilevel analysis of students and schools. *American Educational Research Journal*, 32 (3): 583–625.

Sanchez, J. and Stuckey, M. (1999) From boarding schools to the multicultural classroom: the intercultural politics of education, assimilation, and American Indians. *Teacher Education Quarterly*, 26 (3): 83–93.

Sewell, T. (1997) *Black Masculinities and Schooling: How Black Boys Survive Modern Schooling*. New York, NY: Vintage Books.

Willis, P. (1977) *Learning to Labour*. Farnborough: Saxon House.

Willis, P. (1981) Cultural production is different from cultural reproduction is different from social reproduction is different from reproduction. *Interchange*, 12 (2–3): 48–67.

Willis, P. (1983) Cultural production and theories of reproduction, in L. Barton and S. Walker (eds) *Race, Class and Education*. London: Croom Helm.

Wright, D. (1998) Preparing First Nations students for college: the experience of the Squamish Nation of British Columbia. *Canadian Journal of Native Education*, 22 (1): 85–91.

CHAPTER 12

Naughty boys at school: perspectives on boys and discipline[1]

BOB MEYENN AND JUDITH PARKER

Introduction

In this chapter we explore important issues for teachers/student teachers related to the problem of 'naughty boys' in schools. The public media in Australia has highlighted that boys are being suspended for acts of violence and misbehaviour at 'more than four times the rate of girls and, hence, are more likely to be in trouble for violence' (Raethel 1996). In Western Australia it was reported that 'males top [the] rising suspension list' (Capp 2000). In addition, Lloyd (1995), another journalist, writes that in South Australia 'males account for 82.3 per cent of all suspensions'. However, while these statistics draw attention to an important issue that needs to be addressed in schools, much of this public discourse about boys and discipline feeds and fuels a 'competing victims syndrome' (Cox 1997) which casts boys as the 'new disadvantaged' (see Chapter 1, this volume; Lingard and Douglas 1999). This is further evidenced by Raethel (1996) who writes about boys' suspensions from school in an article for the *Sydney Morning Herald*. Within this frame of reference he claims that:

> The data, compiled for the first time by the Department of School Education, has fuelled parents' concerns about the disadvantages faced by boys in school and comes on top of several reports which show girls have been outperforming boys in many popular HSC subjects.

The problem of 'naughty boys' thus feeds into discourses about girls' interests being set against those of boys with the latter now acquiring the status of the 'new disadvantaged' (see Yates 1997). Such a simplistic position fails to explicate the very significant ways in which dominant versions of masculinity are implicated in boys' social practices and misbehaviours at school. In short, it fails to address the kinds of investment that many boys have in establishing a particular version of *rebel* or *protest* masculinity and the kinds of power relations driving social practices (see Willis 1977; Walker 1988; Connell 1995). Moreover, such competing victim perspectives are not particularly helpful in signalling effective approaches to dealing with this 'boy problem' in schools.

In light of these concerns, we explore in this chapter an alternative framework for addressing the problem of disciplining boys which draws attention to the links between masculinities, violence and schooling. While we do not propose a 'quick fix' solution to a very complex problem, we argue that current research into boys, schooling and masculinities needs to inform:

- the curriculum in teacher training institutions;
- professional development for teachers;
- the development of more effective school policies for managing student behaviour.

Fixing the problem

The focus in this chapter on teacher training and professional development for teachers is situated in response to the New South Wales Education Minister's call for decisive advice on how 'to fix the problem' of violence in schools. This was provoked by a media report in 1996 about a 14-year-old male student who knifed a teacher in an inner city secondary school. Among many headlines, the *Sydney Morning Herald*'s headline of the day read:

Teacher stabbed in schoolyard attack
(By Greg Bearup, Chief Police Reporter SMH 24/10/1996)

The minister turned to his Ministerial Advisory Council on the Quality of Teaching whose role is to provide strategic advice to the minister on issues relating to all aspects of the quality of teaching, including initial teacher education, induction and professional development. Specifically he wanted advice on 'training requirements [needed] to give teachers the capacity to assert, maintain and restore classroom discipline, as well as strategies to cope with bullying and playground violence' (Aquilina: cited in Eltis 1998).

It was stipulated that such advice should seek to identify

- current strategies/practices, policy and support programmes relating to the management of student behaviour as addressed in initial teacher education and in ongoing professional development programmes; [and]
- aspects that student teachers and beginning teachers find most challenging in dealing with the management of student behaviour in and out of the classroom.

A working party was set up to respond to the minister's reference. Information was gained from a variety of sources including teacher educators, teachers and student teachers. Forty-five randomly selected beginning teachers (defined as those in their first three years of teaching) and 42 randomly selected experienced teachers (those who had been teaching between ten and fifteen years) met as focus groups. A final draft of the report to the minister was presented to the Ministerial Advisory Council on the Quality of Teaching in February 1998 as *Teacher Preparation for Student Management: Responses and Directions* (see Eltis 1998).

The report, among other things, examines the key issues to emerge from the investigation and the implications for action around initial teacher education, the induction of neophytes into the profession, in-school support and continuing professional development for all teachers. However, what was significant about this report was that there was no mention of gender, nor was there any reference to the direction of current research and writing on masculinities (Kessler *et al.* 1985; Walker 1988; Mac an Ghaill 1994; Connell 1995; Nayak and Kehily 1996). This is despite the fact that the most remarkable feature of the focus group discussions was that discipline problems were overwhelmingly perceived to be caused by boys. Indeed, the pronoun *he* was scarcely ever replaced by *she* as teachers described their frustrations in trying to engage boys in meaningful learning experiences.

This chapter, therefore, emerges from our concern that discussions of discipline, bullying and playground violence must be embedded in, and interrogated from, positions which acknowledge the complexity of the relationship between boys, schooling and the construction of masculinities (Connell 1995; Nayak and Kehily 1996; Martino 2000; Epstein, this volume), particularly if we are to move beyond the simplistic *hailing* of boys as problems or boys as victims. (Althusser 1992; see also Davies 1993.)

Disciplining boys

We believe that professional development of teachers in schools and teacher training institutions need to incorporate a perspective on boys, schooling and discipline which foregrounds the role that the social practices of masculinity play in how boys learn to relate and to construct their identities at school. This has not been the focus in the past with regards to addressing violence in schools (see Rigby 1996). Such a focus on disciplining boys is important, particularly in light of the comment made by Salisbury and Jackson (1996) who claim that '. . . much of teachers' time, energies and school resources already goes into picking up pieces after boys' routine, daily acts of vandalism, classroom disruption, bullying and harassment of girls and boys'. They further argue that boys have monopolized the linguistic, social, psychological and physical space in mixed secondary schools (see also Spender and Sarah 1980; Mahony 1985). Moreover, they also make the point that boys often do poorly academically because of their identification with hegemonic masculine values and indicate that schools are institutional sites where boys masculinize their bodies – in gyms, playgrounds, sports fields – in conforming with peer pressure to be physically superior (Gard and Meyenn 2000; Gard, this volume):

> Pursuing these traditional modes (of masculinity) traps many boys into severely limited subject, curricular and work choices as well as damaging the range of their emotional lives and social relationships.
>
> (Salisbury and Jackson 1996: 4)

What is significant about this perspective on boys' social practices of masculinity is that it is not organized around problematic oppositions of girl victim/boy problem, advantaged girls/disadvantaged boys. In this sense, we argue that trainee teachers and teachers need to consider the various ways in which masculinities are negotiated in boys' lives at school and the kinds of investment they have in enacting certain versions of masculinity over others (see Kessler *et al.* 1985; Walker 1988; Frank 1993; Mac an Ghaill 1994; Connell 1995). In relation to addressing boys' implication in violence at school, pedagogical spaces need to be created for engaging boys in an active interrogation and exploration of hegemonic heterosexual masculinities and their capacity to impact detrimentally on the ways in which boys learn to relate at school (see Epstein *et al.* 1998; Gilbert and Gilbert 1998). These spaces, we argue, need to be created by sensitive, informed teachers who recognize *hailing* boys as problems will do little to overcome their alienation from schooling or to address the violence that they enact. The anti-social behaviour of many boys 'cannot be reductively read as a product of resistance . . . [it] also acts as a legitimation and articulation of power and subordination' (Skells 1991 in Mac an Ghaill 1994: 162).

In discussions about boys and discipline in schools we argue that there is a need to interrogate the extent to which manifestations of anti-social behaviour arise from what Connell (1995) calls *protest masculinities* (see also Willis 1977; Walker 1988), that is, the way many boys' experience of power-lessness results in 'an exaggerated claim to the potency that European (mid-dle class, dominant) culture attaches to masculinity' (Connell, 1995: 111). Poynting *et al.* (1997: 10), for example, report that for Lebanese-Australian boys:

> Withdrawal of respect, or actively and deliberately behaving disrespect-fully towards such authority figures (as teachers), restores a feeling of power to a less powerful social group.

Their interviews with Lebanese-Australian boys also highlight some interest-ing connections between lack of the dominant language and violence. One of the boys interviewed said, 'Australians have heaps of words that offend us . . . they can't fight for themselves.'

> . . . Violence compensates for the words that are not available; it ameliorates the humiliation of racism. The meaning that youths attach

to this violence *resolves* in ideology, really unresolved contradictions occurring at the intersections of masculinity and ethnicity as well as class relations.

(Poynting *et al.* 1997: 19)

While it is easy for researchers and academics not faced with the diurnal task of helping adolescent boys (and girls) learn in sometimes overcrowded classrooms, with the demands of an often inappropriate curriculum, it is equally easy to see how the expectations of teachers, and the dominant culture that holds that disadvantaged boys are disruptive, perpetuates the hegemonies of class, race and gender in our schools. As Pallotta-Chiarolli (1997: 18) writes:

I have worked with staff who make highly inappropriate cultural assumptions about boys' behaviours. As a means of resistance and challenge, the boys may perform the very cultural stereotypes the school attends to, fears and expects. My brother Tony knew how to perform the tough, spoilt, sexist Italian boy for certain teachers, those who ignored his cultural background, referred to it only in negative contexts, or who made allowances for his disruptive behaviour as being part of his Italianness.

Complex issues of school management and the development of appropriate behaviour protocols cannot be treated in isolation from the larger social context in which they are situated. As McLean (1995: 9) argues:

If we want boys to change, we also need to demand that the world they are expected to enter and survive within changes as well. We need to be turning the spotlight on ourselves and asking what sort of society we want to live in, how schools can contribute to building such a society, and what it is about schools, as they currently are, that gets in the way of creating such a community.

This focus ties in with Wexler's (1992) claim that *becoming somebody* is the primary motivation of boys' and girls' social behaviour at school. For example, many boys learn that they must establish their position in a hierarchy of masculinities to avoid being positioned as the marginalized, feminized 'other' (see Martino 2000). In this regard, the formal curriculum is not nearly as significant as peer and cultural interactions. McLean further suggests (1995: 10) that:

In dominant masculine culture, the need to be somebody is exaggerated and extreme. Competition and the struggle for power are central and school becomes a testing ground for a boy's successful assumption of an appropriate gender identity . . . boys who don't measure up are at best ignored and left out of things, both inside and outside of the classroom. This production of identity manifests in different ways in different class and cultural contexts.

These insights from the literature and research, we argue, need to inform the explanatory framework for understanding the motivations driving the acting out of anti-social behaviour in classrooms. Our involvement in the focus groups for the Ministerial Advisory Council on the Quality of Teaching demonstrated that boys' behaviour was pathologized; boys were often an essential and essentializing category; exclusionary behaviour by boys was permitted; boys were foregrounded, girls remained at the back; issues of gender reached closure and were isolated from the world beginning teachers operate in; classroom management was predicated on control; there is little room for negotiation. The following vignettes, from beginning teachers and students in their final years of their teacher education programmes, are telling examples of our concern that questions of discipline, school culture and classroom organization remain essentially unproblematized.

What the above vignettes highlight is that it is important for teachers to reflect on issues of pedagogic authority and how this might be deployed. Moreover, they need to reflect on motivations driving students' disruptive behaviours in class and to interrogate the limits of behaviouralist models of school-based discipline practices. In teacher education courses there needs to be a critical focus on the exercise of power by teachers; their positioning of themselves; their positioning of boys and of boys in relation to girls; their

---

When I'm telling a story I get all the naughty boys to come up the front.

(Louise)

Louise is a first year out teacher working in a metropolitan primary school on a Grade 1 class. She is enthusiastic, committed and energetic and she wants the best for the children she teaches. She is concerned to develop strategies to overcome disruptive behaviour in her classroom. In a focus group with other beginning teachers, she offered the strategy of bringing the boys closer to her as a way of controlling their behaviour.

This is a classic example of how boys become the focus of the teacher's attention, the effect of which is to keep the girls in the background. Moreover, Louise's pedagogy is built around an imperative to control the boys' misbehaviours as opposed to understanding the motivations behind such social practices of masculinity in the classroom. This results in an exclusive focus on boys with girls moving into the background. What is required is a more active interrogation and problematization of how certain forms of power are being mobilized by the students to mount a challenge to the teacher's authority in the classroom and what this might mean in terms of how to address the problem of disciplining boys.

We've done gender.

(Matthew)

Matthew is a final year DipEd student at the end of his course. He was interviewed as part of an inquiry into a physical fight which took place between two students. When asked whether or not he had discussed issues of gender as part of his course, we were assured by Matthew that he had done gender and in fact there was too much of it.

Here gender is dismissed as an important explanatory framework for understanding violence in schools. This has implications for this student teacher's capacity to deal effectively with the sex-based and gendered dimensions of violence in schools (see Alloway in press; Martino and Pallotta-Chiarolli in press).

He's a real problem, his brother's in gaol.

(Anne)

Anne is a final year primary student who had just returned to the university from an internship programme in a country primary school. Ann had had a *wonderful* time in the school and was feeling very positive about teaching and very confident that she would enjoy her chosen career. She was describing one of the boys in her class whose behaviour was very disruptive.

Anne's explanation of this male student's problem behaviour is grounded in the problematic essentializing presumption that it is somehow a natural consequence of his class location/background. This is further evidence that the kind of discourses which student teachers are drawing on to explain students' disruptive behaviour require some problematization.

---

pedagogical practices; their interactions with students. They need to understand that these are all manifestations of the authority they present. Strategies used by experienced teachers, i.e., those with 10–15 years' experience varied little from those used by the beginning teachers. There was perhaps even greater emphasis on behaviourist approaches with rewards and withdrawals the most significant forms of interventions. The experienced teachers placed more emphasis on a whole-school approach and the importance of rules and systems. They also argued for the need for backup in enforcing these rules

I organize my class by having a demerit system, if anyone gets more than five demerits in a week they are sent to the principal.

(Megan)

Megan is a second year out teacher in an inner city primary school where the strategy she describes is part of school policy on classroom discipline and management. She is pleased that she is able to fit comfortably into existing practices. The scheme, she feels, allows her to control the *naughty* children in her class. On further discussion she indicated that it was only boys that she sent to the principal.

Like Louise, Megan adopts a behaviouralist approach which is superficial in its focus on disciplining boys. Such an approach is grounded in reinforcing a hierarchical system of power and threat rather than encouraging students to take responsibility for their own behaviour. Sending the 'naughty boys' to the principal does nothing to address the socio-cultural and gendered dimensions of students' misbehaviours and the motivation behind such antisocial practices.

and systems. 'The experienced teachers stress the need for executive support for their actions to manage students' (Eltis 1998: 6).

Thus, it is important to emphasize that teachers cannot escape/avoid, any more than can education systems, their role in upholding the dominant culture, of curriculum, of masculinities, of class, of race – and this, as we have seen above, is reflected in their approaches to disciplining students. These values are so often naturalized and are imposed on students, many of whom resist, with such behaviour being interpreted as inappropriate and/or *stupidity*. Unfortunately, schools continue to function according to the belief that *success at school* is about individual abilities rather than about the inequalities inherent in the race, class and gender divides. In this sense, the above beginning teachers do not appear to be equipped with the socio-cultural framework to problematize and to interrogate the nature of power relations at play in their pedagogical relations with their students. In short, there are complex explanations, not only for why 80 to 90 per cent of both short- and long-term suspensions were imposed on boys in NSW in 1996–99 (NSW Department of School Education Annual Reports), but also for why boys tend to engage in disruptive and antisocial behaviour at school. A perspective on boys and discipline, informed by research into schooling masculinities (Mac an Ghaill 1994; Connell 1995; Martino 1999), would equip teachers with the socio-cultural framework for understanding the motivations behind boys' anti-social and disruptive behaviour at school. This is important in light of the fact that absent from many teachers' talk were acknowledgments of the ambivalences in the exercise of power at the level of pedagogical practices. For instance, 'naughty boys' were perceived to be a problem and this was often considered to be an inevitable consequence of their gender.

Productive pedagogies

Gore (1998), drawing on the work of Foucault (1980), studied the disciplinary practices at work in various educational settings: a physical education class in a secondary school; a first-year teacher education group; a feminist reading group; and a women's discussion group. She found that power relations played out in pedagogy took the form of surveillance, normalization, exclusion, classification, distribution, totalization and regulation. But these forms were not necessarily unproductive. What is significant, however, is that they are elements of an explanatory framework which can help us understand the complex relations existing in schools between those who teach, those who learn, those who resist and those who disrupt. Gore writes (1998: 248–9):

> Documenting techniques of power, identifying which seem essential to the pedagogic enterprise and which might be altered is my own contribution to thinking how educators might exercise power differently. In bringing about educational reform, I argue that we must know what we are and what we are doing in order to address adequately how we might do things differently.

We would argue it is such nuancing that prevents discussions about power and pedagogy from solidifying along binary oppositions. It is holding, however tenuously, less determinant and deterministic positions which will support teachers and educational systems in interrogating current taken-for-granted, naturalized practices and discourses. Power can be strategically deployed to effect certain outcomes. In other words, attention needs to be drawn to the productive rather than repressive nature of the workings of power in schools. As Salisbury and Jackson (1996) highlight, work with boys in schools that involves helping them to interrogate the practices of masculinity in their own lives can be quite productive. In fact, Kenway and Willis's (1997) position on why gender reform succeeds in schools is illustrative of a measured teasing out by teachers of the implications for their own specifically situated practices and how these might be deployed to assist students to problematize and to reflect on power relations in their own lives:

> In general, those schools and departments that were most successful were open to and refreshed by new ideas and encouraged energetic intellectual exchange and change from below (from new and junior staff) as well as from outside. Their priorities and practices indicated that they supported, encouraged and celebrated difference and the entitlements of all students,

but that they did not support difference built on dominances or entitlements based on those structures of power noted above. They recognized
the importance for learning and identity of the head, the hand and
the heart. They encouraged all students to accept responsibility for their
behaviour and to take initiatives for change. They recognized that schools
owe girls and boys the right to feel welcome, cared for and safe as well
as the right to be educated about life as it is and as it might become if it
were to fulfil their best hopes. The teachers in these schools recognized
the importance of changing practices and themselves. Their schools
modelled a better society.

(Kenway and Willis 1997: 208–9)

Kenway and Willis, together with Salisbury and Jackson (1996), do not see
men and boys as representatives of an undifferentiated, monolithic system
of power which is static and unchanging. Because of this, they draw attention
to the pedagogical possibilities for engaging boys in schools in an interrogation of hegemonic masculinities. They highlight the transformative implications of variety, difference and plurality, both between men and men and
within individual boys and men. Because gender relations are historical and
always in a state of flux, there are tremendous possibilities for strategically
interrogating gender with students. As Connell (1995: 84) argues, masculinity
is *'a configuration of practice "within" a system of gender relations'*, and such an
acknowledgment signals a role for teachers and schools (as too for other
agencies) to draw strategically on such socio-cultural perspectives in developing productive approaches to dealing with 'naughty boys' in school.

Bullying and violence

It is important that such a socio-cultural perspective on boys and masculinities
be introduced to beginning teachers, particularly in relation to addressing
bullying and violence in schools. Evidence of disruption in schools – disruption expressed as bullying and violence for example – should be made
available to teachers as they develop policies and practices to ensure schools
are sites where all students, not only those attached to hegemonic groups,
have opportunities to learn, to realize their potential, to be positioned to make
choices, not have choices made for them. (See Slee 1995; Teo and Waugh
1997). Rigby's and Slee's (1991) survey of 685 Australian school children
found that approximately one in ten children were subject to bullying (see
also Collins *et al.* 1996). Boys are more likely to be the bullies and girls the
victims. Factor analysis of subjects' responses suggested: '. . . a tendency to
despise the victims of bullies; general admiration for school bullies and avowed
support for intervention to assist the victim' (Rigby and Slee 1991: 615).

Kenway, in fact, indicates that the bullying practices of boys need to be
situated within the broader economic context of changing national and

international labour markets in relation to how they have impacted on boys' attitudes and orientation to schooling:

> Cultural shifts have cut deeply into the foundation of certain sorts of masculinity and arguably this is particularly the case for men whose manual labour is an important source of masculinity and for those whose manhood was tied up in cultural traditions which have been destroyed by colonialism (for example, Australian Aborigines). An increasing amount of literature suggests men and boys who lose power in a given arena look for new ways of reclaiming a sense of manhood, such as violence and scapegoating.
>
> (Kenway 1995: 77–8)

While it is unrealistic to expect schools, school systems and teachers to combat such a trend, it is important to realize the potential for a model of education that is transformative of the status quo. The techno-scientific/technicist curriculum of so many teacher education programmes must be challenged if schools are to be genuinely safe places and encourage diversity for all students and teachers. (Meyenn and Parker 1999)

Implications for teacher education and professional development for teachers

It is clear from the research and our work with beginning teachers that the social construction of masculinities needs to be placed on the agenda in teacher training institutions. In addition, it needs to be made the subject of and focus in professional development forums for teachers. Sociological knowledge about gender needs to be integrated and incorporated into all aspects of the curriculum for students at school and in teacher training institutions (see Connell 1987). The interviews and focus group discussions conducted as part of our work for the Ministerial Advisory Council on the Quality of Teaching, together with discussions we have had with students from our university, suggest quite simply that the prevailing framework of programmes of teacher education is largely technicist, poorly integrated and lacking in the understanding that teachers have a fundamental role in striving to achieve social justice and social transformation as opposed to social reproduction. In other words, it is important to avoid merely reinscribing dominant versions of masculinity in addressing boys and discipline and bullying in schools. In this sense, spaces need to be created for encouraging teachers to explore the pedagogical possibilities for interrogating hegemonic masculinities in their classrooms and schools (see Salisbury and Jackson 1996). However, this needs to be situated within a broader socio-political framework that embraces cultural diversity and is committed to exploring practices of normalization in students' lives (see Martino and Pallotta Chiarolli in press).

This is in line with Giroux's (1992) call for a radical reconceptualizing of teaching, teachers' work and teacher education. He argues that the American public education system is in crisis because the positions educators work from are too narrow, too essentializing, too marginalizing of voices and identities which are constructed as 'other' by the dominant culture (Giroux 1992: 211). He is concerned, in particular, that too little account is taken of difference and further argues that these intellectual positions marginalize notions of agency and develop essentialist, separatist and often totalizing narratives that 'fail to recognize the limits of their own discourse in explaining the complexity of social life and the power such a discourse wields in silencing those who are not considered part of the insider group' (Giroux 1992: 208). For all the care that teachers of the focus groups exhibited, their utterances clearly indicate that there are certain limits to the dominant frames of reference which circumscribe the ways in which they talk about disciplining, teaching and relating to students. In this sense, we argue that there is a need for a critical focus on masculinities and that this needs to be incorporated and integrated into teacher training programmes. This would involve introducing students and teachers to a perspective on boys and schooling that draws attention to the power relations that are implicated in how ascendant and subordinated masculinities inform boys' social relations and practices at school.

However, it is also important that professional development affords teachers the opportunity to reflect on these issues. In this way, an attempt can be made to move beyond a simplistic conceptualization of boys and girls as competing victims to a pedagogical position which interrogates binary categorizations on the basis of gender. This can then form the basis for opening up discussion about the diversity that exists among groups of boys and girls to address issues of race, class, disability, ethnicity and sexuality, geographical location and how these intersect with gender (see Gender Equity Taskforce 1997; Collins *et al.* 2000).

It is in this sense, that we concur with Giroux who posits the need for teachers to encompass a border pedagogy; one which involves analysis of the ways

> the dominant culture creates borders saturated in terror, inequality and forced conclusions. At the same time, students should be allowed to rewrite difference through the process of crossing over into cultural borders that offer narratives, languages, and experiences that provide a resource for rethinking the relationship between the centre and the margins of power as well as between themselves and others.
>
> (Giroux 1992: 209)

In short, the dominant culture needs to be the subject of critical interrogation and problematization in schools and teacher training institutions. An understanding of the relationships between teachers and the cultural and personal histories of their students is essential if homogeneity is to be fractured and students of all backgrounds are to be accorded speaking positions ensuring their experiences of schooling are more inclusive and potentially more able to satisfy their needs as learners – and members of a democracy. Teacher educators must recognize that their programmes of initial teacher preparation are often, too often, perpetuators of an exclusive pedagogy supportive of the status quo. Hence, this border pedagogy would lend itself to exploring the various ways in which gender is policed and patrolled through regimes of compulsory heterosexuality (see Steinberg *et al.* 1997). This is important given the power relations that configure around the ways in which sexuality is deployed to police desirable and, hence, *normal* social relations for both boys and girls at schools (see Mac an Ghaill 2000; Martino 2000).

Thus it is very important that teachers and student teachers be equipped with socio-cultural and critical tools to interrogate and problematize practices of normalization in schools. Grundy and Hatton (1995), in fact, explore in detail the way teacher educators' discourses and consequent practices sustain the status quo and hence reinforce such normalizing tendencies. Building on the work of Beyer and Zeichner (1987), which maintains that conservative ideology is dominant among teacher educators, they contend that teacher education should be 'part of a wider political project . . . directed toward social critique and transformation' (Grundy and Hatton, 1995: 9).

Smyth (1993, 1996) also argues for teacher education to be more socially critical; programmes ought to be about

> developing practices that not only enable, but require, that we empower students to draw upon their own cultural resources as a basis for engaging in the development of new skills and interrogating existing knowledge claims.
>
> (Sultana 1990: cited in Smyth 1993: 159)

He continues:

> we should problematize our work suggesting a need to engage in four forms of action best characterized by several moments which predispose us to describe, inform, confront and reconstruct through asking questions like what do I do? What does this mean? How did I come to be like this? How might I do things differently?
>
> (Smyth 1993: 160)

In other words, teacher education programmes must be more firmly grounded in intellectual dispositions which unsettle. In this regard we argue that it is important for teacher training institutions to equip students with the skills to interrogate masculinities in schools, particularly with regards to exploring the links between boys, schooling and violence.

Giroux (1992), Grundy and Hatton (1995) and Smyth (1993, 1996) all make strong cases for re-examining and reconceptualizing teacher education. It is not sufficient for it to be technicist; it must be transformative if we are to recognize it as 'part of a wider political project' (Grundy and Hatton 1995: 9). Within the context of the debates about the boys as they are outlined in the introductory chapter to this book, this means that teacher educators, and more broadly teachers in schools, need to be committed to destabilizing hegemonic masculinities and reflecting on the normalizing assumptions that inform their own pedagogical practices specifically in relation to how boys and their (mis)behaviours are perceived.

Drawing on socio-critical perspectives, therefore, holds the promise that graduates and teachers may be more inclined to interpret their experiences and their interactions with their students in less constraining and definitive ways. It may mean that they are able to:

- problematize all aspects of social practice, especially those relating to boys' misbehaviour and violence at school;
- locate discussions about professional practice in appropriate theoretical and socio-cultural discourses, particularly in relation to boys' education and gender reform (Collins *et al.* 1996, 2000; Gender Equity Taskforce 1997);
- interrogate and interrupt taken-for-granted practices and policies, especially those related to boys' education and gender equity;
- recognize that everything is dangerous, nothing is innocent (after Foucault 1980).

Such a framework allows for the active interrogation of the social practices of masculinity in schools within the context of teachers' exercising their pedagogic authority to discipline students. More broadly, it enables certain questions to be raised about agency, about who does what? To whom? Who gives what? To whom? Who classifies? Who is classified? Who is the source of causation? Who sees? Who thinks? Who speaks? Who feels? Who acts? In this way, in professional development forums and teacher training institutions, spaces can be created for reflecting on the kinds of discourses upon which teachers draw in their pedagogical practices and relations with boys and girls at school. This will lead to a consideration of issues pertaining to who holds power, who is marginalized and where the silences remain.

Conclusion

In this chapter the focus has been on exploring the important role that teacher training institutions and professional development forums play in providing educators with a framework within which they can interrogate the problematic assumptions about boys, schooling and masculinities, particularly with regards to 'naughty' boys' problematic behaviours in schools. We have emphasized that while the evidence indicates that boys are more often involved in forms of anti-social behaviour, it is simplistic and ultimately destructive to hail them as *the problem*. It is problematizing not hailing that is needed. It is imperative that we provide opportunities for teachers and equip them with the skills to interrogate the complexities of current debates around boys, schooling and the construction of masculinities. In particular, we have argued that both teacher training institutions and professional development forums for teachers need to be committed to an intellectual disposition to interrupt, interrogate, problematize, deconstruct and celebrate uncertainty, ambiguity and ambivalence particularly with regards to exploring issues of masculinity and how these might relate to both exercising pedagogic authority and to understanding the power relations driving boys' anti-social behaviours at school.

Perhaps then teachers might be able to help boys, girls, and boys and girls, play out the possibilities of resisting and transgressing the hegemonies of gender, sexuality, class and race. At the moment we have to agree with Kenway and Willis (1997) when they write that policy imperatives in Australian gender reform 'barely scratch the surface of what it means to be a boy or girl at school'. While ever that remains we would argue that boys will inevitably be *problems* and boys will continue to feature strongly in lists of school suspensions.

Note

1 An earlier version of the chapter was presented at the AERA Conference in San Diego, April 1998.

References

Alloway, N. (forthcoming) *Just Kidding.* Sydney: NSW Department of School Education.
Althusser, L. (1992) Ideology and ideological State apparatuses, in A. Easthope and K. McGowan (eds) *A Critical and Cultural Theory Reader.* Sydney: Allen and Unwin.
Beyer, L.E. and Zeichner, K. (1987) Teacher education in cultural context: beyond reproduction, in T. Popkewitz (ed.) *Critical Studies in Teacher Education: Its Folklore, Theory and Practice*, pp 298–334. London: Falmer.
Capp, G. (2000) Males top rising suspensions list. *The West Australian*, April 15: 3.
Collins, C., Kenway, J. and McLeod, J. (2000) *Factors Influencing the Educational Performance of Males and Females in School and their Initial Destinations After Leaving School.* Canberra: DEETYA.
Collins, C., Batten, M., Ainley, J. and Getty, C. (1996) *Gender and School Education.* Canberra: Australian Council for Educational Research.
Connell, R.W. (1987) *Gender and Power.* Cambridge: Polity Press.
Connell, R.W. (1995) *Masculinities.* Sydney: Allen and Unwin.
Cox, E. (1997) Boys and girls and the costs of gendered behaviour. *Gender Equity: A Framework for Australian Schools.* Canberra: Gender Equity Taskforce, Department of Employment, Education, Training and Youth Affairs.
Davies, B. (1993) *Shards of Glass.* Sydney: Allen and Unwin.
Eltis, K. (1998) *Teacher Preparation for Student Management: Responses and Directions.* Chair, Working Party, Ministerial Advisory Council on the Quality of Teaching. Sydney: Department of Education and Training.

Epstein, D., Elwood, J., Hey, V. and Maw, J. (1998) *Failing Boys?* Buckingham: Open University Press.

Foucault, M. (1980) *Michel Foucault: Power/Knowledge: Selected Interviews and Other Writings 1972–1977*, edited by C. Gordon. New York, NY: Pantheon.

Frank, B. (1993) Straight/strait jackets for masculinity: educating for real men. *Atlantis*, 18 (1 and 2): 47–59.

Gard, M. and Meyenn, B. (2000) Boys, bodies, pleasure and pain: interrogating contact sports in schools. *Sport, Education and Society*, 5(1): 19–34.

Gender Equity Taskforce (1997) *Gender Equity: A Framework for Australian Schools*. Canberra: DEETYA.

Gilbert, P. and Gilbert, R. (1998) *Masculinity Goes to School*. Sydney: Allen and Unwin.

Giroux, H. (1992) *Border Crossings: Cultural Workers and the Politics of Education*. New York, NY, London: Routledge.

Gore, J.M. (1998) Disciplining bodies: on the continuity of power relations in pedagogy, in T.S. Popkewitz and M. Brennan (eds) *Foucault's Challenge: Discourse, Knowledge and Power in Education*, pp. 231–51. New York, NY: Teachers' College Press.

Grundy, S. and Hatton, E. (1995) Teacher educators' ideological discourses. *Journal of Education for Teaching*, 21(1): 7–23.

Kenway, J. (1995) Masculinities in schools: under siege, on the defensive and under reconstruction? *Discourse*, 16(1): 59–79.

Kenway, J. and Willis, S. (1997) *Answering Back: Girls, Boys and Feminism in Schools*. St Leonards, NSW: Allen and Unwin.

Kessler, S., Ashenden, D.J., Connell, R.W. and Dowsett, G.W. (1985) Gender relations in secondary schooling. *Sociology of Education*, 58: 34–48.

Lingard, B. and Douglas, P. (1999) *Men Engaging Feminisms: Pro-feminism, Backlashes and Schooling*. Buckingham: Open University Press.

Lloyd, N. (1995) 9600 suspended for school misconduct. *The Advertiser*, 13 February: 1.

Mac an Ghaill, M. (1994) *The Making of Men: Masculinities, Sexualities and Schooling*. Buckingham: Open University Press.

Mac an Ghaill, M. (2000) Rethinking (male) gendered sexualities: what about the British heteros? *The Journal of Men's Studies*, 8(2): 195–212.

McLean, C. (1995) 'Building bridges'. New directions in boys' education, in The National Council of Women of NSW, *Gender Equity Issues in Schools: Broadening the options*. Report of one-day seminar, Parliament House Theatrette, Sydney, August: 7–17.

Mahony, P. (1985) *Schools for the Boys? Co-education Reassessed*. London: Hutchinson.

Martino, W. (1999) Cool boys, party animals, squids and poofters: interrogating the dynamics and politics of adolescent masculinities in school. *British Journal of Sociology of Education*, 20(2): 239–63.

Martino, W. (2000) Policing masculinities: investigating the role of homophobia and heteronormativity in the lives of adolescent school boys. *The Journal of Men's Studies*, 8(2), 213–36.

Martino, W. and Pallotta-Chiarolli, M. (in press) *So What's a Boy?* Buckingham: Open University Press.

Meyenn, B. and Parker, J. (1999) Necessary but not sufficient: reconceptualizing primary teacher education. *Asia-Pacific Journal of Teacher Education*, 27(3): 173–82.

Nayak, A. and Kehily, M. (1996) Playing it straight: masculinities, homophobias and schooling. *Journal of Gender Studies*, 5(2): 211–30.

Pallotta-Chiarolli, M. (1997) We want to address boys' education but . . . , in J. Kenway (ed.) *Will Boys Be Boys? Boys' Education in the Context of Gender Reform*, pp 17–21. Australian Capital Territory: Australian Curriculum Studies Association.

Raethel, S. (1996) Suspensions from school: boys top class. *Sydney Morning Herald*, 27 July: 6.

Rigby, K. (1996) Bullying in schools: and what to do about it. Melbourne: Australian Council for Educational Research.

Rigby, K. and Slee, P.T. (1991) Bullying among Australian school children: reported behavior and attitudes toward victims. *Journal of Social Psychology*, 131 (5): 615–27.

Salisbury, J. and Jackson, D. (1996) *Challenging Macho Values*. London: Falmer.

Slee, R. (1995) *Changing Theories and Practices of Discipline*. London: Falmer.

Smyth, J. (1993) A socially critical approach to teacher education, in T.A. Simpson (ed.) *Teacher Educators' Annual Handbook*, pp 153–65. Brisbane: Queensland University of Technology.

Smyth, J. (1996) Developing socially critical educators, in D. Bond and N. Miller (eds) *Working with Experience: Animated Learning*. London: Routledge.

Spender, D. and Sarah, E. (1980) *Learning to Lose: Sexism and Education*. London: The Women's Press.

Steinberg, D., Epstein, D. and Johnson, R. (1997) *Border Patrols: Policing the Boundaries of Heterosexuality*. London: Cassell.

Teo, P. and Waugh, R. (1997) Bullying: changing the emphasis for teachers. *Education Australia*, 35: 32–4.

Walker, J.C. (1988) *Louts and Legends: Male Youth Culture in an Inner City School*. Sydney: Allen and Unwin.

Wexler, P. (1992) *Becoming Somebody: Toward a Social Psychology of School*. London, Washington, DC: Falmer.

Willis, P. (1977) *Learning to Labour: How Working Class Kids Get Working Class Jobs*. Farnborough: Saxon House.

Yates, L. (1997) Gender equity and the boys debate: what sort of challenge is it? *British Journal of Sociology of Education*, 18 (3): 337–47.

CHAPTER 13

Boys will be boys (if they pay attention in science class)[1]

WILL LETTS[2]

> And while male sport serves as a representation of the brute
> power and physical strength of the male body loosed on the
> playing fields, mathematics and physical sciences serve as a
> representation of the rational power and mental strength of the
> male mind that dominates in the classroom. It is mathematics
> and physical sciences which still enjoy high institutional prestige,
> and which are still frequently prescribed and recommended by
> university course authorities.
>
> (Gilbert and Gilbert 1998: 19)

Introduction

This chapter is an exploration of the ways in which school science structures
and is structured by norms of masculinity. It arose out of an interest in how
participating in school science can serve as a masculinizing practice – a
practice that helps shape, reinforce and validate the constructions of certain
versions of masculinities – and how students construct identities that are
consonant or at odds with this practice. Following Wolpe (1988), I aim to
examine implicit assumptions that are part of the hidden curriculum of
primary school science. I am interested in how science serves as a masculinizing practice at the level of the implicit – the images of science
presented and the ways that curricula and pedagogies reinforce, mostly
subtly, these gendered notions. I use data from elementary classrooms in the
United States to provide support and examples for the claims that I make.
Although an extensive research base exists about the gendered nature of
science, and a rich research base is accruing about the ways in which schooling
is complicit in the constructions of certain kinds of masculinities, this paper
seeks to examine the intersection of these research programmes – namely

how school science reinforces masculinity in ways that are neither monolithic nor unambiguous. It does not, however, take masculinity as a synonym for boys, men or maleness (Halberstam 1998), but rather it 'is simultaneously a place in gender relations, the practices through which men and women engage that place in gender, and the effects of these practices in bodily experience, personality and culture' (Connell 1995: 71).

My approach reflects on what this gendered school science means for boys – both in terms of opportunities granted and opportunities foreclosed.[3] I am interested not only in why girls reject school science, but also in a different side of the same coin – specifically, why some boys (and some girls) continue to embrace it. I examine not only the curriculum and classroom materials used in school science, but also the ways in which these are deployed pedagogically. I believe it is at the intersections and interplay of curriculum and pedagogy that we can see the allure that school science holds for many students. I am interested in how schools teach science, what science they teach, and how they teach *about* science. To this end, following Davies' (1995) call, I intend this chapter to offer a clearer picture about the ways in which school science fosters the propagation of certain hegemonic masculinities by turning attention to 'the mythologizing practices that create the sciences as hard and male and objective' (p. 9).

School science and *certain* masculinities

Contrary to what many of us have been taught, neither science nor schooling are culture-free, objective, or value-neutral domains. As Rosenthal (1997: 150) writes,

> science classrooms are truly multicultural. The cultures of the students and teacher, as well as the cultures of science and the academy, influence not only the content of the course, but also the teaching and learning processes, interactions between instructor and students, verbal and non-verbal forms of communication, and observable behaviors.

Following Gilbert and Taylor (1991), we need to examine the context of the curriculum, but also the ways in which it is used. As others have noted (Mac an Ghaill 1994; Paechter 1998; Martino 1999), the official curriculum is central in providing a variety of masculinities for students to take up and inhabit. Work has been done in schools on subjects ranging from English (Martino 1994, 1995, 1999; Sanderson 1995) to physical education (Parker 1996; Renold 1997; Wright 1997; Gard and Meyenn 2000). But although the feminist critiques of science are well developed (c.f. Brickhouse 1998), little work has yet interrogated the ways in which school science models a middle-class, white, western, heterosexual academic masculinity of the mind. It encourages competition through rationality and expertise rather than through physical confrontation (Connell 1996).

As Connell (1989) notes about hegemonic masculinities which are constructed in accord with the general school curriculum, they stress notions of responsibility and rationality, which can then eventually translate into social power that is centred on abstract knowledge and authority. In a similar vein, Davies (1995: 8) writes,

> Proper hard, non-subjective subjects like maths, science and technology provide a haven of acceptable (male) knowledges which confirm that true knowledge lies outside oneself, and independent of any subjectivities, independent of those emotions which need to be held in check. They are rational, cool, controllable, abstract, distant, and unquestionably hegemonic.

What's going on in classrooms?

Using data gathered during elementary and middle school science lessons in US classrooms, I examine some of the often subtle ways in which school science serves to recapitulate a vision of and version of hegemonic masculinity. School science serves as a nice example to illustrate how hegemonic masculinity focuses on the rationality of the mind, rather than on the body. In all three examples, it is the interplay of curriculum and pedagogy that I see as crucial to seeing school science as a masculinizing practice which can seduce students to achieve in it. While these examples are from specific classrooms, I believe that they are recognizable to primary science teachers as relatively typical and common classroom phenomena.

The first example is taken from a transcript of a 6th grade lesson in a unit on insects. In this lesson the students were investigating body characteristics and various behaviours of a large species of cockroach. Students worked in groups of four, and each group had a single cockroach that was about 5 centimetres long. This snippet is taken from one 'cooperative' group.

Ashley: Here, do you want it? [to Sam]
Sam: No!
Ashley: Take it – everyone has to.
Carmen: Come on, just take it. *She's* holding it.
[Ashley hands the roach to a visibly nervous Sam. After several seconds, the startled roach starts to run up Sam's arm, and in response he starts flailing his arms, sending the roach flying across the room].
Ashley: Oh my god, what a *baby*!
Lara: Sam!
Mr Wilton: [from across the room] Sam, grow up. It can't be that bad.

Sam is clearly not playing by 'the rules' of the science class. He is not eager for investigation (at least none that involves touching the roach) and when it becomes overwhelming for him, he is chastised rather than helped.

Carmen intones that if a *girl* can hold the roach, then Sam certainly can. This is a very common (misogynist) put-down strategy used against boys – surely there can be nothing worse than being referred to as a girl (Hopkins 1996). And in this case, Sam appears unwilling (unable?) to do what a girl is seemingly doing quite easily – an even bigger put-down. As Carrie Paechter writes, 'By attributing feminine characteristics to already subordinated groups, hegemonic masculinities are able to regard their dominance as being a special case of the power of the masculine over the feminine' (1998: 95). And although it is not clear if he chose to hold the roach or just succumbed to peer pressure, the end result was less than powerful science for Sam. He is derided for being immature (a 'baby' who needs to 'grow up'). I noted elsewhere (Letts 1999) that this treatment of Sam 'seems to work to humiliate him, to police his own enactment of his heterogender,[4] and to coerce him into behaving in ways that boys are expected to behave in science class' (p. 100). This example serves to illustrate the ways in which the hidden curriculum of a subject like science can manifest itself (Wolpe 1988). What is implicit in these criticisms is that Sam is failing to use his mind (the cornerstone of modern western science) to exert control over nature (manifested here as a roach), and is therefore in the dubious position of falling 'victim' to his emotions. If he were really 'doing science' – the mantra goes – he would tame the matter; his emotions wouldn't tame him.

Performing assessment, gendering science

The next segment of dialogue comes from an end of the unit assessment in a 1st grade classroom. The teacher is meeting with each student individually at the conclusion of a sinking and floating unit to do some individualized performance assessment. She was encouraged to try this assessment strategy through her involvement in a state-wide reform effort in science education. This scene takes place between the teacher, Ms Renfrew, and Taurence as they sit at a table in the back of the classroom with a tray of objects and a tub of water.

Ms Renfrew:	Find the penny. Do you think that will sink or float?
Taurence:	Sink.
Ms R:	Would you like to try it?
T:	[Drops penny into tub of water]
Ms R:	Were you right?
T:	[Nods head]
Ms R:	You were right! Great job! Find the ball of clay. Do you think it will sink or float?
T:	Float [Drops it in] Awww
Ms R:	Were you right? What did it do?

T:	[Shakes head] It sank.
Ms R:	It sank. Good try though. Find the string. Do you think it will sink or float?
T:	Float. [Drops it in the water] Float!
Ms R:	Were you right?
T:	Yeah.
Ms R:	Wow! Good job. Find the plastic bottle. What do you think it will do?
T:	Float. [Drops in]
Ms R:	What did it do?
T:	Floated.
Ms R:	Were you right?
T:	Yeah.
Ms R:	Good for you. Find the bottle top. What do you think it's going to do?
T:	Sink.
Ms R:	Let's find out.
T:	Awww. [It floats]
Ms R:	Was your prediction right or wrong?
T:	Wrong.
Ms R:	Wrong. Good try. Good try. Could you find the twist tie? What do you think it's going to do?
T:	Float.
Ms R:	OK. [Taurence puts it in the water]
T:	Sink!
Ms R:	Oh boy! Now I thought that was a floater too. Good try.

Several things appear to be going on here. First, the point of this activity, an end of the unit assessment, seems to be guessing correctly. Taurence is never asked for evidence or reasoning to back up his predictions. Thus, he is guessing what will happen, rather than predicting what will happen when each object is dropped into the water. He just calls his guesses out and rushes on to test them. It's the answer that matters, not why he thinks it is so. This focus promotes a masculinist discourse of objectivity, with the sinking and floating objects acting as the divining rod for that objectivity. By simply placing each object into the water, the 'truth' about its subsequent sinking or floating is revealed. And the focus of the activity seems to be whether or not he has predicted (guessed) correctly for each object. The activity seems to be all about 'right' answers, though Taurence is still praised for guesses that turn out to be incorrect ('good try'); and at one point the teacher admits that she too thought that the twist tie 'was a floater'. Perhaps this admission was intended to make Taurence feel better because he had gotten several predictions 'wrong', but it could also serve to reinforce the point that this entire activity was about guessing as even the teacher didn't know all of the answers!

I also wonder to what extent the science being done (and the teacher helping to do it) are complicit in silencing Taurence both by conversations foreclosed and words never mentioned (Fine 1987). There is silence around both the content and the process of this exploration. He is not pressed (or even asked) to offer evidence or reasons for his predictions about sinking and floating. Instead, he simply picks a choice from a dichotomy, in a task that could be very far removed from the 'big ideas' in science that it appears that the entire unit, and certainly this assessment, are trying to build understanding around. Granted, while this is a Year 1 classroom and we wouldn't expect Taurence to elaborate on his predictions with an extended explanation of density, there still would [should] have been a science concept that this unit was aimed at exploring, and Taurence could have been asked to elaborate on this as part of his explanations.

When talking is not enough

The final segment of dialogue comes from a cooperative group of four students in a Year 4 classroom studying materials and their properties. The four students were charged with coming to consensus about what the results of various tests (for durability, waterproofness, strength) tell them about the fabric they were investigating.

Amy:	What did you get Rachel?
Matt:	I think that it's not very durable, but that it's strong and waterproof.
Amy:	Rachel?
Rachel:	It looks like it's medium-durable . . .
Malik:	Medium?
Rachel:	Yeah, it lasted nine strokes [of the fabric along a concrete surface] before it got a hole.
Matt:	So why is that medium?
Amy:	[under her breath] What else could it be?
Rachel:	Because it could be more or it could be less . . .
Matt:	Nine strokes is not very durable.
Malik:	Yeah. What about waterproof?
Rachel:	I'm not sure . . .
Matt:	It's definitely waterproof.
Amy:	Why?
Matt:	Did you pay attention to the test?
Amy:	*Yes.* I did. I thought it was getting a wet spot.
Rachel:	I think it was too.
Malik:	I didn't see it. Let's say it's waterproof.
Matt:	Yeah.
Amy:	And strong.

Matt: Of course!
Ms Chanson: How are you making out over here?
Matt: Fine. It's strong and waterproof and not very durable.
Ms Chanson: Super. Be ready to talk about that when we report out.

This snippet of classroom talk offers us an important view of consensus building in cooperative groups as they relate to issues of power and authority in the science classroom. Just because the idea of students working in groups seems to start to equalize the power dynamic in the classroom, and just because groups offer the potential for students to work collaboratively in an egalitarian fashion, does not mean that this will happen. As the above example demonstrates, just because students are in a group doesn't mean they will work together; just because they're supposed to share decision-making responsibilities doesn't mean that they will; just because they each have a specific role within the group doesn't mean they'll perform it (Bianchini 1997). Groups, as microcosms of the larger society within which they are formed, run the risk of falling prey to the same exclusionary social practices of homophobia, sexism, classism, racism, etc. that the larger society exhibits. In the instance above, Matt seemed little interested in reaching consensus. His goal seemed to be to assert his power by making his opinions (in the form of his interpretations of the experimental results) heard. This occurred to a large extent at the expense of Amy and Rachel's ideas and interpretations of the test results. Matt's dismissive query, 'Did you pay attention to the test?', asserts the unambiguous manner that the results arise naturally from the test. They don't require interpretation, only report-ing of the 'truths' that are revealed through experimentation. Although the group seems to be working to consensus, when the teacher comes by, Matt asserts his own opinions about the results as if he is speaking for the members of his group. He is not.

Here we can see how regimes of masculine power produce masculine knowledge and reproduce masculine privilege, not only at the expense of Amy, but at the expense of the entire group, and perhaps even the rest of the class. Matt asserted power to dictate the group's answers. In doing so, he not only silenced the others' views, he also foreclosed the opportunities that others were taking advantage of to create 'good at science' identities. The ways in which they were negotiating science, Matt made clear to them, were inferior and insufficient. He presented them with the model of a hege-monic masculinist school science – take it or leave it. Unfortunately, as most of the research suggests, Amy, Rachel and maybe even Malik are likely to leave it.

In group interactions, these points are particularly salient around the issue of language. As Trinh (1989: 52) writes, 'language is one of the most complex forms of subjugation, being at the same time the locus of power and uncon-scious servility'. Just because students are talking does not mean they aren't dominating, silencing and dismissing one another, playing out time-honoured societal scripts where the oppressors maintain power. Talking is not a neutral activity; it is, as described earlier, a mediational tool through which students construct meaning. The mere presence of talk, without further analysis, doesn't offer us clear clues about what meaning is being constructed. The same talk that could be used to understand a science concept better or to discuss differing interpretations of the results of a test could simultaneously be reinforcing classroom norms of submissiveness, obedience or, in this case, hegemonic masculinity. 'Students may have opportunities for group work', writes Ladson-Billings, 'but what teachers deem cooperative behavior more accurately falls under the category of compliance or conformity' (1994: 70). In this vignette language was used both to silence other group members and to hijack the vision of the nature of science that the group was working under – science became about unambiguous results, not informed interpretations. So the issues of power, authority and language that infuse the commonly used grouping approach to science pedagogy must be better theorized and articulated to ensure that grouping does not degenerate into yet another form of hegemonic subjugation of the students in the classroom.

Alternatives in classroom practices

First, when examining the issues surrounding hegemonic masculinities and school science, I think it is important to echo Connell's caution that 'Boys are not, as boys, a disadvantaged group, and the goal of educational work therefore is not to redress a gender disadvantage from which they suffer' (1996: 223). Viewing boys as disadvantaged unnecessarily reinscribes the false dichotomy between boys and girls and sets up an oppositional dynamic (Kenway 1995; Yates 1997; Lingard and Douglas 1999.) Instead, this project has been about examining the ways in which school science can perpetuate – through the interplay of its curricula and pedagogies – certain hegemonic masculinities that disadvantage both girls and boys. Thus, the focus of this work has been an uncovering of some of the ways in which this perpetuation can occur within classrooms.

Schools are undoubtedly the sites of cultural production and reproduction, where students conform, resist, negotiate, and contest identities. I argue that school science should offer more resources to engage in this struggle. School science should work to actively refute the ideology that school science equals hegemonic masculinity. I agree with Sharon Haggerty (1996) that we can't ignore issues of how science is represented in schools, and its interactions with gender. Left unexamined, these beliefs would most likely simply perpetuate themselves in a vicious cycle, as they have for decades. Instead, we need to start to view schools, and specifically in this case school science, as sites of intervention, and as offering resources for the refashioning of gendered, racialized, classed, and heterosexualized identities by explicitly taking up these issues in our instruction.

I think it is worth exploring the possible ways in which a girls/boys dichotomy used in science education, as well as countless other disciplines, may oversimplify reality and in fact reinforce the prominence of science as a masculinist regime of truth. This false dichotomy – captured in a realist tale that naturalizes two sexes – certainly homogenizes all boys (Martino 1997; Pallotta-Chiarolli 1997; Gilbert and Gilbert 1998), erasing many who do not embrace, or fit, hegemonic masculinities. It also allows us as teachers, teacher educators and researchers to perpetuate the 'automatic slippage that super-imposes dichotomous notions of gender – femininity and masculinity – onto 'biological' sex in such a way that it makes gender also seem dichotomous, discrete, polarized and 'natural' – in effect making it heterogender' (Letts 1999: 103). This reliance on the 'biological' distinctions of boys and girls doesn't challenge or disrupt the dichotomy that serves hegemonic masculinist interests. 'Biological explanations of social arrangements remain common', Connell writes, 'because of the general prestige of "science" and because they broadly justify the status quo and the privileges of those who benefit from the status quo' (1999: 451). We must then challenge both the deploy-ment of science to naturalize these categories of 'sex', and the deployment of these categories to essentialize what we see in science classrooms. A simple way to start to do this would be to make these naturalized categories visible, explicitly spelling out how they operate and what our investments in them are. As Smith (1989) poignantly reminds us, this dichotomizing is intricately bound up in a cultural proclivity for misogyny, and this, Epstein (1997) insists, is further reinscribed with homophobias and compulsory heterosexuality. There is a great deal of unpacking that needs to be done around these concepts and their many manifestations within schools. We can start this long process by fostering the conversations that bring these implicit notions to light, eliminating the silence and invisibility that currently surround them.

Another potential for change is to re-view the role of the teacher in the science classroom. Instead of viewing teachers as purveyors of information or even as facilitators of children's learning, let's try viewing teachers as change agents, through even the smallest changes to their practices. Since what is at issue here is not about a static body of content (science), but rather how science content gets enacted by teachers through pedagogy, this stance towards teaching may allow us to think about ways to enact science that are less masculinist. For example, in the vignette above involving Sam and the roach, a teacher as change agent could have seized upon the mar-ginalization of Sam as an opportunity to have a frank but sensitive discussion with the class about the power of language and labelling. One outcome of the discussion could be that the class collectively starts to monitor the ways in which they use language to hurt, denigrate, and silence other classmates (or even the teacher).

A teacher as change agent can also work to thwart the dominant pres-entation of science in school as a grand narrative, one that is universal, unchanging, and historically coherent (Hodson 1993; Brickhouse 1994; Stanley and Brickhouse 1994; Harding 1998). Stanley and Brickhouse (1994: 395) caution that

> excessively narrow definitions of what science is (e.g., science is what Western scientists have produced during the last 200 years) is too exclusionary of multiple perspectives and is ultimately detrimental to both science education and to science. Multiple perspectives should be seen as a rich resource for science and science education.

In the sinking and floating vignette above, if the focus had shifted from correct answers to Taurence's reasoning and evidence, the possibilities within the assessment would have changed drastically. As Taurence worked to build an understanding of sinking and floating, what would have been foregrounded as most important were his reasons for his predictions, not necessarily the final result. Taurence could have begun a journey in school science that explicitly centred his own perspective as important and worth exploration and explanation. A Year 1 science lesson might be the perfect place to start to create such counternarratives (Giroux *et al.* 1996) to the status quo in science. We need to reterritorialize the science classroom with a vision and version of science that is more inclusive. Bentley and Watts (1987) wrote that school science should be re-examined, reshaped, and redefined in terms of the views it has of people in science so that it better reflects the diverse populations that it is serving.

Teachers as change agents and students need to work together to create and sustain more spaces to explore and negotiate diverse identities within the dominant discourses of school science. Science is uniquely configured to offer students a myriad of resources for the construction of 'good at science' or 'I like science' identities. We need to come to terms with how to maximize these opportunities in classrooms, thereby eliminating, or at least minimizing the barriers that school science can erect to the formation of such identities. Schools must refute the ideology that school science equals hegemonic masculinity. A critical reassessment of the gender regimes reinscribed by and propagated through school science could mean that it could perhaps one day function as a critical counterdiscourse that 'speaks out' against hegemonic forms of masculinity. In the snippet from the fourth grade classroom, we can see how regimes of masculine power produce masculine knowledge and reproduce masculine privilege, not only at the expense of Amy, but at the expense of the entire group, and perhaps even the rest of the class. Matt asserted power to dictate the group's answers. In doing so, he not only silenced the others' views, he also foreclosed the opportunities that others were taking advantage of to create 'good at science' identities. The ways in which they were negotiating science, Matt made clear to them, were inferior and insufficient. He presented them with the model of a hegemonic masculinist school science – take it or leave it.

Unfortunately, as most of the research suggests, Amy, Rachel and maybe even Malik are likely to leave it.

Conclusion

My aim in this chapter has been to interrogate some of the manifestations of a hegemonic masculinist science in elementary school classrooms in order to help us better identify and correct its effects. Only in recognizing the myriad of ways in which children (and often times teachers) get silenced and alienated from science can we really hope to bring in all of the outsiders (Brickhouse 1994). My hope is that as teachers, teacher educators and researchers we can improve science education for all children, even those currently succumbing to the seductions of a science that is grounded in and perpetuates hegemonic masculinity.

Notes

1 As Bob Connell notes, 'The research forcibly shows – in contrast to much popular thinking – that "boys" are not a homogeneous bloc, that masculinities vary and change, and that in gender, institutions (as well as bodies) matter' (1996: 230). In light of this, I am using the phrase 'boys will be boys' quite differently from the way it is used in Chapter 1 in that I don't see it as a naturalized process, but rather due to their interactions (or lack of interactions) with school science.

2 Thanks to Jay Lemke, Michael Gard and the editors for helpful comments and critical feedback on earlier versions of this chapter.

3 My focus on boys here is not part of an anti-feminist 'what about the boys' backlash (Chapter I, this volume; Lingard and Douglas 1999), but rather views some boys' successes in science as a starting point to deconstruct the curriculum and pedagogies of school science as sites for the formation and perpetuation of hegemonic masculinities.

4 Following Chrys Ingraham, I take heterogender to be the 'asymmetrical stratification of the sexes in relation to the historically varying institutions of patriarchal hetero-sexuality' (1994: 204), thereby foregrounding the interimplicated natures of gender and sexuality. In this particular instance, I think that Sam's classmates are acting to police his improper embodiment of heterosexual masculinity.

References

Bentley, D. and Watts, M. (1987) Courting the positive virtues: a case for feminist science in A. Kelly (ed.) *Science for Girls*? Philadelphia, PA: Open University Press.

Bianchini, J.A. (1997) Where knowledge construction, equity, and context intersect: student learning of science in small groups. *Journal of Research in Science Teaching*, 34 (10): 1039–65.

Brickhouse, N.W. (1994) Bringing in the outsiders: reshaping the sciences of the future. *Journal of Curriculum Studies*, 26 (4): 401–16.

Brickhouse, N.W. (1998) Feminism(s) and science education in B.J. Fraser and K.G. Tobin (eds) *International Handbook of Science Education*. Dordrecht: Kluwer.

Connell, R.W. (1989) Cool guys, swots and wimps: the interplay of masculinity and education. *Oxford Review of Education*, 15 (3): 291–303.

Connell, R.W. (1995) *Masculinities*. Berkeley, CA: University of California Press.

Connell, R.W. (1996) Teaching the boys: new research on masculinity, and gender strategies for schools. *Teachers' College Record*, 98 (2): 206–35.

Connell, R.W. (1999) Making gendered people: bodies, identities, sexualities in M.M. Ferree, J. Lorber and B.B. Hess (eds) *Revisioning Gender*. Thousand Oaks, CA: Sage.

Davies, B. (1995) What about the boys? The parable of the bear and the rabbit. *Interpretations*, 28 (2): 1–17.

Epstein, D. (1997) Boyz own stories: masculinities and sexualities in schools. *Gender and Education*, 9 (1): 105–15.

Fine, M. (1987) Silencing in public schools. *Language Arts*, 64 (2): 157–74.

Gard, M. and Meyenn, R. (2000) Boys, bodies, pleasure and pain: interrogating contact sports in schools. *Sport, Education and Society*, 5 (1): 19–34.

Gilbert, R. and Gilbert P. (1998) *Masculinity Goes to School*. Sydney: Allen and Unwin.

Gilbert, P. and Taylor, S. (1991) *Fashioning the Feminine: Girls, Popular Culture and Schooling*. Sydney: Allen and Unwin.

Giroux, H.A., Lankshear, C., McLaren, P., and Peters, M. (1996) *Counternarratives: Cultural Studies and Critical Pedagogies in Postmodern Spaces*. New York, NY: Routledge.

Haggerty, S.M. (1996) Towards a gender-inclusive science in schools: confronting student teachers' perceptions and attitudes, in L.H. Parker, L.J. Rennie and B.J. Fraser (eds) *Gender, Science and Mathematics: Shortening the Shadow*. Dordrecht: Kluwer Academic Publishers.

Halberstam, J. (1998) *Female Masculinity*. Durham: Duke University Press.

Harding, S. (1991) *Whose Science? Whose Knowledge? Thinking from Women's Lives*. Ithaca, NY: Cornell University Press.

Harding, S. (1998) *Is Science Multicultural? Postcolonialisms, Feminisms, and Epistemologies*. Bloomington, IN: Indiana University Press.

Hodson, D. (1993) In search of a rationale for multicultural science education. *Science Education*, 77: 685–711.

Hopkins, P.D. (1996) Gender treachery: homophobia, masculinity, and threatened identities, in L. May, R. Strikwerda and P.D. Hopkins (eds) *Rethinking Masculinity: Philosophical Explorations in Light of Feminism*. Lanham, MD: Rowman and Littlefield.

Ingraham, C. (1994) The heterosexual imaginary: feminist sociology and theories of gender. *Sociological Theory*, 12 (2): 203–19.

Kenway, J. (1995) Masculinities in schools: under siege, on the defensive and under reconstruction? *Discourse: Studies in the Cultural Politics of Education*, 16 (1): 59–79.

Ladson-Billings, G. (1994) *The Dreamkeepers: Successful Teachers of African American Children*. San Francisco, CA: Jossey-Bass.

Letts, W. (1999) How to make 'boys' and 'girls' in the classroom: the heteronormative nature of elementary-school science, in W. Letts and J. Sears (eds) *Queering Elementary Education: Advancing the Dialogue About Sexualities and Schooling*. Lanham, MD: Rowman and Littlefield.

Lingard, B. and Douglas, P. (1999) *Men Engaging Feminisms: Pro-feminism, Backlashes and Schooling*. Buckingham: Open University Press.

Mac an Ghaill, M. (1994) *The Making of Men: Masculinities, Sexualities, and Schooling*. Buckingham: Open University Press.

Martino, W. (1994) Masculinity and learning: exploring boys' underachievement and under-representation in subject English. *Interpretations*, 27 (2): 22–57.

Martino, W. (1995) It's not the way guys think!, in R. Browne and R. Fletcher (eds) *Boys in Schools: Addressing the Real Issues – Behaviour, Values and Relationships*. Sydney: Finch Publishing.

Martino, W. (1997) Boys in schools: addressing the politics of hegemonic masculinities. Paper presented at the annual meeting of the Australian Association of Research in Education, Brisbane, Queensland, 30 November–4 December.

Martino, W. (1999) 'It's okay to be gay': interrupting straight thinking in the English classroom in W. Letts and J. Sears (eds) *Queering Elementary Education: Advancing the Dialogue About Sexualities and Schooling*. Lanham, MD: Rowman and Littlefield.

Paechter, C. (1998) *Educating the Other: Gender, Power and Schooling*. Brighton: Falmer.

Pallotta-Chiarolli, M. (1997) We want to address boys' education, but . . . *Curriculum Perspectives*, 17 (1): 65–9.

Parker, A. (1996) The construction of masculinity within boys' physical education. *Gender and Education*, 8 (2): 141–57.

Renold, E. (1997) 'All they've got in their brains is football'. Sport, masculinity and the gendered practices of playground relations. *Sport, Education and Society*, 2 (1): 5–23.

Rosenthal, J.W. (1997) Multicultural science: focus on the biological and environmental sciences, in A.I. Morey and M.K. Kitano (eds) *Multicultural Course Transformation in Higher Education*. Boston: Allyn and Bacon.

Sanderson, G. (1995) Being cool *and* a reader, in R. Browne and R. Fletcher (eds) *Boys in Schools: Addressing the Real Issues – Behaviour, Values and Relationships*. Sydney: Finch Publishing.

Smith, J. (1989) *Misogynies*. London: Vintage.

Stanley, W.B. and Brickhouse, N.W. (1994) Multiculturalism, universalism, and science education. *Science Education*, 78 (4): 387–98.

Trinh, Minh-ha T. (1989) *Woman, Native, Other: Writing Postcoloniality and Feminism*, Bloomington, IN: Indiana University Press.

Wolpe, A. (1988) *Within School Walls: The Role of Discipline, Sexuality and the Curriculum*. London: Routledge.

Wright, J. (1997) The construction of gendered contexts in single sex and co-educational physical education lessons. *Sport, Education and Society*, 2 (1): 55–72.

Yates, L. (1997) Gender equity and the boys debate: what sort of challenge is it? *British Journal of Sociology of Education*, 18 (3): 337–47.

CHAPTER 14

Maths talk is boys' talk: constructing masculinity in school mathematics

ANNE CHAPMAN

Introduction

This chapter explores relationships among language, learning and gender in mathematics, to highlight ways in which boys engage with this subject at school. It describes ways in which language operates to construct gendered identities in what is typically regarded as a 'masculine' discourse. In doing so, the chapter brings a new perspective to the 'What about the boys?' debate which, as Victoria Foster points out in Chapter 1, in the Australian context has been situated in a discursive framework of gender-related disadvantage. For teachers of mathematics, arguments about whether boys are 'more disadvantaged' or 'less disadvantaged' than girls are not particularly helpful in developing good curricular or pedagogical strategies for boys. It is more useful, I suggest, to find out what it means to be a boy in this male-dominated subject. What kind of masculinity is promoted in this discourse? How is that masculinity constructed? The chapter considers the role of language in the construction of masculinity in school mathematics discourse.

The perspective taken here is a social semiotic one, in which all uses of language are understood as forms of social action. To really understand the social action that goes on in the classroom, we need to consider the ways in which people learn; how they construct shared meanings. Social semiotics views meaning as an active process, in which all meanings are made. It focuses on social interaction; on how people construct systems of meaning. Importantly, for the concerns of this chapter, it allows an understanding of both language and other systems (for example, mathematics, art, drama) as semiotic resource systems; that is, systems of possible ways of meaning. It considers too that language operates together with other semiotic systems to produce the meanings of a subject area (Chapman 1997).

My argument is that learning mathematics involves learning its characteristically male patterns of language use; its precise, concise, factual and authoritative way of speaking. 'Doing' mathematics is very much about speaking 'properly': talking a particular style of masculinity. This involves making shifts from 'less mathematical' to 'more mathematical' language, and making mathematical meanings *within* those shifts. Distinctive aspects of mathematical language are its minimal metaphoric content and high modality structure. Metaphoric content refers to all the things that are said, or might be said, to talk about and around a subject in order to elaborate and explain what we mean. In mathematics, it is very common for teachers to use a lot of metaphorical content, especially in early primary years, to introduce new topics and to conjure up images. At higher levels of mathematics schooling, however, much more abstract language is used, and the emphasis shifts to form and grammar, that is, metonymy, rather than metaphor. Modality refers to the use of language to assert truth or factuality. The language of school mathematics tends to be definitive and factual, that is, it has a high modality. Again, this feature is more noticeable in the talk that goes on in higher level mathematics classrooms. These features, elaborated further in later sections of the chapter, are usually associated with boys' talk.

In what follows I will examine the operation of these features to illustrate the shift towards 'more mathematical' language. Working from the notion of mathematics as a constructed, masculine discourse, the analysis demonstrates specific gendered language practices through which mathematical meanings are constructed. A single example of classroom talk shows how boys can be positioned with respect to the curricular knowledge of mathematics; how the subject discourse requires boys to portray a particular kind of masculinity. The implications of this gendered subject production, for boys and for their teachers, are discussed.

Mathematics as a discursive practice

School studies generally agree that mathematics is a masculine discourse in large part because of the kind of rationality and reason it perpetuates within a curriculum that reflects traditionally masculine knowledge values (see, for example, Walkerdine 1988; Mac an Ghaill 1994; Gilbert and Gilbert 1998). Davies (1996: 214) explains:

> Proper hard, non-subjective subjects like maths, science and technology provide a haven of acceptable (male) knowledges which confirm that true knowledge lies outside oneself and independent of any subjectivities, independent of those emotions which need to be held in check. They are rational, cool, controllable, abstract, distant, and unquestionably hegemonic.

The areas of mathematics and science 'serve as a representation of the rational power and mental strength of the male mind that dominates in the classroom' (Gilbert and Gilbert 1998: 19). Mathematics in particular valorizes abstract reasoning, objectivity, factuality, precision, rationality, and other masculine values substantiated in its curricular content (Walkerdine 1988). This situation has led to girls being disadvantaged in participation and performance, to boys making inappropriate learning area choices, and to both girls and boys being subjected to a form of masculinity associated with the inherently gendered discourse of school mathematics. There is no doubt that boys are often disadvantaged by the particular kinds of masculinity constructed for them, indeed, inflicted on them, at school (Mac an Ghaill 1994; Epstein *et al.* 1998). Exploring the gendered language of the mathematics classroom is one way to understand how masculine identity is constructed in the discursive practices of this subject; that is, in the ways we talk and act in order to produce mathematical meanings.

The rules of discursive practices prescribe particular kinds of roles for learners. To take up and maintain a role as a mathematics student, it is necessary to speak and act in a particular way, according to the rules. Certain social relations and ways of speaking must be adhered to. The social semiotic perspective taken here is that mathematics is a 'constructed discourse', the 'language of mathematics' being situated within the discursive practices that produce and maintain mathematical knowledge.

McBride (1989) identifies four discursive practices in mathematics teaching: the use of textbooks; teaching methods or styles; examination processes; and the use of space in the classroom. Following Foucault (1970, 1980), she asserts that these practices are governed by rules that determine the nature of knowledge or truth in mathematics education, and that each of these four domains promotes gender-biased practices. Often, this bias is implicit and unconscious. For example, argues McBride, the language and images of mathematics textbooks privilege 'masculine states of knowledge', and mathematics teachers interact proportionately more with male students in mixed-sex classes. In light of this, I recommend in this chapter that mathematics teachers promote a style of mathematical language that does not reinforce the typically masculine ways in which boys have been, and are presently, positioned in school mathematics.

Mathematical language

Lemke points out, 'Discourse analysis reminds us that comprehension is the ability to speak the pattern, rather than merely copy the model' (1989: 140). It is the pattern that I want to examine here, in particular those typically masculine features of the pattern that characterize the register of mathematical language, and which are valued in school mathematics. This section considers two key features of mathematical language; its highly metonymic form and its high modality (Chapman 1997). These features are the basis for an analysis of classroom talk to follow.

The first part of the analysis, which illustrates the 'metonymic' form of mathematical language, describes the patterns of the linguistic system in two ways; in terms of metaphor and metonymy. The term metaphor refers to the sets of, and selection from, possible alternatives for each word. The term metonymy refers to the combination of parts, or the regular, linear sequencing of words.

Walkerdine (1988) makes use of the terms metaphor and metonymy to specify transformations from non-mathematical to mathematical discourse. She points out that formal statements in school mathematics discourse typically contain little or no metaphoric content. Walkerdine (1982) shows how, in children's play, metaphors are used to 'call up' particular discourses, within which children can take up positions. In mathematics, there is a tendency to 'call up' a discourse, or introduce a concept with the use of metaphor and, once that concept is established, to shift towards a more metonymic form of language.

In the analysis of a transcript of classroom talk in the following section of this chapter I will draw on the work of Walkerdine to examine how language is used to 'strip away' the metaphoric content. Mathematical language is shown to operate mostly metonymically; there is an emphasis on the form, style and grammar of the language, to structure language in a particular way. This does not mean that metaphoric content is disregarded; rather it means 'suppressing' it, in favour of using more 'abstract' language.

The second part of the analysis concerns the high modality, or degree of factuality and certainty, of mathematical language. Certainly, teachers of all subjects use language to show students appropriate ways to talk in subject-specialist classrooms. In mathematics classrooms, for example, teachers model the language of school mathematics. At the same time, they use language to say something *about* mathematics. They might refer to mathematical 'objects', such as angles and units, and other mathematical 'realities', such as 'a hectare is a square measure'. Teachers thus use language to assert certainty about mathematical meanings. The social construction of mathematics depends a great deal on what counts as truth or fact. It is important, therefore, to consider how an utterance is affirmed as true or real.

The semiotic term modality, as developed by Hodge and Kress (1988), refers to the 'truth value' attached to a proposition. The way a statement is made, that is, how it is modalized, determines significantly whether it will be understood by the listener as true or real. If a statement is made in a way that asserts truth or factuality, it is said to have a high modality. Conversely, if it is made in a way that suggests doubt, rather than reality, then it has a low modality. It is important to note that modality does not have only these two forms, high and low. Rather, it operates within a range between the two.

A great deal of the talk that goes on in the classroom works in ways that bear upon the 'truth value' of what is said. The importance of modality for all classroom learning is that it provides a way of understanding how language is used to establish 'truth value'. In subject-area mathematics, it is important to know what is true. Mathematical knowledge can be said to consist of 'truths' or 'facts', realities that form the basis for mathematical operations. Studies of the relation between modality and gender (e.g. Threadgold 1988; Poynton 1990) and the gender effects of modalization in school discourses (Lee 1996) strongly suggest that linguistic modality is gendered, with high modality a feature of masculine discourses.

My earlier study of language and mathematics learning (Chapman 1997) identified high modality and a highly metonymic form as being features of mathematical language; features described here as characteristically male. It is within the transformational shift from less mathematical language to more mathematical language that mathematical meanings are constructed. The next section provides a descriptive and interpretive account of how this shift can happen.

An example of classroom talk

The following example is taken from a Year 9 mathematics class in a Western Australian State Government senior high school. According to the (male) teacher, it was a fairly able group with several very good students. The class was considered within the school to be in the second quartile in achievement.

The transcript and analysis focus mainly on one boy, Stuart, who was described by his teacher as 'competent' in mathematics. He was talkative, always keen to answer the teacher's questions, and often volunteered to participate in classroom discussions. Another boy, David, joins the conversation very briefly. The transcript was selected to exemplify the kinds of discussion that typically took place in this particular classroom. Also, it is representative of the way Stuart uses language in mathematics.

The teacher had written the following questions on the blackboard:

$y = x^2 + 4$ How are these graphs the same?
$y = (x + 4)^2$ Different?

1	*Stuart:*	They're both different when you graph them. They are
2		both quadratic.
3	*Teacher:*	OK. So what does that mean? I'm talking about the graph,
4		so you've got to talk about pictures now. I'm not talking
5		about the rule or, I'm only talking about pictures you end
		up with.
6	*Stuart:*	The first one, ah, intersects at four on the y axis.
7	*Teacher:*	Let me do it systematically. How are they the same?
8	*Stuart:*	Yep. Well they are both quadratic.

9	*Teacher:*	So what does that mean?
10	*Stuart:*	They are both going to have a curve, and they're both
11		going to be a mirror image, on the y axis.
12	*Teacher:*	You happy with that, Linda, David?
13	*David:*	No, they're not, because the x add four squared will touch
14		the x axis at negative four.
15	*Teacher:*	No, well, Stuart was trying to deal with the same. Don't
16		start telling me the difference because I haven't given him
17		a chance on that.
18	*David:*	They both have the same curve and they're both exactly
19		the same sort of pictures. Just in different places.
20	*Teacher:*	So when you said they were both the same did you mean
21		the same curve?
22	*Stuart:*	Oh yeh. They both, they're not the same, but the same
23		curve. The same curve but they intersect at a different point.
24	*Teacher:*	So if we picked one up and put it on top of the other one,
25		would it look exactly like it? Would it be a bit steeper, a
26		bit flatter maybe? You all agree with that? Stuart, you
27		agree with that?
28	*Stuart:*	Yes.
29	*Teacher:*	OK. How are they different, Stuart?
30	*Stuart:*	Well, the first one intersects at four on the y axis, and the
31		second one intersects at negative four on the x axis.

Stuart has volunteered, by raising his hand, to answer these questions. He begins in lines 1–2 by dealing first of all with the difference, 'they're both different when you graph them', and then the similarity, 'they are both quadratic'. There is no metaphoric content in these opening sentences. The placement of the words, the structure of the sentences, provides two closely related metonymic axes. The teacher's response is in less mathematical language, in the sense that it introduces metaphoric elements. He states, 'I'm talking about the graph' (line 3), signalling that he thinks Stuart was talking about the rules and not the graphs. The teacher's response involves several transformations. The message is that Stuart *should* be talking about 'the graph'/'pictures'/'pictures you end up with'. Thus, the nature of the task is clarified and Stuart is required to establish a new, more appropriate metonymic form.

Stuart's reply is tentative (line 6). He now focuses on the graphs, rather than the rules, but again appears to misunderstand the task. He deals with only one of the graphs and the teacher puts him on track by asking, 'how are they (the graphs) the same?' (line 7). This question requires an answer of a particular metonymic form: the linear sequencing of words in the form 'they are both ___.' Stuart immediately adopts this form, and retains it in the following responses:

(line 8)	they are both quadratic;
(line 10)	they are both going to have a curve;
(lines 10–11)	they're both going to be a mirror image.

The metaphoric elements are used to elaborate on the meaning of 'quadratic', that is, to explain the idea contained in the metonymic string. It is this idea, that 'they are both (the same)', that is important. Stuart now has an appropriate style of language to use to make this point. He has read the teacher's signal that speaking 'properly' is, in this episode at least, a matter of replacing the various metaphoric elements, while holding them together with a particular metonymic string. It involves operating language in a metonymic way.

David's two responses follow the same pattern as Stuart's. The first one does not address the set task, as he is dealing with only one of the graphs. The teacher again points out that there are two parts to the task, noting the similarities and differences (lines 15–17). David's next response does just that (lines 18–19). This brief dialogue between David and the teacher indicates that they do not share the same understanding of Stuart's response. David disagrees with Stuart's statement that the two graphs are 'both going to be a mirror image, on the y axis' (lines 10–11). David apparently takes this to mean that both graphs cross the y axis at the same point and are thus the same. The teacher, however, does not consider that Stuart thinks that the graphs are the same. Rather, he considers that Stuart is pointing out what aspects of the graphs are the same.

David's language can be understood as being more mathematical than Stuart's. In lines 18–19, for example, David uses very little metaphoric content and makes only one transformation:

they both have	the same curve
they're both	exactly the same sort of pictures

The teacher does not comment on this response. Instead, he asks Stuart whether *he* thinks that the graphs have the same curve, 'so when you said they were both the same did you mean the same curve?' (lines 20–21). This causes even more confusion, since Stuart has not actually said that the graphs are the same. Nevertheless, Stuart readily takes up this new position. The teacher thus leads him quite explicitly to the statement, 'they're not the same, but the same curve' (lines 22–23). He goes on to point out that the graphs 'intersect (the y axis) at a different point' (line 23). Stuart has now mentioned all of the points made by David, but in precisely the way that the teacher wanted it said, that is, in terms of what is the same and what is different about the two graphs.

The teacher makes a transformation from more mathematical to less mathematical language when he introduces new metaphoric content in lines 24–27. He includes non-mathematical features to elaborate Stuart's previous response. The mathematics of Stuart's answer is now embedded in 'everyday' language. The curves are 'picked up' and put 'on top of' each other. They are described in terms of being 'steep' and 'flat'. Stuart, however, retains the more mathematical style in his final response (lines 30–31) which operates in a purely metonymic way.

The language of this text is transformed in various ways that modify both the metonymic and metaphoric axes. The above analysis has shown that the signals about what is the appropriate form are very subtle, and sometimes contradictory. For example, the teacher introduces metaphoric content in order to help Stuart focus on the set task. Achieving this, he begins to lead Stuart towards a 'correct' metonymic form. There is a problem, though, as David transforms the metonymic axis. The teacher then shifts from more mathematical to less mathematical language to encourage Stuart to elaborate and explain his meanings. However, perhaps in response to the teacher's signals that he has made the 'correct' meaning and is using the 'proper' kind of language, Stuart does not emulate this shift; he is learning to operate the gendered language practices of mathematics.

There are many shifts between levels of modality, or 'truth value', within the text. To begin with, Stuart's opening statements assert truth and factuality; they have a high modality. The use of the present tense indicates factuality: they *are* both different, they *are* both quadratic. This is Stuart's answer. This is what he knows to be true about the two graphs. The word 'when' does not indicate a hypothetical form in this instance. It indicates that Stuart is talking about the graphs of the functions rather than the rule; 'they're both different *when you graph them*' (line 1). Apparently this is not clear to the teacher, who introduces metaphoric elements to point out that it is the 'graph'/'picture' that is important. The teacher's response, 'so what does that mean?' (line 3) has a lower modality. He is suggesting that Stuart's answer is not clear. It may not be correct. He states, 'I'm talking about . . .' and, 'I'm not talking about . . .'. This invites Stuart to substantiate his meanings. He has to show that he understands the task and that he has the appropriate knowledge about the graphs. To do this, Stuart has to re-establish a high modality.

The tentative start to Stuart's response in line 6 indicates a lower modality than his initial response. He works towards establishing a higher modality using the present tense to verify that the first graph 'intersects at four on the y axis'. The teacher encourages Stuart to consolidate this higher modality by asking him for a specific, factual answer, 'how are they the same? (line 7). Stuart follows the high modality structure of this sentence: *they are both* quadratic, *they are both* going to have a curve, *they are both* going to be a mirror image (lines 8, 10–11). The high modality structure has now been established. Stuart is exhibiting the 'correct' meanings as well as the 'proper' kind of language.

David's two responses are operating with a high modality structure. But this is not affirmed by the teacher as an example of good mathematical language, because David has missed the point of the task. Instead, the teacher returns to Stuart. David's response has created some tension in the discussion. If David does not share the meanings that are apparently shared by the teacher and Stuart, then there is a need to elaborate them further. Also, they need to be expressed more mathematically, in the kind of language displayed by David. In order to clarify Stuart's meanings, the teacher uses what is very clearly a less mathematical kind of language. The hypothetical forms 'if' and 'would it', together with the repeated questioning, result in a lower modality. However, Stuart's response is more definite. He maintains his previously established high modality structure.

There is very clearly a correlation between the metonymic/metaphoric forms and the modality structures of the text. For example, Stuart begins the discussion with a mathematical style of language; it operates metonymically and with a high modality. The teacher uses less mathematical language, making transformations in both the metonymic and modality structures, in order to focus on the nature of the set task. He signals the importance of establishing the 'correct' metonymic structure together with a high modality. Stuart follows these signals and maintains these features of masculine discourse. What is happening here is that Stuart is adopting a version of masculinity, through the use of language, that reflects the masculine knowledge values of mathematics.

Implications for classroom teachers

The brief analysis presented above shows that Stuart makes multiple transformational shifts overall towards more mathematical language, features of which are characteristically male patterns of language use. These patterns are minimal metaphoric content and a high modality structure. Moreover, Stuart makes these shifts in response to transformational strategies of the teacher. The broader study, from which the above example is drawn, found that Stuart tends to rely on the teacher's strategies to make the shifts. Stuart is probably the greatest contributor to discussions in his class and so it is clear that having the ability to shift freely between less mathematical and more mathematical language is not simply a matter of talking a lot. Rather, it is about talking in a very particular, gendered way.

This raises important questions about the gendered language practices of school mathematics, and about the role of language in learning mathematics and in promoting a masculinized image of mathematics. Is the shift towards more mathematical language a necessary part of successful mathematics learning? This shift certainly seems to be valorized in school mathematics. If students see that teachers value this style of language use, then they will no doubt strive to achieve and perform it. And what of the transformational strategies of the teacher? To what extent are they deliberate or even conscious? The teacher in the example shown here is seen to lead his students in subtle and intricate ways towards a more mathematical, masculine style of language use. It seems that the teacher's strategies both develop and accommodate the transformational abilities of Stuart and David.

Some implications can be drawn from this brief exploration. Certainly, attention must be paid to the role of language in classroom learning. My argument has been that learning mathematics is very much a matter of learning to speak in a particular style. There is a pervasive and continual requirement, which is often implicit, to shift towards increasingly mathematical language. The features of this language are those usually associated with masculine, or boys', talk. Thus, the language of school mathematics promotes gender-biased practices and knowledge. Language practices are not just important, but integral, to mathematics learning. The language demands of mathematics must therefore be made more explicit to afford students greater control over their meaning constructions.

A focus on gender and language has been shown here to be useful in understanding how gendered identities are constructed through classroom talk. A similar focus in everyday classroom interaction might allow both teachers and learners to rethink their assumptions about what kinds of talk are appropriate in mathematics. When we speak and act in particular ways, we are modelling, and signalling that we value, those ways of saying and doing. We need to accept, model and appreciate a style of mathematical language that is not alienating to students and is gender-inclusive. Indeed, the case can be made for using gender-inclusive language in all curriculum areas, including those, such as English, that value feminized learning practices which may disadvantage boys.

Current trends in language, literacy and classroom mathematics recognize that language use is a fundamental part of the social practice of mathematics. Teachers are encouraged to adopt a 'language-sensitive' approach in order to enhance literacy outcomes as well as learning area outcomes. Such an approach involves allowing students to use the full range of the specialist language features of mathematics, including its distinctive vocabulary, as well as its written symbolic, diagrammatic, pictorial and graphical representations. In this way, teachers can redefine the notion of mathematical language to emphasize features others than those that are associated with dominant forms of masculinity.

Language and literacy strategies that teachers might employ to foster a 'language-sensitive' approach to mathematics include brainstorming, classroom call-out of ideas, group work, mathematical investigations, predictions about the outcomes of mathematical situations, approximating results, retrieval charts for recording information, glossaries of mathematical terms, student-generated questions and journal writing. There is quite a lot of curriculum support material already available in this area, with an increasing focus on inclusivity (O'Neill forthcoming). This kind of approach allows learners to use language to express and try out their ideas, without the rigid concern for correct style exhibited in the example shown in this chapter. This is not to say that learning to operate the register of mathematics is not important, but it should not dominate the curriculum. Not constraining learners' talk with the requirement to use a particular, masculinized style of language will go some way to challenging the 'maleness' that typically pervades school mathematics. For boys this means an opportunity to be 'good at maths' without having to take on the dominant form of masculinity it promotes.

Conclusion

This chapter has considered some ways in which language is gendered in school mathematics. The analysis of one boy's talk in the classroom has highlighted aspects of the relationship between language and mathematics, and the impact of this relationship on the social construction of masculine identity. How gender exists and operates in classroom interactions can help teachers understand their critical role in the social construction of their learners' identities. In the strongly male domain of mathematics, this is especially pertinent for boys.

Granted, many students have learned to 'talk the talk' of school mathematics, and have been successful in mathematics. And, yes, studies show that the majority of those students have been boys. But what does this masculine image and structure of mathematics mean to boys? What 'kind' of boy is most likely to succeed? What does he say? How does he say it? How does he act? Conversely, if a boy cannot or will not 'talk the talk', or construct the world as required by the language of mathematics, how does that affect his opportunities to learn, and his position in the social hierarchy of the classroom? In this chapter I hoped to open up discussion of some of the ways by which boys are positioned in and by school mathematics, and to show that language is a useful avenue for understanding the role of masculine identity in school mathematics.

References

Chapman, A.P. (1997) Towards a model of language shifts in mathematics learning. *Mathematics Education Research Journal*, 9 (2): 152–73.

Davies, B. (1996) *Power, Knowledge, Desire: Changing School Organisation and Management Practices*. Canberra: Department of Employment, Education, Training and Youth Affairs.

Epstein, D., Elwood, J., Hey, V. and Maw, J. (eds) (1998) *Failing Boys?* Buckingham: Open University Press.

Foucault, M. (1970) *The Archeology of Knowledge*. New York, NY: Pantheon.

Foucault, M. (1980) *Power/Knowledge: Selected Interviews and Other Writings 1972–1977*, edited by Colin Gordon. New York, NY: Pantheon.

Gilbert, R. and Gilbert, P. (1998) *Masculinity Goes to School*. Sydney: Allen and Unwin.

Hodge, R. and Kress, G. (1988) *Social Semiotics*. Cambridge: Polity Press.

Lee, A. (1996) *Gender, Literacy, Curriculum*. London: Taylor and Francis.

Lemke, J.L. (1989) Making text talk. *Theory into Practice*, XXVIII (2): 136–41.

Mac an Ghaill, M. (1994) *The Making of Men: Masculinities, Sexualities, and Schooling*. Buckingham: Open University Press.

McBride, M. (1989) A Foucauldian analysis of mathematical discourse. *For the Learning of Mathematics*, 9 (1): 40–6.

O'Neill, M. (forthcoming) Inclusive literacy strategies to enhance learning. CIE Monograph Series, No. 4. Nedlands: UWA.

Poynton, C. (1990) The privileging of representation and the marginalising of the interpersonal: a metaphor (and more) for contemporary gender relations, in T. Threadgold and A. Cranny-Francis (eds) *Feminine/Masculine and Representation*, pp 231–55. Sydney: Allen and Unwin.

Threadgold, T. (1988) Language and gender. *Australian Journal of Feminist Studies*, 6: 41–69.

Walkerdine, V. (1982) From context to text: a psychosemiotic approach to abstract thought, in M. Beveridge (ed.) *Children Thinking through Language*. London: Edward Arnold.

Walkerdine, V. (1988) *The Mastery of Reason: Cognitive Development and the Production of Rationality*. London: Routledge.

CHAPTER 15

Boys, books and breaking boundaries: developing literacy in and out of school

CHRISTINE HALL AND MARTIN COLES

Our aim in this chapter is to pursue two main lines of argument about boys and school-based literacy development. First, we want to argue for the importance of recognizing and respecting in school the range of reading children engage in outside school. Whether or not they inhabit bookish households, children in developed countries live in cultural contexts which routinely require of them sophisticated literacy practices. Our argument is that it is only by recognizing and respecting these popular – we will call them 'vernacular' – reading cultures in school that we can build a properly developmental model of literacy which puts the learner at the centre and acknowledges and responds to the relatively recent and dramatic changes in our contemporary understanding of what it means to be literate. We offer evidence from our own research on the vernacular reading cultures in which 10, 12 and 14-year-old English children live – reading cultures which are highly demarcated by gender. And we consider ways in which evidence of this kind can be used to build better school policy and classroom practice aimed at improving the present literacy disadvantages boys experience in school. We argue that current, officially sanctioned, school definitions of literacy unintentionally undermine many young readers, but particularly boys, inhibiting their development towards the confidence and mastery that are necessary if a reading habit is going to be sustained. Confidence and mastery are built more readily from an acknowledgement of what children can and do read, from trying not to look askance at what they enjoy and from analysing the skills they have which provide the basis for further development. Developing readers need to see reading, and literacy practices generally, situated in as wide a social and cultural context as possible – and certainly one which extends beyond the school boundaries.

Our second main line of argument relates to the fact that the current debate about the teaching of literacy is often unhelpfully polarized around gender issues. The debate is often crudely formulated to suggest that boys' reading is a major national and international problem, and boys themselves are therefore to be seen as deficient and in need of remediation. We recognize, of course, that gender plays an important part in the whole debate about attitudes to literacy and attainment levels. However, our aim here is to suggest ways of conceptualizing the issues around gender and reading which offer an alternative to the current dualistic and often dichotomized terms of the debate. This second strand of our argument intersects with the first. It makes us wary of the totalizing discourse that official school improvement and school effectiveness strategies are currently imposing on British schooling, and leads us to argue for a clearer focus on the importance of pupils' cultures and backgrounds to their achievements and development in school.

Before pursuing these arguments we need to sketch in two aspects of our own social context: national educational concerns in Britain about boys' achievements, particularly in relation to literacy, and findings about children's reading choices from our own research, which provide the foundation on which our discussion about boys' engagement with literacy is based.

The national context: concerns about boys' literacy in Britain

In the 1970s and 1980s the main gender issue in education was the performance of the girls – in particular, girls' performance in mathematics and science. Concerted efforts were made to improve this situation, and in the 1990s girls' performance in these subjects at the official school leaving age of 16 broadly matched that of boys (DfEE, 2000.) The focus in the 1990s shifted to boys and their perceived underperformance across a range of curriculum subjects – but particularly in reading and the subject English – throughout all the years of compulsory schooling.

An official review of research on gender and education performance by the government Office for Standards in Education (Ofsted) summarized the situation thus:

> The pattern of performance in Reading or English at Key Stage I in 1995 seems pretty clear-cut. Girls made a better start at learning to read than boys; 83 per cent of seven-year-old girls were performing at the 'expected level' (level 2) or above compared with 73 per cent of boys . . . The position is similar if one looks at any of the other components of English . . . Girls always out-performed boys and usually by a considerable margin.
>
> (Ofsted 1996)

The report goes on to state that at 16, the official minimum school leaving age, 'girls outperformed boys by some considerable distance in English'. General

Certificate in Secondary Education (GCSE) results in 1997 showed 65 per cent of girls achieving an A–C grade while only 43 per cent of boys matched this performance (QCA 1998). In 1999, English tests for 11-year-olds demonstrated that 50 per cent of boys, compared to 65 per cent of girls, had achieved the expected level of attainment for their age. The differential performance was maintained in tests for 14-year-olds in the same year, with 55 per cent of boys and 72 per cent of girls achieving the expected standard in English.

There is an enormous amount of statistical information available which points towards one set of now very widely accepted conclusions: that boys are more likely than girls to have problems with basic literacy; that boys in all kinds of schools perform markedly less well than girls; that girls dominate numerically in upper groups where there is setting; that girls read more fiction and that girls tend to be better at writing at length (Ofsted 1993, 1996; QCA, 1998).

As Christine Skelton points out in Chapter 1 of this book, nationally within Britain, boys' underachievement in school has been perceived as something of a crisis. The problem has been dramatically 'exposed' in several very high profile television documentaries. It is a regular topic for feature articles in the press. The Secretary of State for Education and junior ministers regularly make reference to concerns about boys' underachievement; there are burgeoning numbers of publications and courses offering advice on strategies which teachers can and should adopt to minimize the problem. There are innumerable local initiatives and projects; a National Literacy Strategy which runs alongside the statutory pupils' national curriculum for English; and a national curriculum for trainee teachers to mandate coverage of aspects of literacy teaching. The National Literacy Strategy, despite its non-statutory status, has been introduced with a high degree of funded support and encouragement, and some degree of coercion. It enshrines a detailed term-by-term literacy curriculum and promotes specific teaching techniques such as the 'Literacy Hour', a structured pattern of whole-class, group and individual teaching, which are perceived as being particularly supportive of boys' development.

The situation in England and Wales is unusual in the degree of centralized control being exerted over the content of the literacy curriculum and, to some extent, the preferred methods of teaching that curriculum. Nevertheless, it is clear that the analysis of the problem – the sense that boys in general are failing to make proper progress in literacy and that their peer cultures and school contexts exacerbate their difficulties – resonates with similar analyses in developed countries around the world (see, for example, analyses of current situations in Australia and the US in Chapter I of this volume).

The research context: boys' and girls' voluntary reading

In 1994/95 we began work on *The Children's Reading Choices Project*. This was a large-scale nationally generalizable survey, carried out in rural, suburban

Table 15.1   Average numbers of books read in the month prior to the survey, 1971 and 1994

Age	Boys 1971	Boys 1994	Girls 1971	Girls 1994
10+	2.68	2.98	3.28	3.71
12+	1.99	1.90	2.48	2.93
14+	1.78	1.45	2.15	2.06

Partial source: Whitehead *et al*. 1977: 51

and metropolitan areas of England. About eight thousand (7976) children aged 10, 12 and 14 completed questionnaires about their reading habits and voluntary, out-of-school, choices of reading material. The survey was followed up by interviews with just over 1 per cent of the sample.

The questionnaire was administered in school, although children knew that their individual responses would not be shared with their teachers. The research yielded an enormous amount of information about contemporary reading habits and choices. Also, since it was a replication study, repeating a Schools Council research project conducted by Frank Whitehead in the early 1970s (Whitehead *et al*. 1977), it allowed comparison of children's reading habits over a period of approximately a quarter of a century. The findings from the research are, therefore, complex. They are reported and discussed at greater length in our book *Children's Reading Choices* (Hall and Coles 1999).

The research findings we wish to focus upon in the light of our current arguments about boys' achievements are those which contribute to our understanding of the gendered nature of reading during these early pre-teenage and teenage years. So, what do the general trends show? Do boys read less than they used to? Do boys read less than girls?

The findings show clearly that popular anxiety about an overall decline in the amount of children's book reading is unfounded. Across all age groups, the average number of books that children reported reading in the month prior to the survey in 1994 was 2.52. This compares with a figure of 2.4 in 1971. Over the last two decades, book reading in England has increased for 10-year-olds of both sexes and for 12-year-old girls. It has remained at the same level for 12-year-old boys and for 14-year-old girls (i.e. there is no statistical significance between the figures for 1971 and 1994). It has declined only among 14-year-old boys (See Table 15.1)

These figures are confirmed by other data from the questionnaire, which suggest that although most children read regularly outside school, there is a tendency towards fewer books being read by children as they grow older. When asked whether they had read *any* book in the month prior to the survey, 91 per cent of 10-year-olds responded positively. This compared with 81 per cent of 12-year-olds and 64 per cent of 14-year-olds.

Table 15.2 Average numbers of periodicals read regularly, 1971 and 1994

Age	Boys 1971	Boys 1994	Girls 1971	Girls 1994
10+	3.13	2.55	3.52	2.69
12+	2.93	3.18	3.25	3.79
14+	2.68	3.34	3.18	4.13

As well as this slight increase in book reading, newspaper and magazine reading has increased among children in these age categories over the two decades. Some 24 per cent of the contemporary sample regularly read five or more periodicals. Whereas in the 1970s the reading of periodicals declined as children grew older, the reverse is now true (Table 15.2).

Among boys a comic (*Beano*), a tabloid newspaper (*Sun*) and football magazines (*Shoot* and *Match)*, are most popular. Among girls one magazine, *Just 17*, had extraordinary dominance of the market at that time – 42.5 per cent of all girls in the sample reported that they read this magazine. Of the children in the sample, 83 per cent report reading periodicals regularly. The interview phase of the project highlighted the fact that children of all three ages regularly reread their periodicals, sometimes a number of times. This seems to demonstrate the importance of such reading, which is not only initially attractive but also offers the child enough in the way of interest for the magazines to be stored and revisited, sometimes on numerous occasions.

What the figures also show, of course, is that boys read less than girls – and that they seem to have been reading less than girls for 25 years. Nor was this a new phenomenon in the 1970s. A survey conducted by Jenkinson in 1940 indicated the same pattern. And Michele Cohen, in her very illuminating work tracing historical perspectives on boys' performance, quotes such seventeenth-century luminaries as John Locke and Daniel Defoe, both of whom were concerned about boys' underachievement over 300 years ago (Cohen 1998).

Vernacular reading cultures

Having sketched in the national educational context and the research project from which our arguments are derived, we want now to develop our argument referring, as we do so, to particular findings in the *Children's Reading Choices* research (Hall and Coles 1999). Our basic arguments are for the importance of recognizing in school the vernacular reading cultures children inhabit in their daily lives; and for the reframing of current dichotomized debates about girls' and boys' attainment in literacy. The school-based and classroom implications of our arguments relate to the need to adopt localized strategies based on teachers developing their understanding of the cultural contexts of the pupils they teach.

It is important that we begin by saying that we accept that there are serious issues about boys' attitudes and levels of achievement in the British school system. These issues need addressing. Government-backed attention to gender-related patterns of achievement is very welcome, and we are supportive of many of the strategies for school improvement which have been drawn from the school improvement and school effectiveness research. These improvement strategies tend to be conceived on a whole-school level with the focus very firmly upon the school context and teacher behaviours. The strategies emphasize action ('Education Action Zones'; 'action planning') and aggressive intervention ('zero tolerance of failure') for whole cohorts of children. They focus upon teaching methods, teacher behaviours which will improve pupils' learning, the collection of statistical data, benchmarking performance against similar institutions, measuring progress and moving up league performance tables.

While not wishing to underestimate the importance of this perspective, we would want to argue that what gets lost in it is a focus on the differences between groups of pupils, and an acknowledgement of the central importance of pupils' cultural as well as their socio-economic backgrounds. In the first instance, as Richard Hatcher points out, 'raising levels of pupil achievement does not necessarily entail reducing educational inequalities – in fact, standards can rise while the equality gap widens' (Hatcher 1997). Within a universal, totalizing discourse about raising standards, difference tends to be simplified – so that the conceptualization of the problem comes to be seen in a simple dichotomized way as being about the relative performance of boys on the one hand and girls on the other. It is, of course, about the achievements of *some* boys and *some* girls, (see for example, Murphy and Elwood 1998a, 1998b). What we know about getting underneath these differences in order to minimize inequalities and improve achievement is that we must take account of cultural disjunctions and dissonances between home and school. It is these disjunctions which raise barriers to the success of so many groups of children.

While we believe this to be true generally, this argument is particularly important in relation to the acquisition and development of literacy. Literacy practices are both highly gendered and highly influenced by cultural background, as the ethnographic studies in this area demonstrate so clearly (Heath 1983; Street 1985; Barton and Hamilton 1998). This being the case, we need to recognize and respect children's vernacular reading cultures in school in order to understand disjunctions and dissonances which impede learning. It is not a matter of appropriating these vernacular cultures to school purposes but of building links from a foundation of everyday literacy practices and understandings, through to the more formal literacy practices of schooling. It is only by building these links from the child's home literacy background to the school literacy environment that we can hope to encourage confident, well-rounded readers who have a strong sense of their own agency and independence.

This is, of course, acknowledged in the everyday home/school reading links which virtually all British primary schools seek to develop. But this is very much a school-to-home link, with literacy defined in school terms. Our argument is for the importance of acknowledging vernacular literacies – those less formal practices linked to the fabric of everyday life – which are so often discounted in the school context by teachers and pupils alike, and for maintaining those links beyond the initial stages of learning to decode and to establish a reading habit, into the secondary school years where such routine partnerships are rare.

The *Children's Reading Choices* research offers some insights into vernacular literacies, albeit on a macro level. The findings demonstrate that when they choose to read books, both boys and girls tend to choose fiction. There is a common misconception in Britain that boys at these ages (10 to 14) read non-fiction almost exclusively. This is not borne out by the survey findings, although it is interesting to note that the overwhelming majority (78 per cent) of those few children who *do* choose to read exclusively non-fiction books are boys. But only 2 per cent of children in our survey chose non-fiction as their exclusive book reading diet.

However, when we consider non-book reading, different patterns emerge. Magazines and periodicals form a very significant part of children's reading diet. In the 1970s children read fewer periodicals as they grew older. The reverse is now true. Boys used to move from reading comics at aged 10 and 12 to showing a more 'adult' interest in sports magazines at the age of 14. Now, two decades later, boys at all three ages share a reading diet of often rather dense statistical and biographical information about football, footballers, league tables, transfer fees, computer games, prices and computer cheats. The sports magazines reflect the language and style of television sports coverage and, in doing so, reinforce a common vocabulary and set of conversational topics which can be heard among boys in playgrounds throughout Britain. The language and style is strongly gender-related, but is not, as in the past, particularly demarcated by age.

Girls' non-book reading, of magazines and periodicals, is also a very significant part of their reading diet. But while the boys' preferences here favour information-rich texts, the emphasis of the girls' magazines has changed significantly since the 1970s. The romantic prose fiction of publications like *Jackie* is long gone (see McRobbie 1984, 1988, 1997 for a very interesting analysis of these changes). Contemporary girls' magazines provide consumer information and guidance of varying kinds, but predominantly the emphasis is on story – sometimes fragmented and reframed as advice or biography – but none the less strongly narrative in focus. From the problem pages with their carefully balanced pot-pourri of condensed narratives to more extended accounts of celebrities' lives or story-based features on issues, the narrative thrust is clear.

In the interview phase of the research, children's reports of the ways in which they use these periodicals are illuminating of the differences between boys' and girls' habits. Both boys and girls report using their periodical reading to cement social relations. But while among boys this reading tends to lead to analysis of information, swapping facts and figures, scores and club histories, among girls magazine reading tends to lead to consideration of life stories, and analysis of motivation and character.

In Britain, the school reading curriculum privileges fiction from the point of children's entry at 4 or 5 to the end of compulsory schooling at 16. Children learn to read through story to the extent that being 'good at reading' often becomes synonymous with being good at reading stories. Research from the mid-1980s onwards has shown that the most highly valued forms of writing in English, the subject which is central to the school writing curriculum, are fictional narrative, varieties of 'creative' description and personal accounts, particularly those that draw strongly upon emotional involvement (White 1986; Moss 1989). These types of writing are most highly rewarded in examinations at 16 (Stobbart *et al.* 1992) and reading in these areas is carefully monitored, most commonly studied in class, and forms the bedrock of what children understand the subject 'English' to be about (Barrs and Pidgeon 1993).

Seen through this lens, it is clear that girls' vernacular literacies as they are revealed in the *Children's Reading Choices* research tend to equip them well for school literacy requirements. In their individual book reading, girls focus upon fiction. They show a particular preference for reading popular series of books which they tend to swap and share with their female friends. Their regular magazine reading is often followed up (in school and at home) by group discussion of a particular story, or analysis of a gobbet of text. These literacy habits serve girls well – they tend to adapt well to the reading curriculum because it matches their tastes and habits and school literacy practices mirror their vernacular practices.

On the other hand, boys as a group are less well adapted to school reading requirements. At all ages, they read less fiction than girls do. Their periodical reading includes more newspapers than girls' does; their magazines tend to be information rich and analytical rather than narrative in style. Interview data suggest that their social interactions around these literacy practices tend to be focused on memorizing facts and figures, rehearsing arguments, comparing and ranking performances and identifying procedures. Boys' vernacular literacies give greater emphasis to taking from the text rather than poring over it, and to analysing information rather than analysing motivation or characterization. Tom Gorman and colleagues, for example, showed in their review of research in this area in the early 1980s that at the age of 15 boys show a far stronger preference than girls do for reading books which give accurate facts, while girls show a preference for reading which helps them 'understand their own and other people's personal problems' (Gorman, 1987; Gorman *et al.* 1988). These differences affect pupils' motivation towards school-based reading, and their attainment in both reading and written response. And these gendered patterns of achievement and inclination are currently problematized as underachievement by boys which is so serious as to require urgent intervention.

But, of course, literacy is not just about an ability to read and write fiction. School definitions of literacy have been slow to change, and slow to acknowledge the changing nature of literacy in society. While there is no shortage of rhetoric on this subject, there is a shortage of practical, well-grounded work in reframing the reading curriculum and rethinking assessment criteria to promote the kinds of literacy which are required in the workplace and in the home. In terms of both the workplace and the home, the reading of non-fiction, information texts is arguably more important – or certainly as important – as the reading of fiction. For example, as computer-based reading becomes increasingly important, in the home and at work, we need to be developing readers who can select relevant information from a huge body of potentially relevant material. We need readers who can be attentive to and skilled in reading associative patterns and making links. Screen reading brings with it none of the features of closure and the sense of an ending which are classic elements of the study of fiction – the links and associations can go on indefinitely, layered one upon the other. And, in some respects, this important aspect of computer screen literacy is related to skills in reading texts on film or television screens. It is clear that the amorphous metaphor of the web is fundamentally different to the patternings of book-based literary forms. Literacy teaching about elements such as style, diction, form, audience and purpose would all need to be approached differently if it was really our intention to value and develop screen reading in school.

This is not to argue that teaching pupils to appreciate literature is unimportant. On the contrary, we regard the teaching of fiction as fundamental to the development of literacy and to establishing a sense of cultural heritage and cultural continuity. But we do need to broaden the focus of the school literacy curriculum beyond its current emphasis upon the literary and the narrative, with its tentative nods in the direction of non-fiction, media and computer literacies. It is commonplace to observe that technological change has revolutionized literacy and information supply in recent years, and it is hardly surprising that school systems are finding it difficult to accommodate to these changes, to predict future needs in the work and leisure lives of the population and to conserve what is best in the former traditions of literacy. But educationists at all levels – teachers, policy makers, administrators, researchers – need to be actively engaged in analysing what the younger generation will need to know, understand and be able to do in terms of literacy, and it is our contention that this must involve a change in the current balance and set of emphases within the curriculum.

If we were to broaden current definitions of school literacy, we might find that boys' vernacular literacies are actually serving many boys rather well, although the school system is failing to recognize or to capitalize on this. Many boys who in fact read voraciously in texts and forms unrecognized by official school curricula see themselves as non-readers. Large numbers of boys are being labelled as having literacy problems, either in their skills or attitudes, or both. Yet outside school, in their home contexts, many are able to demonstrate competence and motivation in reading, discussing and applying information which they see as relevant to their lives. On the other hand, for girls the concentration on narrative reading might actually be failing to educate them for the wide range of reading required outside the school curriculum.

The current conceptualization of the 'problem' of boys' underachievement meshes with the focus on raising achievement across the board and 'improving' whole schools; it has resulted in a great deal of activity in analysing attainment and modifying teaching strategies. But the school improvement sweep also diverts attention: away from curricular and assessment issues, away from the social and cultural background of family, peer group, class, gender and ethnicity. While it is admirable to seek to ensure that social or ethnic background are not used as excuses for underachievement in school, it is too crude to attempt to ignore them altogether. In Britain, information on pupils' social and economic backgrounds tends to be factored in to calculations of comparative results and 'value added' by the school. While this information might, in part, account for performance, it can only really *affect* performance if it is used proactively to make decisions about the curricula and teaching strategies which are appropriate to the groups of children being taught. At the level of the individual school and the individual classroom, this means beginning by investigating the reading backgrounds and habits of the pupils. It means taking these vernacular reading cultures seriously, respecting rather than disparaging what children and their families enjoy reading and writing about. The developmental work is then in building learners' self-concepts, helping them see what kind of reader and writer they already are, helping them make the links from one form of reading and writing to another, and helping them interrogate their own practices. Sustained literacy habits are based on the confidence and independence which come from seeing yourself as a reader and writer, someone who has the power to use literacy as a tool, as a means of self-expression and as a means of enjoyment.

Conclusion

A fundamental principle for us, then, is that school literacy practices should complement and enhance home and community literacy practices. When vernacular literacy practices are devalued or ignored, the child's self-concept as an independent reader and writer is damaged, and a fundamental principle of effective learning is violated. When they are acknowledged and respected, they provide the foundation of prior knowledge and experience necessary for effective teaching and learning to take place. Broad brush analyses, such as those about the 'problem' of boys' literacy levels across the school sector, are then forced to give way to more sophisticated accounts of what different groups of boys and girls can do, and of the multiple factors which intersect with gender to determine performance. One of these intersecting factors is the definition of literacy we are currently employing in our school systems.

References

Barrs, M. and Pidgeon, S. (eds) (1993) *Reading the Difference*. London: Centre for Language in Primary Education.

Barton, D. and Hamilton, M. (1998) *Local Literacies: Reading and Writing in One Community*. London: Routledge.

Cohen, Michele (1998) 'A habit of healthy idleness': boys' underachievement in historical perspective in D. Epstein, J. Elwood, V. Hey and J. Maw (eds) *Failing Boys? Issues in Gender and Achievement*. Buckingham: Open University Press.

Department for Education and Employment (2000) *Statistical Volume: Statistics of Education – Public Examinations in England 1998*. London: The Stationery Office.

Gorman, T.P. (1987) *Pupils' Attitudes to Reading*. Windsor: NFER-Nelson.

Gorman, T.P., White, J., Brook, G., Maclure, M. and Kispal, A. (1988) *Language Performance in Schools: Review of APU Language Monitoring 1979–1983*. London: HMSO.

Hall, C. and Coles, M. (1999) *Children's Reading Choices*. London: Routledge.

Hatcher, R. (1997) New labour, school improvement and racial equality. *Multicultural Teaching*, 15 (3): 8–13.

Heath, S. Brice (1983) *Ways with Words: Language, Life and Work in Communities and Classrooms*. Cambridge: Cambridge University Press.

McRobbie, A. (1988) *Feminism and Youth Culture*. London: Macmillan.

McRobbie, A. (1997) Pecs and penises: the meaning of girlie culture. *Soundings*, 5: 157–66.

McRobbie, A. and Nava, M. (1984) *Gender and Generation*. London: Macmillan.

Moss, G., (1989) *Un/Popular Fictions*. London: Virago.

Murphy, P. and Elwood, J. (1998a) Gendered experiences, choices and achievement: exploring the links. *International Journal of Inclusive Education*, 2 (2): 95–118.

Murphy, P. and Elwood, J. (1998b) Gendered learning outside and inside school: influences on achievement in D. Epstein, J. Elwood, V. Hey and J. Maw (eds) *Failing Boys? Issues in Gender and Achievement*. Buckingham: Open University Press.

Office for Standards in Education (1993) *Boys and English*. London: The Stationery Office.

Office for Standards in Education (1996) *Gender Divide: The Performance Differences between Boys and Girls at School*. London: The Stationery Office.

Qualifications and Curriculum Authority (1998) *Can Do Better: Raising Boys' Achievement in English*. London: QCA.

Stobbart, G., White, J., Elwood, J., Hayden, M. and Mason, K. (1992) *Differential Performance in Examinations at 16+: English and Mathematics*. London: Schools Examination and Assessment Council.

Street, B. (1985) *Literacy in Theory and Practice*. Cambridge: Cambridge University Press.

White, J. (1986) The writing on the wall: beginning or end of a girl's career? *Women's Studies International Forum*, 9: 561–74.

Whitehead, F., Capey, A.C., Maddren, W. and Wellings, A. (1977) *Children and their Books: The Final Report of the Schools Council Research Project on Children's Reading Habits, 10–15*. London: Macmillan.

CHAPTER 16

'I like smashing people, and I like getting smashed myself': addressing issues of masculinity in physical education and sport[1]

MICHAEL GARD

Introduction

The presence of a chapter about physical education and school sport (PE and SS) in this book may seem surprising. Certainly, apart from some elite and/ or independent boys schools[2], PE and SS have rarely, if ever, enjoyed high educational status. Research generally shows that teachers and parents feel that physical activity provides an important counterbalance to the 'real' academic work of learning to read, write and add up (Kirk *et al.* 1989; Hickey 1992; Tinning *et al.* 1993).[3] However, this implies that both physical education and school sport are only seen as valuable in terms of their effect on other school subjects. And although teachers generally support the inclusion of PE and SS, they are often the first things sacrificed to make way for 'more important' work.[4]

For their part, physical educators have struggled to agree upon a rationale for physical activity in schools (see Green 1998 for a discussion). While I stop well short of proposing a unified rationale for PE and SS in this chapter, I do make suggestions which are intended to contribute to discussions about their educational value. In particular, I argue that alternative approaches are emerging out of relatively recent school-based research and theorizing about physical education and school sport, and that these approaches have the potential to connect constructively with current concerns about boys. In this sense, PE and SS are important sites for interrogating gender in schools.

However, as the introductory chapter to this volume suggests, it is important that one states precisely which 'concerns' about boys one sees as worthy of attention. I do not hold the view that boys, as a unified group, are disadvantaged in schools, least of all in PE and SS. Rather, I take up the point made in Chapter 1 that masculinity involves the *expectation* of power and superiority over femininity, and that it is this expectation which is reinforced in dominant approaches to this subject. I argue that PE and SS can address 'concerns about boys' by providing boys and girls spaces to think and talk about the expectations and meanings they attach to certain forms of physical activity.

In the first part of the chapter, I draw on recent research which shows how PE and SS are implicated in the problems some boys create (for girls, for other boys, for teachers and for themselves) and experience in schools. For example, it is clear from this work that violent, sexist and homophobic words and actions are often rewarded and encouraged during PE and SS. And as a number of scholars have pointed out (Martino 1995a, 1995b; Haywood and Mac an Ghaill 1996; Jackson and Salisbury 1996; Gilbert and Gilbert 1998; Letts 1999), it is the *ways boys learn to be male* which presents teachers in all subjects with one of their greatest challenges.

In the second part, I present some findings from my own research with boys in order to explore further the connections between physical activity and violence, sexism and homophobia. I look at two particular types of physical activity, contact sport and dance, and suggest that the acutely gendered meanings boys associate with these activities present us with valuable clues about how we might approach the 'trouble with boys'.

I conclude by advocating the use of PE and SS in pedagogically strategic ways which explicitly take up these meanings in order to help boys find new ways of being male. In short, I argue that gender, violence, sexism and homophobia are important influences on the ways all students experience PE and SS at school, and that they need to be central to the ways educators approach these curriculum areas if they are to connect with the movement aspirations of more students.

But before discussing the part PE and SS might play in concerns about boys, I need to make two important qualifying points. First, this chapter focuses on day-to-day social interactions among students and between teachers and students during PE and SS. While I would maintain that the nature of these interactions can influence academic achievement, the suggestions I offer are in no way remedies for the profound structural inequalities experienced by socially disadvantaged children in schools. As Gilbert and Gilbert (1998) have pointed out, socio-economic class is a much better predictor of academic success than gender.

Second, in advocating a socially informed approach to PE and SS, I am not suggesting that less emphasis should be placed on *doing* physical activity or that we should abandon trying to help children develop motor skills and enjoy an active life. However, I do claim that in devoting most of our attention to a narrow range of 'traditional' games and pedagogical approaches, we invite an escalation of the problems outlined in the various chapters of this volume. To illustrate this point, I begin with some recollections from my own teaching career.

'Managing' masculinity

My first teaching job was as a secondary Personal Development, Health and Physical Education teacher at a school on what was then Sydney's far western perimeter in the early 1990s.[5] In official terms, the school was known as 'difficult to staff', presumably because of the low socio-economic status and ethnic diversity of the surrounding suburbs. The label 'difficult to staff' is one that is still used and suggested to me then, as now, something about the school's students or its location; a place where teachers are reluctant to go.

Like many early career physical education teachers, I knew a great deal about the physiological and mechanical workings of the human body. I also had at my disposal an array of practice drills, games and class formations for teaching motor skills to children. Since I was expected to teach classroom lessons on health, I had learnt the latest in fitness training, nutrition for sports performance and a little first aid. While I felt comparatively comfortable about teaching 'physical education' and 'health', the objective of 'personal development' instruction was much less clear to me, and certainly not something my teacher training had helped to clarify. In short, I saw myself as an expert in sports and fitness.

My early classroom lessons on topics like the 'healthy diet pyramid', the 'health risks of smoking', sexuality (read reproduction) and the human skeletal and muscular systems were not well received. Often they were dominated by small groups of loud, and sometimes aggressive, male students. They struggled to see the value of memorizing health facts and used discussions about reproduction as an opportunity to embarrass less assertive students. Others, equally bored, battled on heroically and quietly, often in chaotic circumstances, almost pitying my predicament. Students who attempted to engage with the material were often ridiculed, particularly if they were female or one of the quieter boys.

The story was rather different when the class moved outside or into the gymnasium. Here, the wrath of the dominant group was reserved for students who failed to show interest or skill in the sports-dominated physical education programme. As well as laziness, inferior sporting skill was attributed to sex ('girls are hopeless!'), alleged sexual orientation ('he runs like a poof!') or lack of physical courage ('don't be a wuss!'). As well as I tried to plan sports classes, physically and socially powerful children tended to dominate, tempers often ran high, and verbal and physical confrontations between students were common.

I detested the way my classes became places in which the power of certain students over others was reinforced, and yet I felt unable to stop it. Needless to say, I was also concerned about teaching the official curriculum, which I understood to consist mainly of games (which I enjoyed and had been good at) and teaching students about a 'healthy lifestyle' (which, coincidentally, seemed to match my own middle-class lifestyle). In fact, there seemed a vast gap between what I was supposed to teach and the things my students seemed to be 'learning' in every single lesson.

These memories do not simply recall the plight of a struggling first-year teacher. I eventually learnt to 'manage' my classes using discipline techniques I copied from other teachers. But the verbal and physical intimidation simply happened in less obvious ways, and continued more or less unchecked during school sport and in the playground. These memories also highlight the folly of treating the use of power by students solely as a classroom management problem, as something that was preventing me from implementing the curriculum, rather than an important part of it.

They also show that my students brought certain beliefs to classes. For my dominant boys these appeared to include the belief that boys are physically stronger and more skilful than girls, physical aggression and intimidation are legitimate ways of achieving success, and that boys who don't enjoy sports are 'gay'. For some of the other students, their behaviour seemed to be informed by the belief that it is better not to attempt something than to risk the stinging ridicule of peers, and that physical education classes can be physically and emotionally dangerous places (see Parker 1996a).

It is clear to me now that my classes were being used as 'performance spaces' in which hierarchies of power decided what kinds of performances students felt safe to give. Girls and boys, whom I had watched playing during recess and lunch breaks, would often show no interest in similar activities during physical education classes. I have no doubt that this was partly because their position in the 'movement hierarchy' called for a display which minimized the potential for derision from other students. More fundamentally, PE and SS provided the 'terrain' in which male 'performances' of aggression and contempt for others met with success and approval, particularly by other similarly inclined boys. When I attempted to teach activities like dance, which arguably place far less value on aggression than team sports, I was accused of 'favouring the girls'. A boy once told me that dance was 'boring' and that physical education should be fun, to compensate for the boredom of all the other subjects.

The gendered terrain of schools

Regardless of what conclusions readers might make about my teaching skill, it is clear that my experiences have been shared by many other teachers. Numerous studies (see below), using a variety of research methods, have shown how PE and SS can produce, maintain and legitimize the domination of symbolic and physical school space by particular groups of mostly male students. Unfortunately, this research is often misinterpreted as suggesting that sports and games, or even boys, are inherently bad. What it actually shows is that schools are similar to other places were people interact; they have their own cultures, which are never identical from one school to the next, and which are not experienced in the same ways by the people within them.

For example, Thorne (1993) and Renold (1997) have shown how the domination of school-organized sport and playground games in primary schools can position some boys as feminine or 'gay' if they aren't part of the dominant sporting groups. At the school Renold studied, male staff members colluded with the soccer-playing boys to define other boys who didn't play soccer as weak or 'gay'. In both Renold's and Thorne's work, girls' activities were seen as less important than boys' sport and received much less recognition within the school.

In Australia, Wright (1996) has argued that the practices of PE and SS help to construct boys as active and physically competent, and girls as passive and unskilled. Based on detailed analysis of interactions between teachers and students during PE and SS instruction, Wright concludes that: '(p)hysical education and sport seem to be powerful sites for the visible demonstration of male and female differences as the antithesis of one another' (1996: 76). Parker's (1996a) research in an English boys' school found that physical education lessons provided opportunities for dominant groups to enact ritualized violence against other groups. He also found that many boys 'equate lack of sporting prowess with homosexuality' (p. 149).

In the United States, Hasbrook (1999) has shown that, even among very young children, boys are aware of the pressure to demonstrate superior physical strength and sporting prowess, while denigrating girls'. In fact, Hasbrook's work found boys avoiding challenges with girls whom they knew to be physically superior, and girls hiding their own physical capacities, partly to avoid embarrassing male students. Writing in the Canadian context, Kidd (1987, 1995) argues that many children's experience of sport is marked by physical abuse and prejudice on the grounds of gender, race and sexual orientation.

It would obviously be dangerous to conclude from this research that PE and SS are responsible for generating violence, sexism, racism and homophobia where none previously existed. However, a robust case now exists for recognizing sport's 'exemplary status' (Connell 1995: 30) in the construction of western masculinities. That is, the behaviours of male students that many schools are currently finding most problematic are an integral and valued part of sport and, by extension, physical education. This is not to argue that PE and SS have to be this way. Rather, it is to draw attention to the ways PE and SS are currently *practised*. It is also to acknowledge that students bring a great deal of 'knowledge' about sport to school, and that some of this knowledge is potentially harmful.

In 1999 I went 'back to school', this time as a researcher with my colleague Robert Meyenn.[6] We wanted to get underneath the categories of 'physical education' and 'sport' and to know more about the gendered meanings boys associate with different forms of physical activity. In the next section I present two aspects of the research findings; the ways these boys talked about contact sport and dance. My purpose here is to build upon the research summarized above, and to point to potential new directions in PE and SS pedagogy which I take up in the chapter's conclusion.

Talking and performing masculinity

'Enough' contact

The research took place in two New South Wales secondary schools and involved small focus group interviews with 23 boys aged between 12 and 14.[7] Both schools were well known for producing successful male contact sports teams. The boys were asked to comment on video-taped footage of various sports and dance forms and to discuss their own physical activity preferences.

A great deal of the discussion focused on physical safety. Some boys avoided sports in which they felt the risk of injury was too high. Others, like Tom, initially talked with relish about brutal body contact within his favourite sport, rugby league:

MG: What do you like about rugby league?
Tom: I like being in a sport but contact sport, 'cos I like smashing people, and I like getting smashed myself and [pause]
MG: Why do you like being smashed?
Tom: I dunno I just do, um [pause]
MG: Does it hurt?
Tom: Sometimes.
MG: Is that fun?
Tom: Not really.
MG: So I'm interested to know why you like being hurt.
Tom: Oh well I don't really I just, if I get hurt I get hurt, if I don't, I don't. That's just well, rugby league. You can get hurt fairly easily, but if you do you just, bit of bad luck but if you don't you just, it's all right.

In the next passage, Shane and Laurie demonstrate a clear understanding that inflicting a certain level of pain is an important part of success in contact sport, in this case rugby league:

Shane: Well if you just like hurt 'em enough so that they don't wanna run it again, that way you can just build up enough that you win the game.
Laurie: You sorta . . .
Shane: But like if you hit 'em, if you stop, hit 'em hard enough then they don't wanna run it again and then they start runnin' soft and they don't wanna score tries.[8]
Laurie: Yeah you, you intimidate them sorta.

One reading of these two passages is that the boys are, in fact, very concerned about safety when playing rugby league, both for themselves and for other players. All three boys imply that injury is not desirable. Tom says he likes 'being smashed' but doesn't want to get 'hurt', which I interpret here to include physical injury as well as pain. Shane says he wants to hurt his opponents 'enough', while Laurie only wants to go as far as intimidating them. The problem that arises is that the line between 'enough' and 'too much' body contact and intimidation is impossibly blurred. It is likely to be different for children with different body shapes and sizes, levels of motivation, reasons for playing and knowledge of the game. It might also change according to the standard of the game or whether it is being played indoors or outdoors. Furthermore, most people involved in contact sports understand that serious injuries are common even when all players respect the laws of the game. So knowing how much body contact is 'enough' doesn't guarantee safety.

If we put to one side the possibility of players deliberately setting out to injure one another, the sporting contests these boys describe involve making rapid and complex decisions about appropriate levels of body contact and intimidation. My experience as a teacher and a coach of young people is that some get the level right and others don't. It is also worth remembering that the words 'aggression' and 'intimidation' are freely used in non-contact as well as contact sports. The crucial point here is that, as we saw earlier, success at sport is a significant factor in determining hierarchies of power in schools, particularly for boys. This raises the stakes in sports participation for many boys and becomes a crucial factor for 'deciding' how much body contact, intimidation or aggression is appropriate. Given the high stakes, we should not be surprised when many boys get the level wrong. We should also not be surprised when boys fail to realize that aggressive behaviour which is encouraged and rewarded on the sporting field is inappropriate off it. After all, our world is full of images and stories of men using aggression and intimidation to achieve success in many other fields of endeavour besides sport.

In terms of teaching practice, these passages remind us that many physical education and sports teachers impress upon their students the need to play safely and respectfully, but far fewer explicitly address the construction of socially powerful male identities as an obstacle to achieving this goal. That is, despite the apparently close relationship between aggressive masculinity and sport, aggressive masculinity is more likely to be seen as an obstacle to curriculum implementation, rather than an issue to be addressed by it.

Dance and homophobia

One potential approach to the issues raised by discussing contact sport is to offer a broader range of movement options, particularly in physical education. Some educators have argued that including dance in physical education programmes brings some much needed balance to the range of movement experiences children are offered. But while most official physical education syllabus documents include dance strands, it is clear that school programmes are usually dominated by sports, and that some include little or no dance.

While a number of explanations for this have been suggested, it is apparent that sports-minded physical education teachers have tended to feel uncomfortable about teaching dance.[9] Talbot (1997) has argued that this has been compounded by teacher anxieties about adverse male students' reactions towards learning dance. On one level, these anxieties seem to be well founded. Consider the following passage taken from the same research described in the previous section. In this passage the boys have just seen some footage of male ballet dancers and agreed among themselves that they look 'stupid':

MG:	So like the guy with the ballet, the ballet guys in the tights they look stupid?
Murray:	Mmm.
Jeremy:	You look like something out of the Gay and Lesbian Mardi Gras if you're wearing tights.
MG:	Mmhm, so what's the problem with that?
Murray:	Gays (all laugh).
MG:	Mmhm, so the ballet, wearing the tights in the ballet makes you look gay?
Jeremy:	Yep.
Terry:	Yep.
MG:	OK, let's take away the tights; does it still look gay?
Terry:	Yep.
Murray:	Yep.
MG:	And what is it about it that makes it look gay?
Murray:	It just looks like, it looks, you look like a girl sort of thing like . . .
Terry:	Yeah 'cos it, you're sort of associated with women's sports and . . .
Murray:	Yeah, it's, twirling round like little, yeah, little oh . . .
MG:	No, I understand what you're saying.
Murray:	Twirling round like little girlies sort of thing.
MG:	Mmhm.
Murray:	That's what you . . .
MG:	OK, so is, um, looking gay the same as being gay?
Terry:	Probably not.
MG:	So if you go . . . if you're doing the ballet in the tights and you just say that looks gay, is that the same as being gay?
Murray:	It just depends if they're gay or not, like, 'cos if they were gay they would look gay as well. [Jeremy laughs]
Murray:	Yeah.
MG:	So all gay people look gay? [All laugh]
Terry:	Sometimes you can usually tell.
MG:	Huh?
Terry:	Sometimes you just [unclear] can tell.

MG: Right, 'cos, um, a lot of the ballet dancers are gay, but a lot of
           them are straight as well, but they all wear the tights. So how
           can you tell the straight ones from the gay ones?
Terry: Oh it's probably like . . .
Jeremy: The way they talk and that.

As the transcription indicates, this section of my interview with Terry,
Jeremy and Murray included a lot of laughter. The boys were friends, played
sport together and rarely disagreed with each other's comments during the
interview. Often they would look and smile at each other before and after
speaking. In particular, they struggled to find the words to discuss homosexuality, despite their apparent 'knowledge' about it ('you can usually tell',
'the way they talk and that'), and regularly stopped mid-sentence and looked
to one another for support. It was as if they wanted to explain everything by
saying 'you know what I mean', 'surely you understand', but hesitated,
because they knew, by this stage of the interview, I would ask them to
explain what they meant. My failure to laugh when Murray said 'gays'
seems to have positioned me outside their 'circle of knowledge', knowledge
which they communicated with looks, laughter and by simply using the
word 'gay'.

It is very difficult to know how much reflects the boys' 'true' opinions
and how much was part of a 'performance' for each other and for me. But
performance or not, it is clear that the boys share 'knowledge' which relates
how bodies move and how they are dressed to the sexual orientation of the
mover. In this case, the boys associated ballet movements and tight clothes
with male homosexuality. It is equally clear that, as a group, they have
decided that homosexuality is a bad thing and that it is 'written' upon the
bodies of 'gay' people. Jeremy's final comment ('the way they talk and
that') suggests that the way a male speaks is also an important factor when
boys decide who is 'gay' and who is not.

These comments would seem to offer rich material for physical educators
who want to challenge these 'knowledges' and offer students more than a
diet of sport, but who may be concerned about student resistance. In the
past, some educators have suggested trying to overcome this resistance by
offering boys 'non-sissy' dance experiences (Lloyd and West 1988; Crawford
1994), that is, dance that does not 'indicate' homosexuality. The result of
this tends to be dance that looks like sport, or dance that looks like fighting,
or dance that presents the dancer as sexually attracted to females. These
approaches simply restate the association of sports with heterosexual 're-
spectability' and dance with homosexuality and deviance. It is no surprise,
then, that many forms of dance such as ballet and creative dance are still
not popular among boys, and that homosexuality is still viewed by many
boys as outside the limits of 'normal' sexuality.

I would argue that these comments, plus the existing research cited above,
leave us with little choice but to acknowledge that different forms of physical

activity 'carry' meanings for many, if not all, students. Of course, these meanings will not be the same for every student. Three of the boys in our research said they would like to dance in physical education, but thought other boys would probably object. But the fact that not all boys agree offers scope for engaging students in discussions about this issue.

Therefore, in order to make a wider range of activities available to students, we might ask them to think about and talk about *why* certain activities are or are not acceptable. As researchers such as Wright (1996), Parker (1996b), Martino (1999) and Ingham and Dewar (1999) have clearly shown, boys and girls know a great deal about these issues. For example, some of the boys in Martino's study (1999) were able to articulate how the 'cool boys' use sporting prowess to consolidate their power *within* their own peer groups, and power *over* other groups. The crucial point is that having students discuss issues related to masculinity, femininity and PE and SS has the potential to draw on knowledge that students *already have*. And it is precisely these kinds of discussions, where they engage in critical self-reflection, which many boys find most difficult; not because they have nothing to say but because being a boy is so much about performing for others, rather than talking about and reflecting on the performance.

Finally, the passage also offers possibilities for discussions about gender-appropriate physical activity. The boys repeatedly associate ballet with females as a means of emphasizing their dislike for the activity. This is significant because most (though not all) of the boys in the study agreed that females should be allowed to play traditionally male sports, including contact sports. Far fewer were prepared to be involved in an activity like ballet which, as Terry says, were seen as 'women's sports'. This suggests that some boys see 'women's sports' as inferior and therefore not appropriate for boys. I would argue that they indicate an underlying belief in inherent female physical inferiority and contribute to the continued marginalization of women's sport. It is also not difficult to see how these kinds of views might severely restrict the sorts of activities teachers feel confident to offer students or that boys and girls feel confident to try.

In summary, I am suggesting something that many physical educators will find controversial. I am suggesting that by providing safe and supportive classroom environments in which the kinds of discussions I have described can take place, teachers may be doing far more to broaden the 'movement horizons' of *all* students than simply by doing physical activity. In fact, I suspect that simply offering students a variety of activities, in the hope that the activities themselves will appeal to students, will alter the views of very few students. We need to remember that physical activity *always* happens within a social context; a context which is shaped, to a large extent, by the meanings students bring to different activities. Put simply, I am suggesting that we need to help boys and girls feel that it is 'OK' to use their bodies in ways which do not conform to gender stereotypes, and that very often this will involve more than simply doing physical activity during class time.

Conclusion

Although physical education is not always explicitly tied to 'personal development' strands of study as it is in New South Wales, there is general agreement that 'well being' is a multifaceted concept, and that the emotional, social and spiritual aspects of health and physical activity are as important as knowing *how* to move one's body. There is growing awareness that for children to enjoy and learn from physical activity, it must be physically and emotionally safe and connect with children's more general aspirations in life. These might include fun, friendship, success or fitness. There can be no doubt that for a significant proportion of children, PE and SS has not fulfilled these requirements, and that this is true for far more girls than boys. This is partly because PE and SS have been areas of school life in which certain kinds of boys have dominated and in which certain behaviours have been rewarded. I well remember teaching colleagues suggesting to me that teaching physical education must be easy because the 'kids' enjoy it. The reality is that physical education teaching can be a very demanding job because many students don't enjoy it, and would prefer to be somewhere else. Therefore with these points in mind, I offer the following suggestions.

First, I suggest we be clear with students that the purpose of physical education is more than learning how to do physical activity so that we can incorporate it into our lives. We need to teach explicitly about the ways physical activity is not enjoyed equally by all members of society, discuss the various reasons why this is so, and to make addressing these inequalities a stated purpose of physical education. This way, addressing violence, sexism, homophobia and racism in physical education are less likely to be seen as the 'mission' of particular teachers. Instead, they become an embedded rationale for the subject's existence.

Second, 'personal development'[10] should be practised as an inextricable part of physical education, whether it exists as an official syllabus component or not. In the past, 'personal development' has tended to be thought of as a series of *separate* topics, such as 'decision making' and 'lifestyle choices'. I propose that discussion of the ways students experience physical education, the physical activity itself and the social interactions which surround it, should be an explicit part of the official or unofficial 'personal development' work we do with children.

Third, since sport is a highly significant institution within western societies, I propose that we avoid *simply playing sport*; that, as much as possible, the act of doing sport is embedded within a broader pedagogy, not simply a thing done by itself and for its own sake. We should provide children with the opportunity to talk about sport, think about it, write about it, draw about it, and reflect on the whole experience of it, and not just the skills needed to do it better.

Fourth, if students are invited to reveal their feelings about physical education and school sport, it is vital that this happens in a safe environment. For example, for a boy to voice his dislike of sport may be an invitation to homophobic abuse from other students. This is why ongoing discussions with students about the purpose of physical education becomes an important first step. It may be that open discussion is not the most appropriate way for these matters to be raised. But whatever methods teachers adopt, the important point is that students need to know that it is 'OK' to dislike or be less skilled at particular forms of physical activity. Indeed, this may be the one message that makes the biggest difference to the amount of pleasure students derive from physical activity at school.

Readers will notice that I have said very little in this chapter about the specific problems boys are creating and experiencing in schools. This is partly because most popular concern about boys has focused on classroom-based subjects, particularly mathematics and English, topics which are covered elsewhere in this volume. I have been more intent on showing that the ways PE and SS are currently practised tend to favour certain forms of masculinity (interested in sport, aggressive, heterosexual) and that this has implications for all students and teachers. Therefore, my final suggestion is that physical education be used as a means of highlighting human diversity, as opposed to glossing over it. For example, this could include pedagogical consideration of events and issues which make obvious connections between physical activity and human diversity, such as the Women's Olympics, the Gay Games and the enduring presence of racism in sport. As the interview excerpt with Terry, Jeremy and Murray (above) suggests, many students (and adults) do not even have a vocabulary to talk about topics such as sexual diversity. As King and Schneider (1999) argue, while these topics remain silenced, insults like 'gay' and 'wuss' will retain their power to limit the range of acceptable ways of being a boy or a girl.

Of course, there are teachers who already teach in ways that critically examine the social meanings and consequences of PE and SS. The suggestions I make here are inevitably a synthesis of the work and ideas emanating from a community of students, teachers and researchers. My hope is that this chapter will play a small part in the process of disseminating ideas and stimulating discussion.

The search for a coherent and unified educational rationale for physical activity in schools has probably been an unrealistic and, in some senses, unnecessarily time-consuming preoccupation. It may well be that we are best served in accepting that human societies are constantly changing and that the purpose of education will be a similarly dynamic and highly contested process. Therefore, I have attempted to make the case here that physical education and sport teachers should be involved in the daunting but important task of helping students to make sense of the complex and changing social world they inhabit, and of making connections with people who are unlike themselves.

Notes

1 I would like to acknowledge and thank Mark Falcous for his insightful comments during the preparation of this chapter.

2 Here, sporting success rather than physical education has tended to be seen as an important part of the institution's reputation and prestige, or as a means of building 'character' among upper middle class white males. Both Chandler (1996) and Kirk (1998) provide excellent discussions of the 'games ethic' which emerged out of the English boys' public schools of the nineteenth century.

3 This is not to deny the existence of less mainstream approaches which explicitly use movement to teach numeracy and literacy to children, outside the classroom, without pencils or paper. However, these approaches remain marginal to more traditional pedagogies.

4 For example, there are anecdotal signs that the recent intensification of concern for primary school literacy levels in England has resulted in less time being devoted to physical activity (see Goodbody 1999).

5 Personal Development, Health and Physical Education is a discrete and, in theory, integrated key learning area in New South Wales, Australia's most populous state.

6 Some of this research has been published in Gard and Meyenn (2000).

7 All the names used here are pseudonyms.

8 The object of the game of rugby league.

9 This appears to be more of a problem for male teachers than females (Brennan 1996).

10 I am conscious of critiques of the term 'personal development', particularly those which argue that it suggests that problems can be overcome simply by individual effort to be a 'better person'. I use it here strategically to indicate that it can be 'co-opted' and that the suggestions I make here can be accommodated within existing curriculum frameworks.

References

Brennan, D. (1996) Dance in the Northern Ireland physical education curriculum: a farsighted policy or an unrealistic innovation? *Women's Studies International Forum*, 19 (5): 493–503.

Chandler, T.J.L. (1996) The structuring of manliness and the development of rugby football at the public schools and Oxbridge, 1830–1880, in T.J.L. Chandler and J. Nauright (eds) *Making Men: Rugby and Masculine Identity*. London: Frank Cass and Co.

Connell, R.W. (1995) *Masculinities*. St. Leonards: Allen and Unwin.

Crawford, J.R. (1994) Encouraging male participation in dance. *Journal of Physical Education, Recreation and Dance*, 65 (2): 40–3.

Gard, M. and Meyenn, R. (2000) Boys, bodies, pleasure and pain: interrogating contact sports in schools. *Sport, Education and Society*, 5 (1): 19–34.

Gilbert, R. and Gilbert, P. (1998) *Masculinity Goes to School*. St. Leonards: Allen and Unwin.

Goodbody, J. (1999) Why PE is in decline. *The Times*, 6 April.

Green, K. (1998) Philosophies, ideologies and the practice of physical education, *Sport, Education and Society*, 3 (2): 125–43.

Hasbrook, C.A. (1999) Young children's social constructions of physicality and gender, in J. Coakley and P. Donnelly (eds) *Inside Sports*. London: Routledge.

Haywood, C. and Mac an Ghaill, M. (1996) Schooling masculinities, in M. Mac an Ghaill (ed.) *Understanding Masculinities: Social Relations and Cultural Arenas*. Buckingham: Open University Press.

Hickey, C. (1992) Physical education in Victorian primary schools: a review of current provision. *ACHPER National Journal*, 138: 18–23.

Ingham, A.G. and Dewar, A. (1999) Through the eyes of youth: 'deep play' in peewee ice hockey, in J. Coakley and P. Donnelly (eds) *Inside Sports*. London: Routledge.

Jackson, D. and Salisbury, J. (1996) Why should secondary schools take working with boys seriously? *Gender and Education*, 8 (1): 103–15.

Kidd, B. (1987) Sports and masculinity, in M. Kaufman (ed.) *Beyond Patriarchy: Essays by Men on Pleasure, Power, and Change*. Toronto: Oxford University Press.

Kidd, B. (1995) Inequality in sport, the corporation, and the state: an agenda for social scientists. *Journal of Sport and Social Issues*, 19 (3): 232–48.

King, J.R. and Schneider, J.J. (1999) Locating a place for gay and lesbian themes in elementary reading, writing and talking, in W.J. Letts and J.T. Sears (eds) *Queering Elementary Education: Advancing the Dialogue about Sexualities and Schooling*. New York, NY: Rowman and Littlefield.

Kirk, D. (1998) *Schooling Bodies: School Practice and Public Discourse 1880–1950*. London: Leicester University Press.

Kirk, D., Colquhoun, D. and Gore, J. (1989) Teachers' perceptions of the effects of daily physical education on their students. *ACHPER National Journal*, 123: 13–16.

Letts, W.J. (1999) How to make 'boys' and 'girls' in the classroom: the heteronormative nature of elementary-school science, in W.J. Letts and J.T. Sears (eds) *Queering Elementary Education: Advancing the Dialogue about Sexualities and Schooling*. New York, NY: Rowman and Littlefield.

Lloyd, M.L. and West, B.H. (1988) Where are the boys in dance? *Journal of Physical Education, Recreation and Dance*, 59 (5): 47–51.

Martino, W. (1995a) Boys and literacy: exploring the construction of hegemonic masculinities and the formation of literate capacities for boys in the English class-room. *English in Australia*, 112: 11–24.

Martino, W. (1995b) Deconstructing masculinity in the English classroom: a site for reconstituting gendered subjectivity. *Gender and Education*, 7 (2): 205–20.

Martino, W. (1999) 'Cool boys', 'party animals', 'squids' and 'poofters': interrogating the dynamics and politics of adolescent masculinities in school. *British Journal of Sociology of Education*, 20 (2): 239–63.

Parker, A. (1996a) The construction of masculinity within boys' physical education. *Gender and Education*, 8 (2): 141–57.

Parker, A. (1996b) Sporting masculinities: gender relations and the body, in M. Mac an Ghaill (ed.) *Understanding Masculinities: Social Relations and Cultural Arenas*. Buckingham: Open University Press.

Renold, E. (1997) 'All they've got in their brains is football.' Sport, masculinity and the gendered practices of playground relations. *Sport, Education and Society*, 2 (1): 5–23.

Talbot, M. (1997) Physical education and the national curriculum: some political issues, in G. McFee and A. Tomlinson (eds) *Sport and Leisure: Connections and Controversies*. Aachen: Meyer and Meyer Verlag.

Thorne, B. (1993) *Gender Play: Girls and Boys in School*. New Brunswick: Rutgers University Press.

Tinning, R., Kirk, D. and Evans, J. (1993) *Learning to Teach Physical Education*. Englewood Cliffs, NJ: Prentice-Hall.

Wright, J. (1996) The construction of complementarity in physical education. *Gender and Education*, 8 (1): 61–79.

Index

n indicates an endnote.

Aboriginal students, *see* indigenous boys
(Australia)
adolescence
changes in, 13
risk taking in, 54–5, 57–8
uses of humour, 110
see also boys' comments
African American boys
at Haverford School, 49–50
inequalities in schooling, 140–1
school expulsions, 59
see also black boys; black masculinities
Afrocentric models of masculinity, 143
aimlessness
curriculum, 163
post-school, 159, 160
America, *see* United States (US)
Asian boys, 34, 48–9
assertiveness
in group work, 192–3
in sports classes, 224–5
see also power
Australia, 5, 7–11, 14, 29, 82, 203
New South Wales (NSW)
gender equity strategy, 67–8
Ministry of Education, 10, 170–1,
174, 176, 179

studies, *see* discipline; indigenous boys
(Australia); physical education and
school sports (PESS); risk taking

bad behaviour, 169–70
discipline, 171–8
girls' perceptions of, 131–2
Bergh, M. *et al.*, 49
Bhabha, H.K., 51
Biddulph, S., 54–5
bikers, 56, 59
biographies, 68–76
analysis, 76–8
see also boys' comments; interviews
biological explanations, 12–13, 194
vs cultural, 17–18, 55
black boys
interviews, 144–6, 149
middle school project, 143–4
popular, 145, 146
specific characteristics, 141–2
teachers' influence on, 148–50
victims of labels, 147–8, 150
see also African American boys
black masculinities, 60, 142–3
Bleach, K. *et al.*, 5, 6
'boy code', 13–15
boyhood, as therapeutic opportunity,
13–16

boys' comments
  Aboriginal, 159–64
  African American, 144–6, 149
  on heterosexuality, 98–9
  on homophobia, 97, 100–1, 102–3, 104
  on masculinity, 55–6, 57, 83–91
  on peers, 43, 44–5, 46
  on physical education, 227–8, 229–30
  on school practices, 40–3
  on showing emotions, 83, 84
  on subjects, 14
  on teasing, 57
  see also biographies; interviews
'boys will be boys' discourse, 4, 5
bullying, 178–9
Butler, J., 31, 32–3, 97
Byers, S., 2

Canaan, J., 56
Canada, 155, 226
childhood, conceptions of, 29–30
Children's Reading Choices survey, 213–15, 217, 218
collaboration, 132, 192
comics/magazines/periodicals, 215, 217–18
'competing victim syndrome', 58, 82–3, 96, 169, 170
computer screen literacy, 219
'conformist-blindness', 156
Connell, R.W.
  bikers, 59
  on boys' programmes, 38, 193
  'emphasized femininities', 99
  on gender relations, 7, 31, 178
  'masculinity therapy', 8
  'protest masculinity', 172
  on school science, 187–8, 194
  on schools and teachers, 26, 28, 38, 39, 43
  sports, 226
'cool' masculinity, 69, 70
Cox, E., 58, 96, 169
cultural influences, 88–9, 141
cultural perspectives, 177–82
cultural support, 158–9, 160–3
cultural transformations, 25–31, 178–9
cultural *vs* biological explanations, 17–18, 55
'culture of cruelty', 13, 14–15

curriculum
  aimlessness, 163
  hidden, 189
  inappropriate, 173
  UK, 3
  see also subjects
'cussing matches', 112–13, 114

dance, and homophobia, 229–32
David, M., 3
Davies, B., 133, 187, 188, 200
discipline, 171–8
Donaldson, M., 41

Education Acts, UK, 2–3
education journals
  Australia, 8, 10
  UK, 2, 5, 7, 9, 10
educational restructuring
  Australia, 10–11
  UK, 2–3, 25–7, 28, 30–1
educational underachievement, 2–4
  and disadvantage, 7–8, 9–11
  'failing boys' discourse, 4–6, 14, 25
Eltis, K., 176
emasculinization
  feminization of boys, 12, 14
  of risk taking, 62–3
  of work, 120–1
emotional display, 83–5
emotional literacy, 47–9
England, *see* United Kingdom (UK)
entrepreneurism, 27–8
Epstein, D. *et al.*, 4, 5, 25
ethical and moral issues, 11
exclusion/suspension from school, 59, 60–1, 169

'failing boys' discourse, 4–6, 14, 25
family support, 160–1
fathers, 84–5
femininity, accusations of, 188–9, 224, 225, 226
feminism/feminists, 4, 5, 13, 17–18
  backlash, 7, 8, 11, 12
  research, 6, 35
feminization of boys, 12, 14
  see also emasculinization
football, 5, 87–8
Francis, B., 125
Franklin, B., 29

games, 225, 226
  punch 'n' run, 114–15, 122*n*
gay issues, *see* homophobia; homosexuality
gender awareness programmes, 46–50
  see also programmes for boys
gender differences, 133
  literacy, 212–13, 216
  mathematics, 207–9
  physical education, 225–7
  uses of schooling, 9
  see also science
gender relations, 31, 132–4, 178
Gerwitz, S., 29
Gilbert, P., 8
Gilbert, R. and Gilbert, P., 186, 201
Gilligan, J., 17
girls, 132–4
  cultural expectations of, 89–91, 99–100
  deficit framework, 10
  dominance of/superiority over, 56–7
  emotional literacy, 83
  gender awareness programme, 47
  lesbian, 35
  literacy, 212–13, 218
  needs, 6
  opinions of boys, 126–8, 129, 131–2
  resistance, 125
  risk taking, 62
  sensibleness of, 134–7
  successes, 8–9, 14
  'tomboys', 102
  uses of schooling, 9
  white, attitudes of black boys to,
    145–6
Giroux, H.A., 49, 180
Gore, J.M., 177
Greene, M., 51
group work, science, 191–3
Grundy, S. and Hatton, E., 181–2
Gurian, M., 12, 13

Hatcher, R., 216
Haverford School, The
  'Haverford Man', 42, 45
  interviews, 39–46
  'lifers' *vs* 'recruits', 44–6, 49–50
  programme for boys, 46–51
hegemonic masculinity, 41, 171–2, 188,
    192, 193
heterosexism, 97–106
'heterosexual matrix', 32–3, 97

heterosexualization of learning cultures,
    126–8
Hey, V., 92
homophobia, 33, 57, 62, 63, 86
  and dance, 229–32
  and heterosexism, 100–2
  in humour, 119–20
homosexuality, 35
  accusations of, 86, 147–8, 224, 226,
    233
  biography, 73–6
  interviews, 100–1, 102–4
  Section 28 (Local Government Act
    1988), 30, 36*n*, 97, 108*n*
  support for students, 102–4
  teachers, 105–6
humour
  'classic stories', 115–20
  girls' opinions, 127, 128, 129
  global/local context of study, 111–12,
    121–2
  and masculinity, 112–15
  uses of, 110–11, 120–1

identity, 5
  black masculinities, 60, 142–3
  formation, 32, 33, 173
  and image, 42
  indigenous boys, 156–7, 160–1
  marginalized groups, 35
  and power, 41, 173
  teachers, 27–8
indigenous boys (Australia)
  arrest rate, 59
  interviews, 159–64
  school participation and retention,
    155–6
  theoretical underpinnings, 156–9
infants, 98–9
insults, 112–14
interviews
  black boys, 144–6, 149
  girls, 126–8, 129, 130, 131–2
  Haverford School, 39–46
  homosexual boys, 100–1, 102–4
  indigenous boys, 159–64
  teachers, 105–6, 112, 174, 175, 176–7
  see also biographies; boys' comments

Johnson, R., 28
Johnson, W., 7–8

Kenway, J., 4, 53, 178–9
Kenway, J. and Willis, S., 177–8, 183
Kindlon, D. and Thompson, M., 13, 14–15

'lads' movement', 4
Ladson-Billings, G., 193
language, 30–1
    'cussing matches', 112–13, 114
    mathematical, 200–9
    and power, 192–3
    and violence, 172–3
    see also literacy
Lebanese-Australian boys, 172–3
Lees, S., 101–2
Lemke, J.L., 201
Letts, W., 194
Levinson, M., 47
Lingard, B. and Douglas, P., 5
literacy
    concerns, 212–13
    fiction *vs* information texts, 218–20
    voluntary/vernacular reading, 213–20
    see also language

Mac an Ghaill, M., 101–2
    Redman, P. and, 33–4
McLean, C., 58, 62, 173
magazines/comics/periodicals, 215, 217–18
male disadvantage discourse, 7–8, 9–11
male role models, *see* role models, male
male stereotypes, 86–8, 173
male teachers, 6, 40, 41, 86
    homosexual, 105–6
Manhood (story), 86–7
Maori students, 155
marginalized groups, *see* homosexuality;
    race
market economics, 26
    and entrepreneurism, 27–8
Martino, W., 14, 43–4
masculine practices, 43–4, 46
masculinity
    Afrocentric models, 143
    black, 60, 142–3
    boys' comments on, 55–6, 57, 83–91
    'cool', 69, 70
    and cultural transformations, 25–31,
        178–9
    different/multiple, 31–2, 34–5, 44–6,
        63–4, 106–7
        lessons in, 150–1

hegemonic, 41, 171–2, 188, 192, 193
    and humour, 112–15
    indigenous boys, 156–7
    and physical education, 224–5, 227–32
    problems of, 8, 12
    protest, 172
    and race, 34–5, 58–61, 63
    'real' boyness, 16–17, 32–4
    and school science, 187–8
    and school sport, 224–5, 227–32
    and sexuality, 30–1
    social organization of, 55–6
    subordinated, 157
    traditional, 13–15, 28, 69–70, 83–5, 172
    and violence, 16–17, 55–6, 171–2,
        178–9
    working class, 56, 59, 110–11, 120,
        121–2
    see also assertiveness; biological
        explanations; emasculinization;
        power; remasculinization
'masculinity therapy', 8
mathematics
    classroom talk, 203–7
    language-sensitive approach, 207–9
    as masculine discourse, 200–1
    metaphor/metonymics/modality, 201–7
media
    children's reading, 215, 217–18
    'queer ads', 107
    reports, 2, 8, 9
        of violence in schools, 169, 170
    see also education journals
metaphor/metonymics/modality of
        mathematical language, 201–7
middle-class boys, *see* privileged boys
middle-class girls, 126–8
    vs working-class girls, 128–31
middle-class masculinity, 59–60
    occupations, 58
middle school project, black boys, 143–4
Mills, M., 29, 86
misogyny, 57, 62, 63
modality/metaphor/metonymics of
        mathematical language, 201–7
moral and ethical issues, 11
moral panic, 2, 7, 30, 97
mother insults, 112–14

National Curriculum, UK, 3
national league tables, UK, 3–4

National Literacy Strategy, UK, 213
'nerds', 127
New South Wales (NSW), *see under* Australia
New Zealand, 155

Office for Standards in Education (Ofsted),
    212

Paechter, C., 189
Pallotta-Chiarolli, M., 173
pathologizing of normal boys, 12
pedagogies
    challenging, 76–8, 91–3
    competitive, 126
    productive, 177–8
    see also teacher(s)
peer(s)
    'boy code', 13–14
    hypermasculine behaviours, 83, 85
    insults, 112–14
    mock fighting, 114–15
    out of school, 159, 163
    post-compulsory years, 161–2
    responses to homosexuality, 73–5
    and risk taking, 55–8, 62
    rivalries, 43–6, 49–50
    support, 47–9
    see also humour
Penn, H., 6
'performance spaces', 225
periodicals/comics/magazines, 215, 217–18
personal development, 232–3
physical education and school sport
        (PESS)
    and gender, 225–7
    and masculinity, 224–5, 227–32
    see also sports
Pollack, W., 13
'poor boys' discourse, 4, 5, 91
popular boys
    black, 145, 146
    'sexy', 127, 141
populist discourses, *see* media
post-colonial countries, 155, 165
post-compulsory years, 156, 157, 158–9,
        160–3
post-school aimlessness, 159, 160
post-school rewards, 9, 10
power, 84, 85, 91, 92
    and identity, 41, 173
    and language, 192–3

and resistance, 35, 174–6
    techniques of, 177
    theories of, 32
    see also assertiveness
power relations, 177–8
Poynting, S. *et al.*, 172–3
presumptive equality, 7
primary school study, UK, 124–39
privileged boys, 67–8
    biographies, 68–76
pro-feminist approaches, 6
professionalism, new, 27–8, 29
programmes for boys
    birthday cards, 53–4, 55
    Haverford School, 46–51
    race issues, 48–50, 142–3, 149–50
    'recuperative masculinity' strategies, 5,
        6, 7
    resources, 7–8, 63
protest masculinity, 172
punch 'n' run, 114–15, 122*n*

'queer ads', 107

race, 2, 4, 16
    Asian boys, 34, 48–9
    black masculinities, 60, 142–3
    and gender stereotypes, 99, 100
    Lebanese-Australian boys, 172–3
    and masculinity, 34–5
    and risk taking, 58–61, 63
    see also African American boys; black
        boys; indigenous boys
racism, 100, 104
Raethel, S., 169
rapes, 56, 85
reading, voluntary/vernacular, 213–20
'real' boyness
    crisis, 16–17
    search for, 32–4
'real' lads, 56, 77
'recuperative masculinity' strategies, 5, 6, 7
Redman, P. and Mac an Ghaill, M., 33–4
religious differences, 44
remasculinization
    of public work sector, 25–7
    of schooling, 26–7, 29
    of teacher hierarchies/identities, 27–8
remedial strategies
    violence, 170–1
    see also programmes for boys

resistance
  and cultural support, 158–9
  girls, 125
  indigneous students, 156–9
  and power, 35, 174–6
resources, teaching, 7–8, 63
Rigby, K. and Slee, P.T., 178
Riseborough, G.F., 156
risk taking
  effects of, 54–61
  rearticulating, 61–4
role models, male, 84–5
  black, 142–3
  teachers, 6, 41
role reversal, 5
Rosenthal, J.W., 187
rugby, 100–1, 227–8

Sadker, M. and Sadker, D., 63–4
Salisbury, J. and Jackson, D., 6, 55, 56,
    61, 76, 77
  on discipline, 171, 172
Sampson, E., 134
SATs (Standard Assessment Tasks), 3
schooling
  crisis, 25–31
  different uses of, 9
  masculinizing practices, 39–43
  remasculinzation of, 26–7, 28
  sex/gender system, 31–5
schools
  failing, 4
  management and discipline, 173
  normalization in, 181
  physical design, 40
  shootings in, 16
science
  assessment performance, 189–91
  and certain masculinities, 187–8
  classroom interactions, 188–93
  classroom practices, alternative,
    193–5
  group work, 191–3
  multiple perspective of, 187, 195
secondary school study, UK, 110–23
Section 28 (Local Government Act 1988),
    30, 36*n*, 97, 108*n*
Seidler, V.J., 28
sex/gender issues, critical approaches,
    31–5
sexual relationships, interracial, 145–6

sexuality
  and masculinity, 30–1
  popular boys, 127, 141
  see also homosexuality
shame, 163, 166*n*
Shame (film), 84, 85
Skeggs, B., 35
Smyth, J., 181
social organization of masculinity, 55–6
social transformations, 25–31, 178–9
socio-critical perspectives, 177–82
socio-economic groups, 4, 16, 70
  and academic success, 223
  and risk taking, 58–61, 63
  see also privileged boys; *and headings
    beginning* middle-class; working-class
sports
  football, 5, 87–8
  Haverford School, The, 42, 43
  indigenous males, 60, 163–4
  magazines, 217
  rugby, 100–1, 227–8
  violent, 60
  see also physical education and school
    sport (PESS)
Standard Assessment Tasks (SATs), 3
Stanley, W.B. and Brickhouse, N.W., 195
stereotypes
  challenging, 63
  female, 89–91, 99–100
  male, 86–8, 173
  racial/sexual, 145
subjects
  choice of, 69, 164
  'masculine' and 'feminine', 14, 33
  see also curriculum
support
  from families, 160–1
  from girls, 133–4
  for homosexual students, 102–4
  post-compulsory years, 160–3
  and resistance, 158–9
  for teachers, 175–6
suspension/exclusion from school, 59,
    60–1, 169

teacher(s)
  accountability, 148–9
  approaches to discipline, 170, 171,
    174–6, 177–8
  expectations and assumptions, 173

experienced *vs* new, 175–6
hierarchies/identities, 27–8
homosexual, 105–6
influence on black boys, 148–50
interviews, 105–6, 112, 174, 175, 176–7
leadership role, 49–50
male, *see* male teachers
mathematics, 207–9
physical education, 228–9
post-compulsory years, 162–3, 164
practices, 29–31
professional development, 170, 179–82
resources, 7–8, 63
science, 194–5
support for, 175–6
training, 170, 179–82
types, 27
see also pedagogies
teasing, 57, 104
TES, see Times Educational Supplement
testosterone, and violence, 12, 13, 17–18
therapeutic opportunity, boyhood as,
     13–16
Times Educational Supplement (TES), 2, 5
'tomboys', 102
transgression, 147–8
     teaching, 148–50
Trinh, M.T., 192

'understanding', 130, 131
United Kingdom (UK)
     boys' underachievement in, 2–4
     Education Acts, 2–3
     physical education, 226
     primary school study, 124–39

secondary school study, 110–23
Section 28 (Local Government Act
     1988), 30, 36*n*, 97, 108*n*
suspension/exclusion of black boys,
     60–1
vs Australian situation, 10–11
United States (US), 12, 38, 39, 56, 59
American Indian students, 155
physical education, 226
science classes, 188
see also African American boys

victim status, 5
black boys, 147–8, 150
bullied children, 178
'competing victim syndrome', 58, 82–3,
     96, 169, 170
violence
and language, 172–3
and masculinity, 16–17, 55–6, 171–2,
     178–9
punch 'n' run, 114–15, 122*n*
remedial strategies, 170–1
and testosterone, 12, 13, 17–18
towards homosexuals, 73, 75

Walkerdine, V., 99–100, 130, 202
Weiner, G. *et al.*, 9
Woodhead, Chris, 2
Woods, P., 120
working-class masculinity, 56, 59, 110–11,
     120, 121–2
working-class *vs* middle-class girls, 128–31
Wright, C. *et al.*, 60–1
Wright, J., 226